The EFT MANUAL
Third Edition

by Dawson Church

www.EFTUniverse.com

Energy Psychology Press
3340 Fulton Rd., #442, Fulton, CA 95439
www.EFTUniverse.com

Library of Congress Cataloging-in-Publication Data
Church, Dawson, 1956– author.
The EFT manual – Third edition / by Dawson Church, PhD.
    pages cm.
Revision of: The EFT manual / by Gary Craig. 2011.
ISBN 978-1-60415-214-2
    1. Emotional freedom techniques. 2. Emotion-focused therapy. I. Craig, Gary,
1940- EFT manual. II. Title. III. Title: Emotional freedom techniques manual.
    RC489.F62C48 2013
    616.89'147—dc23

2013038886

Cover design by Victoria Valentine
Editing by Stephanie Marohn
Typesetting by Karin Kinsey
Typeset in Cochin and Adobe Garamond
Printed in USA by Bang Printing
Third Edition

10 9 8 7 6 5 4 3 2 1

Important note: While EFT (Emotional Freedom Techniques) has produced remarkable clinical results, it must still be considered to be in the experimental stage and thus practitioners and the public must take complete responsibility for their use of it. Further, Dawson Church is not a licensed health professional and offers the information in this book solely as a life coach. Readers are strongly cautioned and advised to consult with a physician, psychologist, psychiatrist or other licensed health care professional before utilizing any of the information in this book. The information is based on information from sources believed to be accurate and reliable and every reasonable effort has been made to make the information as complete and accurate as possible but such completeness and accuracy cannot be guaranteed and is not guaranteed. The author, publisher, and contributors to this book, and their successors, assigns, licensees, employees, officers, directors, attorneys, agents and other parties related to them (a) do not make any representations, warranties or guarantees that any of the information will produce any particular medical, psychological, physical or emotional result, (b) are not engaged in the rendering of medical, psychological or other advice or services, (c) do not provide diagnosis, care, treatment or rehabilitation of any individual, and (d) do not necessarily share the views and opinions expressed in the information. The information has not undergone evaluation and testing by the United States Food and Drug Administration or similar agency of any other country and is not intended to diagnose, treat, prevent, mitigate or cure any disease. Risks that might be determined by such testing are unknown. If the reader purchases any services or products as a result of the information, the reader or user acknowledges that the reader or user has done so with informed consent. The information is provided on an "as is" basis without any warranties of any kind, express or implied, whether warranties as to use, merchantability, fitness for a particular purpose or otherwise. The author, publisher, and contributors to this book, and their successors, assigns, licensees, employees, officers, directors, attorneys, agents and other parties related to them (a) expressly disclaim any liability for and shall not be liable for any loss or damage including but not limited to use of the information; (b) shall not be liable for any direct or indirect compensatory, special, incidental, or consequential damages or costs of any kind or character; (c) shall not be responsible for any acts or omissions by any party including but not limited to any party mentioned or included in the information or otherwise; (d) do not endorse or support any material or information from any party mentioned or included in the information or otherwise; (e) will not be liable for damages or costs resulting from any claim whatsoever. The within limitation of warranties may be limited by the laws of certain states and/or other jurisdictions and so some of the foregoing limitations may not apply to the reader who may have other rights that vary from state to state. If the reader or user does not agree with any of the terms of the foregoing, the reader or user should not use the information in this book or read it. A reader who continues reading this book will be deemed to have accepted the provisions of this disclaimer.

Please consult qualified health practitioners regarding your use of EFT.

Contents

About EFT and *The EFT Manual* xv

    Roots in Modern Psychology xvi

    Acupoint Tapping.. xvi

    Combining Acupoint Tapping with Exposure xvii

    Clinical EFT xix

    APA Standards for Evidence-Based Treatment xx

    Listing Statistical Significance.. xxi

    Developing EFT xxii

Chapter 1: Inspiring Stories and Compelling
    Evidence 23

        Fear of Flying by Karen Ledger 23

    EFT for Psychological Disorders That Resist
    Treatment 24

        From a Downward to an Upward Spiral by Olli 25

        How EFT Helps Active-Duty Warriors by Constance
        Louie-Handelman, PhD, Captain, USAR..................... 27

Breakthroughs in Healing.. 28

Anxiety and Depression... 30

Getting His Life Back by Susitha P. 30

*Battling a Giant with Really Small, Surprisingly
Effective Rocks* by Kari Reed 31

Pain and Physical Symptoms.. 34

*Chronic Fatigue Syndrome and the Energy Level of an
87-Year-Old* by Sarah Marshall 34

*"I'm Never Good Enough"—Addressing the Roots of
Barbara's Fibromyalgia* by Clay LaPorte 36

A Flu Shot Gone Wrong by Chuck Gebhardt, MD 39

Online Delivery of EFT 42

Surprise at Quick Pain Relief by Ruth Ruddock 42

EFT for Blood Sugar Levels by Kate Flegal........................ 44

Three Key Reasons for EFT's Efficacy................................ 45

Learning the Basics Thoroughly 47

Not a Panacea.. 49

The Dark Side of EFT 51

How to Use This Book... 51

Chapter 2: The Science Behind EFT..................................... 53

How EFT Is Able to Address Such a Wide
Variety of Problems.. 53

The Brain's Ability to Detect Threats 55

Brain Waves: Beta, Alpha, Theta, and Delta...................... 57

Exposure, Cognitive Change, and Conditioned
Responses 59

Electromagnetic Energy and Acupoints 61

Evidence-Based Practice 63

Lifting the Weight of PTSD by Ingrid Dinter.........................65

EFT and Performance 72

Mechanisms of Action..72

Counterconditioning..74

Neural Plasticity 76

Dr. Callahan's First Experience 78

Chapter 3: How to Do EFT: The Basic Recipe 81

Testing..85

The Setup Statement..87

Psychological Reversal 88

Affirmation 89

Secondary Gain 92

How EFT Corrects for Psychological Reversal..................93

The Sequence..94

The Reminder Phrase..96

If Your SUD Level Doesn't Come Down to 0.................97

EFT for You and Others...98

The Importance of Targeting Specific Events...................98

Tapping on Aspects...100

Finding Core Issues...101

The Generalization Effect..103

The Movie Technique and Tell the Story Technique..................104

Constricted Breathing 108

The Personal Peace Procedure 109

Is It Working Yet?...111

Saying the Right Words...112

The Next Steps on Your EFT Journey...........................113

Chapter 4: How People Use EFT for the Five Major
Life Areas: Relationships, Health, Work, Money,
and Spirituality.. 115

    Removing the Blocks to Love's Presence
        by Fraeda Scholz.. 115

  Families 118

    *EFT Is Instrumental in Bringing a Couple Back
        Together by Carey Mann*.. 118

    Counselor Uses EFT to Improve Math Abilities
        by Syandra Ingram.. 120

    Tapping for the Aftermath of Domestic Violence
        by Ann Peck.. 121

    *EFT Improves Memory in Mother with
        Alzheimer's by Debra Trojan* 122

  Pain and Physical Symptoms 124

    The Bowling Ball in My Intestines................................. 124

    Tapping for Cervical Cancer Pain
        by Krysti Wesley 126

    EFT Eliminates Searing Burn Pain
        by Rebecca Snyder 126

  The Health Care System 128

  Emergencies 129

    Step on a Bee, Use EFT by Linda Compton 129

    *EFT for Child's Foot Injury Reduces Swelling
        in Minutes by Angela Seaman* 130

  Weight Loss.. 131

    The Chocolate Dream Pie 132

    Cinnamon Rolls... 132

  Work.. 133

The Man Who Was Afraid to Imagine Success
    by Aileen Nobles.. 134

Workplace Session Addresses Grief and Pain
    by Yair Halfon 135

Money and Abundance 137

Clearing Inner Blocks to Successful Stock Trades
    by Steve Wells and James 138

Manifesting Money with EFT
    by Annette Vaillancourt.................................... 140

Spiritual and Moral Development 141

Uncluttered Mind and a Feeling of Calm
    by Colin Carter...141

Spirituality, Stress, and Thoughts of an Affair
    by Aileen Nobles.. 142

Deeper Meditation, and a Prostate Bonus
    by Jonas Slonaker... 143

Chapter 5: Common Questions, Comments, and
Problems.. 147

How do I find the right words?.................................... 147

Do I need to tap on the exact points?........................... 148

Is it essential that I tap every point? 149

What if I don't feel a change in my SUD scores?........... 149

What if I can't figure out my SUD?............................. 150

*Do I measure my SUD level right now or at the time of
    the event?*.. 150

What if my SUD level doesn't go down to 0?............... 151

What if I can't remember a specific event? 153

*What if I have many similar traumatic events
    in my history?* 154

What if an event is too big or scary for me to deal with? 155

Can EFT work if my problem has existed for many years? 155

What if I have physical as well as psychological problems? 156

Do the positive effects last? 157

How do I know if a loved one has or I have a mental health diagnosis such as depression or PTSD? 158

When should I work with an EFT practitioner? 158

How do I find a practitioner? 160

How do I know if a practitioner is competent? 161

How do I explain EFT to friends, family, and colleagues? 161

Can I tap on a family member? 162

What if I begin, or someone I'm working with begins, to cry uncontrollably? 163

Can I combine tapping with my regular psychotherapy? 165

Should I tell my doctor I'm doing EFT? 166

How does EFT work with medical prescriptions? 166

If I feel better after using EFT, should I reduce my dose of medication? 167

Can EFT be harmful? 168

Are there cases where EFT should not be used? 169

Why does EFT focus on negative problems rather than positive thinking? 170

Why is drinking water during a session helpful? 171

How do I find other EFT users with the same problem as mine? 172

Just Get Started 173

Chapter 6: The Gentle Techniques 175

The Need for Gentle Techniques 177

The Four Characteristics of a Traumatic Event......................... 178

The Trauma Capsule 182

Cognitive Processing: Shifts and How to
 Identify Them... 184

Dissociation... 189

Inducing Dissociation 190

Tearless Trauma Technique... 191

 Using the Tearless Trauma Technique in a Group
  by Steve Wells 193

Further Layers of Therapeutic Dissociation 193

Exceptions to the Rule of Being Specific 195

Sneaking Up on the Problem 196

Chasing the Pain 199

Sneaking Away from the Problem 200

Touch and Breathe (TAB) 202

Posttraumatic Growth 203

Chapter 7: Breaking the Habit of Being Yourself 205

Finding Core Issues... 208

Identifying the Writings on Your Walls 211

The Characteristics of Effective Affirmations 214

Identifying Tail-Enders... 216

 Doubts about Her Holistic Health Practice
  by Paul Zelizer 217

Daisy Chaining, and Talking and Tapping 218

 Little Louise and Taxes.. 220

The Generalization Effect: Identifying It, and
 Adjusting the Setup Statement... 222

The Apex Effect 223

 A Skeptic's Use of EFT for a Burn by Carol Look, LCSW ... 224

Client Forgets Symptoms of Fibromyalgia
  by John Digby, PhD 225

Shifting the Setup Statement as the Client
Rapidly Shifts Aspects 227

Customized Setup Phrasing 228

Using "It's in Here" in the EFT Setup Phrase
  by Timothy J. Hayes, PsyD 229

Flowing Setup Statements 231

*Experiments with the Setup and a Urinary Tract
Infection* by Christine Cloutier 231

Techniques for Working on Your Own Issues 233

Interrupting Your Tragic Story 236

From Abandonment to Engagement
  by Alina Frank 237

Chapter 8: Special Populations 241

Age-Appropriate Techniques for Using EFT
with Children 241

Daily Releasing with Children 243

The Daily Peace Procedure for Children 245

Borrowing Benefits 247

*Simultaneously Resolving Childhood Issues
in Three People* 248

Working with Groups 249

Cravings and Addictions 251

Multiple Phobias 254

EFT for Physical Symptoms: How the Approach Differs
from EFT for Psychological Symptoms 255

Wrist Fracture Pain Tied to Resentment 255

Techniques to Use When Regular EFT Does
Not Reduce SUD Level 258

Emphatic EFT Clears More Blocks Than I Imagined
by Rex Jantze 261

Mental Tapping 264

Mental EFT Stops Migraine in 10 Minutes by Eswar 264

Secret Tapping 265

EFT for Sports and Business Performance 266

Chapter 9: Professional Practice Techniques 269

Maintaining Client-Centered Focus 269

Self-rating versus Observer-rating 270

When Self-acceptance Is the Problem 271

The Role of Insight 273

Collarbone Breathing Exercise 275

The Floor to Ceiling Eye Roll 276

Reframing 276

Preframing 277

Identifying Tables and Legs 278

Tabletop: "I'm Unlovable" by Jan L. Watkins, JD, MSW 281

Becoming Extremely Specific 284

Targeting the Problem from All Angles 285

In Vivo Testing and Confrontive Questions 286

When Your Client Feels Worse 287

Energy Toxins and Allergens 291

Massive Reversal 292

Physical Symptoms That Resist Healing 294

Guidelines for Serious Diseases 295

Professional Standards in a Coaching Practice 300

Chapter 10: Confronting Massive Human Suffering:
Humanitarian Work and Research 303

Highly Traumatized Populations 304

The Veterans Stress Project.. 305

    Vulcan Voodoo with Marilyn by David S 306

    From Rwanda to Newtown: Our Shared Vision for
        Humanity by Lori Leyden, PhD, and Nick Ortner 309

    Children of the Haiti Earthquake
        by Yves Wauthier-Freymann 314

    EFT in Nuevo Laredo by David MacKay 317

Change Is Possible: The San Quentin Death
    Row Project 319

Volunteering for Humanitarian Projects.................................... 321

Future Research.. 322

A World Without Trauma?.. 324

Appendices

Appendix A: The Full Basic Recipe 329

Appendix B: Easy EFT... 339

Appendix C: A Format Diagram for Using EFT 345

Appendix D: The 48 Clinical EFT Techniques 347

Appendix E: Acupuncture Meridians of the Frontal Torso 351

References 353

Index... 367

EFT on a Page 374

About EFT and
The EFT Manual

Welcome to the world of EFT and to *The EFT Manual.* You're about to go on a grand adventure with a technique that has helped millions of people worldwide. Just how many millions? A review of Google Analytics showed that in June of 2013 there were 9,143,000 searches worldwide for terms such as "EFT tapping, EFT therapy," and related terms (Google Trends, 2013). Analysis of traffic to the five most-visited EFT websites showed 6,965,000 unique visitors that month (Traffic Estimate, 2013). Over a million people suffering through natural or human-caused disasters have been treated with EFT, according to charities that offer aid to these victims (Capacitar, 2013; TREST, 2010; Veterans Stress Project, 2013).

All this activity involves grassroots connection, with people telling other people about EFT. There's no government organization dedicating to delivering EFT, no corporate promotional department advertising EFT, no brilliant social media guru creating buzz about EFT, and no drug company pushing EFT. Those millions of people tell their friends each month for one simple reason: EFT works. This manual exists to show you the many ways in which EFT helps those millions of people, tell a few of their stories, show you how EFT can help you, and train you in the basics of Clinical EFT, the science-based EFT method that has been validated by dozens of clinical trials.

As you discover EFT, and how it can benefit you and everyone around you, you're likely to have questions about where EFT came from and why it's set up the way it is. This first section of *The EFT Manual* addresses those questions. If you'd like to dive straight into using EFT, start with Chapter 3, EFT's Basic Recipe, which gives you step-by-step instructions in how to use EFT.

Roots in Modern Psychology

EFT has deep roots in modern psychology as well as the ancient science of acupuncture. The two approaches from psychotherapy from which EFT draws most are cognitive therapy and exposure therapy. Cognitive therapies address how we see the world through thoughts or "cognitions" that also shape our behavior. Exposure therapies focus on the therapeutic value of remembering traumatic life events. Chapter 2, "The Science of EFT," covers in detail the contribution of cognitive and exposure therapies to EFT.

Acupoint Tapping

EFT is often called "tapping" because a central feature of EFT involves tapping with your fingertips on acupuncture points on your body. These acupuncture points are usually referred to as "acupoints." Research has shown that pressure on acupoints, or "acupressure," can be as effective as acupuncture itself (Cherkin, Sherman, & Avins, 2009). Acupuncture theory teaches that energy flows through our body through pathways called meridians. Disease can be caused by a blockage or interruption of that flow, and acupuncture or acupressure can be used to remove those blockages. Chapter 2 has more information on how and why acupressure can be so helpful in healing.

The idea that stimulation of the physical body (also called "somatic stimulation") could play a role in psychological healing arose gradually in the second half of the 20th century. In the 1920s, a colleague of Sigmund Freud, psychiatrist Wilhelm Reich, coined the term "muscular armour" based on his observations that emotional trauma can result in rigidity in certain regions of the body (Reich, 1927). A pioneering psychiatrist named Joseph Wolpe (1958) treated veterans of WWII who had posttraumatic stress disorder (PTSD), searching for a cure. He tried various forms of physical stimulation and eventually found that diaphragmatic breathing (breathing deeply using the diaphragm muscle below your lungs) while recalling a traumatic memory such as a combat experience (exposure) could remove the emotional content from the memory. You still have the memory, but it no longer triggers a big emotional reaction.

In the early 1960s, an American chiropractor named George Goodheart was introduced to acupuncture. He discovered that he could treat physical conditions successfully by tapping on acupuncture points or stimulating them manually, without the use of needles (Adams & Davidson, 2011). He called his method "Applied Kinesiology" (Goodheart, 1991).

Combining Acupoint Tapping with Exposure

A breakthrough occurred when a clinical psychologist called Roger Callahan combined tapping on acupoints with exposure. Callahan studied Applied Kinesiology, and along with other pioneers such as psychiatrist John Diamond, began to apply acupoint tapping to psychological problems. Callahan first discovered that it could cure phobias. Later, he applied it to other psychological conditions including anxiety, depression, and PTSD. His method is called Thought Field Therapy or TFT (Callahan, 2000). Other therapists also experimented with the stimulation of acupressure points and developed various methods. Clinical psychologist Fred Gallo, PhD, made a notable contribution with his method EDxTm (Gallo, 2000). He coined the term "energy psychology" to describe all the modalities that use acupressure and similar techniques to correct energy imbalances in order to treat psychological disorders.

One of Callahan's students, an engineer and performance coach named Gary Craig, simplified Callahan's TFT method and called it Emotional Freedom Techniques or simply EFT. While TFT uses elaborate diagnostic methods to determine which acupoints to tap and in which order, EFT simply taps on 12 points in any order. It dispenses with the diagnostic part of TFT. In collaboration with colleague Adrienne Fowlie, Craig published an online manual from which increasing numbers of people learned EFT. This was the first edition of *The EFT Manual* (Craig & Fowlie, 1995). It was later published in book form (Craig, 2008/2010). After Craig announced his retirement in 2009, the same configuration of EFT became available as a free online download in the form of *The EFT Mini-Manual* (Church, 2009/2013).

Between the first online publication of the manual (1995) and the first book edition of the manual (2008), an abbreviated form of EFT's Basic Recipe came into widespread use by practitioners. The second edition of the manual (2010) reflected this change. The Full Basic Recipe appeared as Appendix A in the second edition, with the abbreviated Basic Recipe the primary method taught. Many practitioners find the original Full Basic Recipe very useful, especially for treatment-resistant conditions like PTSD, so it continues to appear as Appendix A of this third edition of the manual.

This current edition also incorporates a number of EFT techniques previously described only in the curriculum for Level 1, 2 and 3 workshops, and in the Tutorial section of the online EFT archives. The first of these four chapters focuses on psychological trauma. It describes three methods called the Gentle Techniques that are useful when working with memories that are too traumatic to recall directly. These are described in Chapter 6. Chapter 7 shows how to apply EFT to common personal challenges, like identifying your core issues, interrupting your habitual patterns, and counteracting the self-sabotage that gets in the way of your best intentions. Chapter 8 summarizes professional techniques used with special populations such as children, athletes, and addicts. Chapter 9 covers techniques useful for the experienced practitioner such as reframing, insight, different methods for testing your results, and guidelines for working with clients with serious diseases. Packaging these techniques in this manual rather than in the supplementary materials brings them all together in a single handy reference guide.

Clinical EFT

As EFT became more popular in therapy and coaching circles, it attracted the attention of researchers. They conducted studies of EFT and found that it was extremely effective for mental health problems such as phobias, depression, anxiety, and PTSD (Lane, 2009). Because the manual was freely available, all this research was conducted using a uniform version of EFT, which we call Clinical EFT. This is the form of EFT taught in this manual.

The use of a manual is necessary to ensure that a treatment is applied uniformly from study to study. The Clinical Psychology division of the American Psychological Association (APA) has published guidelines for research. These guidelines determine whether or not a therapy is "empirically validated" (Chambless & Hollon, 1998). There are seven "essential" criteria that are required in order for a study to be considered valid, and one of these is the use of a written manual. This ensures that when a scientific study is replicated, researchers are comparing apples to apples. Studies usually contain a sentence similar to this: "The EFT protocol is described in *The EFT Manual* (Craig, 2008); fidelity to the method was assessed by means of written checklists submitted by coaches to investigators" (Hartung & Stein, 2012). In this way, researchers confirm that they are using the same manualized form of the method that has been tested in other studies.

Uniformity is particularly important in the case of EFT. As it has become more popular, and because the basics are so easy to use, hundreds of websites have sprung up and thousands of YouTube videos have been posted demonstrating EFT. A few use EFT as described in the manual, but most introduce variations and innovations developed by those who created them. Some of these EFT variants are probably as effective as the original method while others may not be. Few of them have been tested in research studies, so it is difficult to determine their effectiveness.

It is possible, however, to assess the effectiveness of Clinical EFT, the method taught in this manual, because it carefully adheres to the same version of EFT that has been used in the studies that validate the method. When you use this manual to learn EFT, you can rest assured that you are learning a tried and true technique that dozens of scientific studies have shown to be effective. You're not using a variant that may or may not be effective. There are 48 techniques described in Clinical EFT. This manual gives you a basic understanding of all 48. More detailed descriptions can be found in *The Clinical EFT Handbook, Volume 1* (Church & Marohn, 2013).

To ensure that users always get the same proven EFT formula validated in research, all EFT books in this series have the same "common chapter" on how to perform EFT's Basic Recipe, found here in Chapter 3. Whether you're a fibromyalgia patient reading *EFT for Fibromyalgia and Chronic Fatigue* (Church, 2013b) or a dieter reading *EFT for Weight Loss* (Church, 2013d), you're guaranteed to get the same successful formula demonstrated in all those studies.

APA Standards for Evidence-Based Treatment

All the books in the EFT Series embrace the evidence-based standards defined by the American Psychological Association Division 12 (Clinical Psychology) Task Force ("APA standards" for short). These define an "empirically validated treatment" as one for which two controlled trials have been conducted by independent research teams. For a treatment to be designated as "efficacious," the studies must demonstrate that the treatment is better than a placebo or an established efficacious treatment.

To be designated as "probably efficacious," a treatment must meet these criteria in one study, have been shown to be better than a wait list in two studies, or meet these criteria in two studies that were conducted by the same research team rather than two independent teams. The APA standards advocate that studies contain sufficient subjects to achieve a level of statistical significance of $p < .05$ or greater, which means that there is only one possibility in 20 that the results are due to chance. This threshold is the level of proof most commonly accepted in the scientific community.

The current status of EFT as an "evidence-based" practice is summarized in this statement published in the APA journal *Review of General Psychology:*

> A literature search identified 51 peer-reviewed papers that report or investigate clinical outcomes following the tapping of acupuncture points to address psychological issues. The 18 randomized controlled trials in this sample were critically evaluated for design quality, leading to the conclusion that they consistently demonstrated strong effect sizes and other positive statistical results that far exceed chance after relatively few treatment sessions. Criteria for evidence-based treatments proposed by Division 12 of the American Psychological Association were also applied and found to be met for a number of conditions, including PTSD. (Feinstein, 2012)

This manual and other Energy Psychology Press publications use the APA's style guidelines (American Psychological Association, 2009).

Listing Statistical Significance

Each chapter quotes the scientific studies on the material that is the subject of that chapter, with references listed at the end of the book. Often, the percentage of change in a symptom is listed, as in "pain dropped by an average of 68%." Every percentage quoted in this manual is "statistically significant" at the level of $p < .05$ or better.

I do not, however, quote the degree of statistical significance in the text. The reason for this omission is that this manual is intended primarily as an introduction to EFT, rather than a professional textbook. So while it is based on sound science, technical details such as p values are omitted. They can be found in professional publications such as *The Clinical EFT Handbook, Volume 1* (Church & Marohn, 2013).

Developing EFT

EFT continues to grow and evolve. Over the past decade, thousands of users have reported their experiences with EFT, contributing to a large archive of case histories and stories. Some 5,000 in the English language are posted on the user archive at EFT Universe (www.EFTUniverse.com), and thousands have been translated into other languages, including French, German, Spanish, Portuguese, Bulgarian, Russian, Chinese, Japanese, Arabic, Dutch, Hebrew, Korean, Polish, Turkish, and Italian. An online conference called the Tapping World Summit (ClinicalEFT.com) attracts over half a million participants each year. Over two million people have downloaded *The EFT Manual* (Craig & Fowlie, 1995) or *The EFT Mini-Manual* (Church, 2009/2013). The numbers continue to grow.

On the solid foundation of Clinical EFT, EFT is now being extended to other areas of psychology such as marriage and family therapy, dreamwork, and organizational development. It is making its way into primary care facilities such as hospitals and veterans centers. It is likely to have a major impact on health care as the 21st century progresses. It is so proving to be so effective in treating emotional and physical disorders that it promises to make a large difference in health care costs (Church, 2010a).

Now that you understand where EFT and this manual came from, let's get started with EFT itself. First we'll explain the scientific underpinnings of Clinical EFT, showing that it's a stable and reliable method grounded in solid science. Then we'll clearly explain how to do EFT yourself. We'll then show you how it is applied to various problems, and how you can get the most out of it in your own life. We hope you'll experience the same health and performance benefits as the millions of others who have used EFT as their gateway to emotional freedom.

Resources

• ClinicalEFT.com

Inspiring Stories and
Compelling Evidence

The way most people are introduced to EFT is through stories. There are literally tens of thousands of stories posted online about how well EFT works, and the chances are good that you've had a friend or family member tell you about their astonishing success with EFT. Throughout this book, I'll let members of the global EFT community tell you their heartwarming and inspiring stories, as a way of showing the difference EFT makes in their lives. I'll also share the wealth of scientific evidence that underlies these accounts. To start with, let's examine how EFT can help with a very common phobia, the fear of flying.

Fear of Flying
by Karen Ledger

I helped the mother of client who has such a huge fear of flying that she drives across Canada every year rather than take a plane. Well, she had to go to Ireland and didn't have time to take a boat, and was already getting nauseated 3 weeks before the event, just thinking about it.

I suggested we try EFT and she agreed. We spent about 40 minutes exploring and tapping on all the aspects that might come up for her around flying. We started with thinking about it, the drive to the airport; sitting in the cramped seating and smelling the airplane smell;

takeoff; fear of the pilot being inept; turbulence; and the plane dropping out of the sky or down thousands of feet. Interestingly, there was no fear around landing, as she felt that once they were on their way down she would be okay, even though she realized intellectually that landing could be risky!

Well, she returned from her trip this week and reported that she had "no further worries prior to the flight" even though she tried to make herself worry just to test the technique! She stated. "It was a lovely trip! My husband couldn't believe it…I enjoyed the food, the music the movie and the view!…and I have already booked another flight to Prince Edward Island for later this year! It's really unbelievable!"

* * *

If this were just an isolated story, it would be interesting but inconclusive. But it's one of thousands of such stories found in the international EFT story archive at EFT Universe (EFTUniverse.com). Not only are these stories impressive by themselves, they're mirrored by solid scientific research. For instance, three randomized controlled trials of EFT for phobias showed significant results in just one session (Wells, Polglase, Andrews, Carrington, & Baker, 2003: Salas, Brooks, & Rowe, 2011; Baker & Siegel, 2010). Like Karen Ledger's client, participants in those studies recovered from their phobias, and follow-up showed the improvements to be lasting.

EFT for Psychological Disorders That Resist Treatment

EFT works for far more than phobias. Research shows that it is effective for other psychological conditions, such as anxiety and depression (Church, 2013a). Even PTSD, which is usually very tough to treat by other methods, can be remediated with EFT. Several studies show that PTSD symptoms normalize in four to six sessions (Karatzias et al., 2011; Church et al., 2013; Nemiro, 2013). Here's a story of a veteran who came back from combat in Iraq with PTSD, then used EFT.

From a Downward to an Upward Spiral
by Olli

I deployed with 10th Mountain Division, 2nd BCT, to Baghdad from September 2006 through June 2007. I performed a variety of jobs including guard, medical lab, medic, and pharmacy work. My experience was a typical mosaic of long days, stress, and a variety of emotionally powerful events. In short, I was exposed to the following experiences (some face-to-face and others indirectly through my comrades): IED explosions, small arms fire, rocket attacks, sniper attacks, wounded and dead Americans, allies, and Iraqis (military, enemy, and civilians—including women and children), mass casualty, suicide, self-mutilation, divorce, infidelity, fist fights, rape, captured and beheaded U.S. soldiers, imprisoned terrorists, smell and sights of bloody, decomposing, and burnt tissues, booby traps, destroyed vehicles, and a persistent fear of being attacked.

Upon my return from deployment, I began my first year of medical school. Even though I completed the first academic year with good grades, I noticed that my quality of life had diminished significantly. I recognized that I was no longer able to be present in the moment and was always observing whatever was happening in my life from a "witness" perspective. I also replayed many situations in my mind, often thinking of how I could have done them differently. I no longer laughed much and felt burdened by my past, reminiscing my days when ignorance was bliss.

A year went by and I had spoken about my experiences to a variety of people in attempts to "release" them or find peace from their recurrent nature. Talking about the experiences helped me a bit, but only on an intellectual level. I understood that what I was feeling was "a normal reaction to an abnormal situation." I knew that I had done my best and was a force of good in this world. But I also knew that my symptoms persisted even after talking about them. Otherwise I was doing "fine" and identified my symptoms as recurring emotions that were independent of my intellect. They were in a way unreachable, no matter how I tried to resolve or release them. I concluded that this was the price I had to pay, and continued to live my unrewarding life to the best of my ability.

About a month ago I had a powerful experience. I met an old acquaintance who knew me before I deployed to Iraq. Nancy asked if I was open to letting her try something called EFT to help me gain freedom from my recurring emotions. She said it was an "emotional" tool and not a mental one. I agreed and we spent a total of 4 hours doing the work over 2 days. The results were immediate and I literally "fell back" into my body from a defensive posture that I had unknowingly created in my mind. I could feel my body again and could not stop crying and laughing. I could now be present in the moment and not have half of my attention observing the situation as it was happening. I also became less reactive to whistle sounds and sirens that used to initiate in me a fight-or-flight response, as incoming rockets had done in Iraq. Overall, I regained the quality of life that I had prior to deployment.

It was truly an "emotional freedom" technique. Since then, I have been on a constant upward spiral and have been able to transform my past into a great strength. We worked through every single memory and emotion that I was not at peace with and "tapped them out." I also learned how to "self-administer" EFT and have been practicing it on myself whenever something new has emerged from my past.

* * *

Rather than the downward spiral that so many veterans with PTSD fall into, one that ends in alcoholism, domestic violence, hospitalization, joblessness, or even homelessness, this veteran has now gone on to become a psychiatrist. He has been instrumental in getting EFT to many other veterans suffering from PTSD.

Many therapists have discovered the same effects when they use EFT. Here's an open letter by clinical psychologist Constance Louie-Handelman, PhD, a former captain in the U.S. Army Reserve, who was in charge of a forward operating base in Kandahar Province. She writes how after just one round of EFT tapping, soldiers were noticeably more relieved and calmer.

How EFT Helps Active-Duty Warriors
By Constance Louie-Handelman, PhD, Captain, USAR

I began investigating Emotional Freedom Techniques (EFT) when a friend told me about tapping. Although I have a PhD degree in clinical psychology, I was continually searching for other effective techniques that could help clients. I studied EMDR, Neuro-linguistic Programming, and hypnotherapy.

However, after studying and practicing EFT, I found it worked quickly in eliminating fears, limiting beliefs, pain, and releasing traumatic events. Every opportunity I had, I used EFT with family, friends, and clients and achieved excellent long-lasting results. I was so confident in EFT that I felt I had something to offer when I read about the high rate of suicide among U.S. soldiers.

I was commissioned as a captain in the U.S. Army Reserve on March 2010, and was deployed to Afghanistan from July 2011 to May 2012. As a psychologist, I was in charge of a forward operating base in Kandahar Province and officially saw 199 individual soldiers (574 sessions).

Once I established rapport, understood their problems and needs, I used EFT primarily for anger, sleep, depression, and stress.

After just one round of tapping, soldiers were noticeably more relieved and calmer. Soon thereafter, soldiers added more details about their problems, or expressed issues that they had kept to themselves for years. When they felt the profound positive result, it was then easy to encourage soldiers to learn how to tap, something they could do themselves in a matter of minutes, in order to release past, current, or anticipated problems, or "pre-emptive tapping," as one soldier called it.

The ease to learn and to apply the tapping was an important element of EFT since I often saw a solider just for one session.

I realized the success of EFT when soldiers were able to return to full duty, wanting to learn more about EFT, or referring other soldiers to my office. Since returning home, I am disheartened to learn that EFT is not an accepted technique in the U.S. Department of Veterans Affairs (VA). Fortunately, there is the Veterans Stress Project (www.stressproject.org) that offers free EFT sessions for returning vets.

I can only hope that the VA's powers-that-be will soon realize the effectiveness of EFT in order to help thousands of suffering vets, thus making a dramatic dent in the suicide rate.

* * *

While Dr. Louie-Handelman's wish for the VA to recognize the effectiveness of EFT hasn't come true yet, I'm happy to say that progress has been made. When she returned from deployment, she was hired by the San Francisco Veterans Center where she now offers EFT to veterans.

Breakthroughs in Healing

EFT represents a genuine breakthrough in healing. The history of medicine and psychology is punctuated by similar breakthroughs, such as William Harvey's discovery of the circulation of blood in 1628 or Marie Curie's discovery of the diagnostic usefulness of X-rays in 1898. When a breakthrough such as Jonas Salk's discovery of the polio vaccine occurs, big changes in society may result. A scourge like polio is eradicated, improving the lives of millions of people. There were many diseases that were fearful threats just a century ago, such as cholera, typhoid, diphtheria, and polio. Today, they are little more than historical curiosities.

Like the field of medicine, the subfield of psychology has had its share of breakthroughs. Sigmund Freud's insight that the subconscious mind could drive behavior shaped the thinking of subsequent generations. Ivan Pavlov's discovery that dogs could be conditioned to salivate at the sound of a bell introduced us to the concept of conditioning. Psychiatrist Joseph Wolpe sought methods of changing that conditioning, a process called counterconditioning, in the 1940s and 1950s. He wondered how, after a behavior is strongly and repeatedly conditioned, it could be reversed or counterconditioned. Wolpe sought ways of counterconditioning the suffering of war veterans. He found that diaphragmatic breathing could countercondition PTSD symptoms such as flashbacks and intrusive thoughts (Wolpe, 1958).

EFT is a breakthrough on the same order of magnitude. Just a decade ago, most research showed PTSD to be an incurable condition (Benedek, Friedman, Zatzick, & Ursano, 2009). A long-term study of veterans with PTSD found that even after a vigorous intervention, "the treatment program's impact on the course of illness had been negligible" (Johnson, Fontana, Lubin, Corn, & Rosenheck, 2004). Veterans who go into Veterans Administration hospitals for treatment often report lack of success, and some are even retraumatized by having to talk about and relive their combat experiences (McFarlane & Van der Kolk, 2009). Research shows that PTSD isn't just a psychological problem with a start, middle, and end, like many kinds of depression. Depression usually lasts around 8 months (NIH, 2008), but PTSD symptoms often worsen over time and are associated with adverse changes in the structure and function of the brain (Vasterling & Brewin, 2005). One study found that of every 10 veterans that start a prescribed 1-year course of mental health treatment at a VA hospital, only one completes it (Seal et al., 2010).

The children and spouses of veterans with PTSD bear a terrible burden. Studies find that domestic violence is more likely in the homes of veterans (Orcutt, King, & King, 2003). The spouses of veterans have a higher-than-average likelihood of developing PTSD themselves, a phenomenon called "transferred PTSD" (Nelson & Wright, 1996). There are more veterans in prison than other demographic groups (Greenberg & Rosenheck, 2009). In all these ways, the effects of PTSD radiate out to affect the whole community.

Against this bleak backdrop of prolonged and hopeless human suffering, EFT stands as a beacon. With an investment of just six sessions, and without drugs or harsh treatments, 86% of veterans in one study experienced a dramatic reduction of their PTSD symptoms. Follow-up assessment shows that the improvements are permanent (Church et al., 2013).

Anxiety and Depression

EFT is effective for many other conditions besides phobias and PTSD; it works well for other mental health problems too. Many EFT studies have investigated its effectiveness with anxiety. Anxiety takes various forms, such as public speaking anxiety, test-taking anxiety, performance anxiety, and generalized anxiety. EFT has been shown to reduce such anxiety dramatically, and it often takes just a few sessions (Sezgin & Özcan, 2009; Jones, Thornton, & Andrews, 2011; Jain & Rubino, 2012; Karatzias et al., 2011). Consider the following story by one of our EFT practitioners.

Getting His Life Back
By Susitha P.

Venkat (name changed) approached me for his problem with ongoing anxiety. He was constantly in a state of tension, the physical symptoms being pounding of the heart, tightness in the left leg, and also tightness in the head. These symptoms worsened when he had to meet people, and in crowded places.

Previously an extrovert, he was forced to change his lifestyle because of this constant anxiety. He stopped driving, partying, and going out on trips and even avoided going shopping.

I asked him when this anxiety first surfaced and if there was any particular incident that triggered it. He told me this started 2 years ago when he had a dizzy spell at his workplace. He fainted and even though people were there to help him, he felt helpless, out of control, and weak.

After this incident, he had constant fear and anxiety that he would faint again. It often happens that people dismiss such feelings with words like "It is all in the mind," and "You just need more willpower." As practitioners we know better. We know how a disruption in the energy system can make a person feel helpless and weak.

I figured it was an intense issue for him and used the Tearless Trauma Technique. We labeled the incident as "dizzy incident," and after some rounds of tapping, he was more in control and ready to talk about the details.

We then worked on the incident using the Movie Technique until the intensity dropped to a 0 out of 10. Venkat felt that tapping for "I take my power back" felt uplifting, so we did a lot of tapping using these words.

The level of intensity on a scale of 0 to 10 for the pounding heart, tension in the left leg, and also tension in the head were constantly between 8 and 10 before we started the EFT sessions. The intensity level started dropping after a few sessions and came down to a 4 out of 10. Venkat also tapped between sessions and he was very dedicated and determined to clear this problem.

The feedback I received from him a month after our last session included many success stories. He now meets people comfortably, he has started driving again, he has made two business trips, and he is no longer terrified of crowds. He is very happy that he has his life back and I am very happy that I could part of this wonderful healing.

* * *

Anxiety can be characterized as stress about the future, and depression as stress about the past (Dispenza, 2013). They may be two sides of the same coin, and research shows that EFT is effective for both. Kari Reed, who suffered from depression, worked with author and practitioner Karin Davidson. Kari wrote the following account of her slow but sure recovery from depression. Though it's hilariously funny, you can sense the pain and despair beneath the humor.

Battling a Giant with Really Small, Surprisingly Effective Rocks
By Kari Reed

Tapping is the stupidest thing you'll ever do.

I realize that I just potentially offended an entire, ever-growing community of people, but it's true. Tapping is probably the stupidest thing you'll ever do. Think about it—there are "special places" all over your face and body and if you bang on these enough, while saying some words and imagining some stuff, all your problems will go away. To make it even more ridiculous, you can imagine banging on the face of an imaginary younger version of yourself and your problems will go away even faster. And let's face it, you know that when you're sitting there, eyes closed, trying to picture your inner 4-year-old, touching your face like a crazy person with a nervous tic, and mumbling that you truly and deeply love and accept yourself anyway, you probably look pretty stupid. In fact, we can go ahead and remove the "probably"—you look stupid.

The problem with this stupid thing is that it actually works. That isn't to say that it feels any less silly or ridiculous while you're doing it, and that isn't to say that you'll suddenly stop feeling the urge to sigh and roll your eyes every time your practitioner asks you to "ask your little self how they feel," and it certainly doesn't mean that all of your issues, problems, and troubles will disappear in a cloud of magic tapping dust tomorrow, but it is to say that you will be involved in a process that will help you slowly but surely move forward once and for all. And what's even better is that you will start to feel a difference, see changes in yourself and various parts of your life, and you will get better—it just takes some time and a whole lot of looking stupid.

Everyone who taps gets to go through the "this is so stupid, I can't believe I'm doing this, this thing can't possibly actually work" phase—and for some it's longer than others—but for those dealing with heavy and complex issues like depression, the experience is a little more complicated. You see, depression isn't something that happens overnight—and I speak from experience. Depression is something that creeps in slowly, almost elusively, like putting ink in a jar of water. It creeps. It blurs reality. It affects everything. And when it finally settles, everything seems a little darker—actually, it all seems a lot darker. And you find yourself looking around at all the inky, cloudy water—complete with black ink-sludge on the bottom—and you think "Holy !!##&*@. There's no way I can clean this up. I don't even have the energy to think about where to begin, I think I'll just sleep instead. This is utterly and terribly hopeless." So you sit inside of your little inky jar, feeling depressed, and sad, and hopeless, and unmotivated, and wishing things weren't like this and having no idea if you'll have to live like this forever. Meds might help. Talking to someone might help. Seeing a therapist might help. All of these things help you cope with and rationalize the situation, but none of them makes the darkness—the depression—go away.

Enter tapping (cue glorious music from the sky, a video montage of clouds opening, and maybe even the voice of Morgan Freeman!). Tapping is supposed to be able to help! There's a success rate and testimonials from other people who couldn't get out of their inky, water-filled jars and got better from doing this stupid thing, and suddenly, even though you can hardly believe it (even though you're terrified to believe it because what if it doesn't work on you??!), there's some hope. A glimmer through the muck and mire. And so you resolve yourself, as difficult as resolve feels most of the time, that you're going to try it. You read all of the success stories and watch all of the near-miraculous videos and YouTube clips and talk to as many people as you can and when you finally try this miraculous, godsend of a cure, you realize how stupid it feels, how you don't really wanna talk to any *#%! younger version of yourself, let alone bang on their faces, you don't feel like doing work on your own between sessions even though your practitioner highly recommends it, and my god it's taking so long, why is it taking so long????

Depression can be defeated. Again, I speak from experience. Think of tapping like this (I really like metaphors): Tapping is like fighting giants with stones. Some giants are bigger than others (depression is huge; a spider phobia?—not so huge), and some stones are bigger than others. At first, it's totally natural to look at the pile of stones that you have and think, "There is no way in #@!! these will ever take down that whole giant," but you lob one at him anyway, just because, well, you've tried everything else and you may as well cross this stupid tapping stuff off your list too. The stone you threw (not very zealously, I might add, because you were too busy being skeptical and convincing yourself that it wouldn't work anyway), hits the giant's little finger. Not exactly deadly, but to your surprise, his little pinky finger disintegrates. Poof. Gone. Just like that. You stare at the space where his finger once was in shock. It worked! These stones may seem small compared to the giant, but they're surprisingly effective. It's easy to get hung up on how huge the giant seems—your depression giant is a big one—he's been bingeing on choco-late and carbs to make himself feel better and spending most of his days lying in bed—but if you keep lobbing stones, knowing that if you just hit him again, another piece of him will disintegrate, and then another, and another, and so on. If you feel motivated to tap on your own and you throw some extra stones, great! But if not, it really doesn't matter. As long as you keep going in some fashion, the giant will slowly, but surely, break down, until there's nothing left but a foot, maybe an ear, and you'll think, "Hey, I can live with that!" and it'll be over and you'll be moving on with the rest of your life before you know it.

It takes time. And you'll feel stupid. And it'll feel so long and ridiculous and impossible. But when the giant's gone, all the stupid rock throwing will have been totally worth it.

* * *

Stories like these put us right inside the experience of someone using EFT, giving us a personal sense of what it feels like, while the statistics in studies quantify its effects. Behind those numbers are people like Venkat and Kari, and when you read the results of a study, it's worth keeping in mind that back of every dry statistic is a group of people whose lives have been dramatically changed for the better.

Pain and Physical Symptoms

EFT is effective for more even than psychological problems such as phobias, anxiety, depression, and PTSD. Many people report relief from physical problems too. Here's the case of a chronic fatigue syn-drome (CFS) patient who recovered completely after using EFT for her fears around her symptoms.

Chronic Fatigue Syndrome and the Energy Level of an 87-Year-Old
By Sarah Marshall

I struggled with myalgic encephalomyelitis or ME (the more com-monly used term for CFS in the United Kingdom) for 6 years and was unable to work for over 4 of those years. At the age of 27, I was having days of unrelenting dizziness, I felt as though I had a flu that wasn't getting better, I couldn't concentrate (even just making a cup of tea seemed a challenge at times), and I didn't have the energy to do anything more than sit around waiting for it to pass. I felt as though a plug had been pulled and all of my energy with it. It didn't feel like normal tiredness and I was frightened. All my GP had to say was that I couldn't expect to have the energy I had as a 17-year-old. I desperately needed answers or at least my doctor's support and this is what she offered me. I remember thinking...actually I can't repeat exactly what I thought, as it involved a number of strong phrases! But I do remember thinking, "I might believe you if I was 87 not 27!"

This was one of numerous events that triggered a strong anxiety, which I experienced for the majority of my illness. I was anxious about the confusing symptoms, the inability of my doctors to diagnosis what was wrong, my inability to convince some of the medical doctors I consulted that I was ill at all. I felt helpless and panicked about the unrelenting fatigue and the fact that for a number of years whatever I did just seemed to make it worse.

In hindsight, I can see that anxiety and panic were the two main factors perpetuating many of my symptoms such as dizziness, breathlessness, and visual disturbances. These, for me, were more disabling than the more physical symptoms such as fatigue and joint and muscle pain. I was anxious about my symptoms, the fact I didn't know what was causing them—all I knew is that if I did anything more than 10–15 minutes of physical or cognitive activity I would feel worse—my fears around the future, and my fears at being able to cope if I lost my financial support. I became frightened of life and my ability to cope with it. I'd also lost all trust in my body and its ability to be healthy.

I started using EFT on my fears around my symptoms. This helped reduce my anxiety level. As I worked through the emotional component of the issue, my symptoms began to subside. I worked on my future fears, related to "doing too much" or overdoing it. I did this by tapping on the emotional charge I felt around past times when I had engaged in a physical activity and felt worse afterward. I then moved onto what I feared would happen in the future and what impact it would have, again always tracing it back to the earliest event of when I had experienced each specific fear. This again helped with the anxiety I felt around trying something again in the future. Slowly, I found I was able to do more.

I am fully recovered and have been for around 7 years. EFT is the technique that ensured I fully overcame the condition.

* * *

CFS shares many symptoms in common with fibromyalgia. It's often difficult for even experienced physicians to make a differential diagnosis between them since they're so closely related. Not surprisingly, there are also many case histories in which sufferers or practitioners describe recovery from fibromyalgia. In this one, EFT practitioner Clay LaPorte tells of success with one of his clients.

"I'm Never Good Enough"—Addressing the Roots of Barbara's Fibromyalgia
By Clay LaPorte

When Barbara came to me for help she was in her late 50s and had been suffering with fibromyalgia for the past 6 years. Her pain intensity on the day of her session was only a 3 because she said the weather was in her favor (the right amount of humidity and air pressure). Maybe so, maybe not, but right then I decided to skip working on the fibromyalgia pain and go strictly for one of her core issues. Even though she had several easily definable ones that I could have worked on, I went with the earliest one, as we are taught in EFT.

From the age of 5, whatever Barbara did, it was not good enough for her mother. This is still true today. Barbara feels she is not good enough, no matter what she does. Even though I skipped working on the fibromyalgia symptoms, I did address the symptoms she was experiencing by just thinking about working on the "mom" issue. These were a tight throat, weak shaky hands, and weak shaky legs.

With several rounds of EFT, these decreased and finally ceased by the end of the session.

We worked on one specific incident when her mother told Barbara that she had done something terrible to Barbara's teddy bear collection. Here's what happened: They lived out in the country with very few neighbors. At age 5, Barbara did not have any friends that came to her house. So her collection of teddy bears became her beloved friends. One day, a woman came to visit her mother and brought her young daughter with her. Since Barbara never had friends come over, she did not understand the concept of sharing toys. When she refused to share, her mother decided to teach her a lesson. After their company left, she took Barbara aside and told her she had bagged up all her bears, took them outside, and set them on fire in their burn barrel. To Barbara, he mother had just "killed" her only friends. This had to be devastating to a 5-year-old. Then, after letting Barbara suffer for a few minutes, her mother told her she hadn't really burned her bears, and hoped that she had learned her lesson well.

We addressed all the aspects of this event, jumped around to a few other mom issues, and finally ended the session. But before we did, I followed the EFT advice to always, always test the results. About half-way through the session, I had Barbara say this statement out loud and asked how true it sounded: "My mother has never loved me the way I needed and wanted her to."

Here is where I believe the turning point, and core issue, came into play in the session. I say this because Barbara started sobbing. Obviously, she was at a 10. I immediately started tapping on all her hand points to pull her out of it. This took only about 30 seconds to do.

I retested the statement at the end of the session and she was fine. During the entire session, we never once worked on the fibromyalgia or its pain.

About a week later, Barbara called me and asked how long it takes for EFT to start working. My first thought was, "Oh no, it didn't work at all." So I asked what she meant by "start working." She explained that the next morning after our session, all of her fibromyalgia pain was gone, or maybe at a rating of 1, and has not returned. She was sleeping better, was able to work more, her nose was less runny, and her IBS (irritable bowel syndrome) was mostly gone.

What Barbara wanted to know was if this rapid cessation of physical symptoms was "normal." EFT had done it again! I told her everything was normal and to remember to tap at the first sign of any pain, which might return as the days went by, and not wait until the pain became intense.

Even if you don't have as dramatic a response to EFT as Barbara did, keep tapping. It is also "normal" for it to take a while to clear all the emotional trees in your forest.

* * *

When writing the book *EFT for Fibromyalgia and Chronic Fatigue* (Church, 2013b), I read many such stories. I was struck by how deeply fibromyalgia and chronic fatigue patients suffer. I was also struck by how misunderstood many of them feel. Family members and work colleagues are often impatient with them; they don't look sick on the outside, and the debilitating lack of energy they experience is often condemned as laziness or lack of willpower. Looking from the outside in, those who haven't been afflicted can't easily empathize with how devastating these diseases can be.

In the course of research for the book, I went on the website of the National Institutes of Health, which described fibromyalgia as "incurable" (NIH, 2009). The website of the Mayo Clinic, one of America's leading research hospitals, states that "there is no cure for fibromyalgia" (Mayo Clinic, 2013). Yet stories like Sarah's show that fibromyalgia and chronic fatigue can indeed be cured, at least for some sufferers. Again, Clay LaPorte's story is backed up by research. Dr. Gunilla Brattberg of Lund University in Sweden performed a randomized controlled trial of EFT for fibromyalgia (Brattberg, 2008). She found that those treated with EFT experienced significant improvements in pain, depression, and anxiety. They didn't even have to visit a doctor or psychotherapist. Dr. Brattberg's whole EFT program was delivered as an 8-week online course. We 've now built a program called FibroClear (www.FibroClear.com) that embodies the lessons of that study and of *EFT for Fibromyalgia and Chronic Fatigue* (Church, 2013b) in a powerful online course for fibromyalgia patients.

I've presented EFT workshops at many medical and psychology conferences and noticed that doctors usually take readily to EFT. They are very aware of the contribution that stress makes to physical disease and adopt EFT as an adjunctive technique when appropriate. I've had several doctors tell me that, after tapping, patient issues resolved without further need for conventional allopathic treatment. As Chuck Gebhardt, MD, observed in the following account after seeing swelling subside immediately after acupoint tapping, "Nothing in my traditional medical training in anatomy, physiology, or pathology even hinted at what I am now witnessing."

* * *

A Flu Shot Gone Wrong
By Chuck Gebhardt, MD

I am a traditionally trained American physician who has been using a somewhat modified version of EFT for about 6 months. As readers would expect, I have been seeing great success and tremendous value to my patients.

I will start with a story about a patient of mine. I will call him Bill and entitle the story: "A flu shot gone wrong." Before I get into the details, though, it might be helpful if I describe how I incorporate EFT into my practice. I specialize in internal medicine and I am one of six physicians in a private practice in southwest Georgia.

I typically treat my patients as I always have, but if they are experiencing acute discomfort during our visit, I will try to treat the discomfort with tapping or pressure on acupoints (if circumstances allow). Before I introduce this technique, though, I examine, diagnose, and treat all important problems, as I usually do, including their acute problems that

I am about to target with a new and unusual intervention after the traditional work is done. Now for the story.

Bill received a flu shot from my very able assistant with no initial problem. He is a 60-year-old gentleman whom I treat for hypertension and hypercholesterolemia. He is otherwise completely healthy, well balanced, and down to earth, with no psychological problems of any kind.

Early the next morning, he called and reported that within hours of the shot his left arm began to throb with pain and swell. He did not call earlier because he didn't want to bother us and he figured it would go away after he took some ibuprofen. The pain was severe enough that he didn't get much sleep that night and he was even worse when he finally decided to call. The swelling he described was dramatic enough that I became concerned about the possibility that it might compromise the blood flow or nerves supplying his left arm (technically termed a "compartment syndrome") so we asked him to come right in to be examined.

In my office, the area of swelling was the size of about a half of a hard-boiled egg (very dramatic indeed). It throbbed and hurt him so much he couldn't stand for his shirt sleeve to touch it. It was intensely red and very warm to touch. His temperature was 100.5 and he had beads of cold sweat on his forehead (called diaphoresis). He also now felt bad like he actually had the flu (this is called malaise).

Thankfully, his blood flow and neurological function was fine, along with his breathing and ability to swallow. His blood pressure was good, but his pulse was up a bit at 105 bpm. I diagnosed the obvious: an acute localized reaction to yesterday's flu shot that was acutely painful but not life threatening. I prescribed an antihistamine, pain medicine, and a steroid dose pack to be started immediately and instructed him to call us right away if he had any trouble breathing or felt like he might pass out.

As he was about to leave with his prescriptions in hand, I decided to tap on some of the meridians on his head, left shoulder, and left arm to see if I could relieve his discomfort somewhat until the medications would take effect. I used my usual bridge about "acupuncture without needles" and he responded, "Sure doc, anything that might help, I trust you."

Tapping on several spots seemed to help a little, but when I tapped on the inside of his left elbow at a spot that acupuncturists call L5 he said: "Wow! That is helping a lot." Over the next 30 seconds, while I continuously tapped on L5, the inflamed, swollen lump shrunk to about one 10th its initial size, the redness faded and it stopped hurting.

His low-grade temperature and diaphoresis resolved and his feeling of malaise was also gone. This response was jaw-dropping amazing for both me and for him. He even pounded on the previously exquisitely tender spot with his fist to show how well it now felt. His grin was ear to ear. When I saw him again about a month later, he said the pain and swelling never came back so he didn't see any need to fill the prescriptions I had written for him.

This was one of the most dramatic responses to acupoint stimulation I have witnessed, but it is only one of many I see on a daily basis in my practice. I think it is important to emphasize that Bill had never even heard of energy therapy or any similar technique and his only expectation before this response was that I thought my tapping might help with his pain.

Nothing in my traditional medical training in anatomy, physiology, or pathology even hinted at what I am now witnessing. As you know, anyone who watches these dramatic improvements knows immediately that our previous understanding of how our bodies and our minds work is in need of important revisions and redirected research. This is very exciting.

* * *

Dr. Gebhardt is one of many physicians using EFT for physical ailments. At one conference, a doctor came up to me, grasped my hands, and expressed his gratitude at training in EFT from me at that same conference 2 years earlier. He told me that at his clinic they now use EFT with every new patient during the intake process. This typically clears the emotional aspects of the presenting problem and, after that, the doctors can address what's left—the parts of the problem that are truly medical.

Online Delivery of EFT

By showing that EFT could be successfully delivered online, Dr. Brattberg offered fibromyalgia patients another breakthrough. Online programs can reach many more people at much lower cost than doctor and hospital visits. Inspired by her example, a group of volunteers then designed an online PTSD course for veterans and family members, called Battle Tap. It's available through the nonprofit organization the Veterans Stress Project (www.StressProject.org). This means that veterans who want to see a therapist in person can do so, and those that prefer online tapping can get immediate help through Battle Tap. The extension of EFT through online courses promises a series of breakthroughs for other mental health disorders as well.

EFT is very effective for all kinds of physical pain, not just fibromyalgia pain. The book *EFT for Back Pain* (Church, 2014b) contains dozens of stories written by people who used EFT for pain, with dramatic success. Here's one contributed by a newcomer to EFT.

Surprise at Quick Pain Relief
By Ruth Ruddock

I am one of the "newbies" who has been delightfully surprised at the success achieved using EFT with some of my friends. Recently, I was talking on the phone with a friend, Marilyn, and she mentioned having pain and stiffness in her knee and hip for quite some time. It had gotten to the point of creating great difficulty for her in getting out of bed in the mornings to the point of not being able to stand up straight. She found that she had to have something nearby to pull herself up out of chairs, because the pain and stiffness was getting so bad.

I suggested that we try EFT over the phone, and I told her that she would be my first attempt to use it with someone other than on myself. She agreed and we began to tap, after I explained the tapping points, etc.

She said that the pain and stiffness was at a 10 on her level of intensity scale. We did three tapping rounds and I told her to get up out of her chair. There was a pause and I heard her squealing on the other end of the phone. She said, "I can't believe this! I got right up from the chair, no pain and no stiffness."

So I asked her to walk around a little bit, and I could hear her continuing to laugh and exclaim, "Oh my goodness, I can't believe this!" She then said that she wanted to try this with her daughter, who has severe migraine headaches. I encouraged her to do that and let me know how it went.

For a first-time EFT experience, I was thrilled with the results we had over the phone! I have gone on to help others using this marvelous "tool," but will never forget that initial success!

* * *

Again, we don't rely only on stories to make the case for EFT's effectiveness for pain. Several studies quantify it. A randomized controlled trial performed at the Red Cross Hospital in Athens, Greece, found that headache pain was reduced significantly with EFT compared to a control group (Bougea et al., 2013). A study of 216 healthcare workers including nurses, psychotherapists, doctors, and chiropractors found that their physical pain was reduced by a startling 68% after about 30 minutes of EFT (Church & Brooks, 2010).

A randomized controlled trial of veterans who received EFT found that their pain dropped by 41%, even though they were being treated for PTSD, not for pain (Church, 2014e). The reductions in pain were simply a fortunate side effect of their PTSD treatment. When we talk about side effects, we aren't talking about the long list of warnings that might be printed on the side of a bottle of prescription drugs. With EFT, side effects are usually of the happy kind, such as improvements in skin tone, less conflict in marriages and family relationships, and increased fulfillment in the workplace.

Other research on EFT for physical symptoms includes a pilot study of psoriasis (Hodge & Jurgens, 2010). Psoriasis, a painful skin condition, is the most common autoimmune disease in the United States. As many as 7.5 million Americans suffer from it. The researchers found that after EFT, the psychological health of study participants improved by 50%, and on follow-up, their psoriasis symptoms improved by 75%. A case study found EFT to be effective for dyslexia (McCallion, 2012), and another for traumatic brain injury or TBI (Craig, Bach, Groesbeck, & Benor, 2009). A randomized controlled trial found reductions in TBI symptoms of 41% after six sessions of EFT for PTSD (Church & Palmer-Hoffman, 2013). Dr. Paul Swingle (2010) found EFT useful in the treatment of seizure disorders. There are also many accounts on EFT Universe of people who've used EFT for diabetes. Here's one of them.

EFT for Blood Sugar Levels
By Kate Flegal

Oh, my goodness! I just had the most amazing experience with EFT. I have type I diabetes (aka juvenile diabetes), and recently my blood sugars have been running very high, often close to 300 mg/dl, which is in the danger zone for things like diabetic ketoacidosis and long-term complications like blindness and kidney failure if the level stays elevated for long periods.

It finally occurred to me to try tapping for my blood sugar this morning. Guess what? My blood sugar is back down to 115—in the good range! I started out by saying, "Even though my blood sugar is high, I deeply and completely love, accept, and forgive myself." And then I did the full routine several times, focusing on the phrase "blood sugar." It probably took a total of 5 minutes, and it didn't take time away from my job; I tapped as I worked.

It's such a huge relief to have my blood sugar back to normal, and not just physically; the emotional toll of high blood sugar is big, too. It's hard not to feel like a failure when you can't keep your blood glucose in a good range. I'm confident that with EFT and healthy behavior, I can keep my blood sugars normal. Whew!

You can bet I'll keep using EFT for all of my life, which will be much longer and healthier now that I know how to use EFT to help control my diabetes!

* * *

Three Key Reasons for EFT's Efficacy

How is EFT able to make such dramatic and permanent changes, even for "incurable" conditions like type 1 diabetes and fibromyalgia, and in cases where people have tried other therapies without success?

There are three key reasons for EFT's efficacy, and they work hand in hand. One is that EFT reduces stress. The second is that EFT diminishes the intensity of emotional trauma. The third is that EFT modifies the way the brain processes emotional information. We'll look at each of these three mechanisms in turn.

When you think about an experience that produces negative emotion, such as a rivalry with a colleague at work, a fight with a family member, or a miserable childhood event, you increase stress. You have an emotional response to the experience. You feel emotions like anger, fear, shame, resentment, or guilt. When you use EFT, the intensity of those emotions diminishes, often to nothing, and often in just a few minutes.

This reduction in emotional intensity indicates that your stress level is going down. Stress involves your whole body, from your heart rate to your breathing to your blood pressure to your degree of muscle tension. Your body, brain, and emotions function as a whole. When you feel an emotional response, your body translates this into physical changes in circulation, respiration, digestion, and every other organ system.

This is also why EFT works with such a wide range of problems. Besides the mental health issues and physical symptoms covered earlier, people use EFT to improve their athletic performance, trade stocks and bonds, enhance their love lives, and deepen their spiritual practices. The reason that EFT is beneficial in so many life domains is that they're all affected by stress. A world-class athlete might have the skill to win a game, but if that skill is impeded by stress, the athlete's performance is compromised. A stock trader might be excellent at reading the stock market, but the emotions generated by manipulating large amounts of wealth can produce stress that degrades the trader's ability to make rational decisions.

As EFT reduces stress, all our other resources become available to us. When our emotions are calm and positive, even though our life circumstances may not have changed, then our bodies are no longer receiving those stress signals. As we become calm, our bodies respond by shifting all our systems to a relaxed state of functioning. That's why EFT works on such a wide variety of seemingly dissimilar problems. Stress usually plays some role in our problems, so I encourage you to try EFT in addition to your other strategies for solving them.

Our brains evolved to associate emotions with experiences. Your distant ancestors learned to associate the emotion of fear with tigers, wolves, and other predators. This helped them survive. Their brains created an emotional tag saying "danger" to attach to the image of a predator. You still have all that neural wiring in your brain even though you no longer face an environment full of dangers. It now works to your disadvantage, in the form of irrational fears and worries. Perhaps you had a bad experience with a schoolteacher with bushy eyebrows when you were 5 years old. You now have an unconscious fear of male authority figures, and whenever you have a job interview, you become so nervous that you make a fool of yourself. You don't know why, and you think that your reactions are normal, caused by the external world. They're actually just old neural tags in your brain.

Psychologists used to think that these strongly encoded memories were permanent, that "learnings formed in the presence of strong emotion" could not be changed, because "the brain threw away the key" (Ecker, Ticic, & Hulley, 2012, p. 3). However, recent research in a field called "memory reconsolidation" shows that there is a brief period just after a memory has been reawakened when its emotional content can be "untagged." The neurological wiring governing our old response can be rewired during this window. If such reconsolidation occurs, we may still have the memory, but it will no longer evoke a strong emotional response.

This is exactly what those who use Clinical EFT report. After tapping, they can still recall the traumatic life events that occurred, but those events are no longer associated with strong emotion. Before tapping, they report a high subjective units of distress (SUD) level. After tapping, recalling the same event, they report a low SUD score. When followed up weeks, months, or years later, their SUD levels when recalling the traumatic event are still low. Not only are they no longer emotionally triggered by the old event, they are also less troubled by all similar events that occurred in their lives. In this way, EFT appears to be permanently rewiring the neural network of those who use it. EFT may be more than psychology, working on the mind and emotions. Although we can't peer into the workings of the neural circuits of the brain, the experiences of practitioners and clients suggest that memory reconsolidation is taking place in the brain circuits that conduct the signals of trauma.

Learning the Basics Thoroughly

It's worth learning Clinical EFT thoroughly. One reason for the proliferation of websites with hundreds of versions of EFT is that newcomers try EFT and often have great results immediately. With only the most superficial knowledge of the method, they then believe they "know" EFT and might incorporate it into a coaching or psychotherapy practice. The creativity unlocked by EFT also quickly leads newcomers into introducing innovations to the method. Sometimes, not understanding the breadth of techniques encompassed by Clinical EFT, they fail to understand that an innovation that has just occurred to them has already been extensively developed by others in the practitioner community. They may make a trivial change to the method and then believe that they have invented a "better" form of EFT.

They're correct in their discovery that EFT produces great results quickly. But to get consistent results requires a thorough understanding of the approach. And to make progress with difficult issues and difficult clients requires knowledge of all of the 48 methods that comprise Clinical EFT. The basic acupoint tapping routine utilizes only six of these methods. Though your first experiences with EFT may make it seem beguilingly simple, unlocking its full power requires diving deeper.

My brother-in-law and his wife came to our home recently for a delightful visit. She's from Mexico City, and the last time we stayed at their house they served us carnitas, a Mexican delicacy. I decided to reciprocate for their visit. A Mexican chef friend who worked at a local gourmet catering company taught me how to make carnitas many years ago, so I knew the basics. After our visit to our in-laws, I was inspired to make the dish several times, recalling my dusty skills. When I knew they'd be visiting us in return, I made carnitas several times to practice.

The first night we ate together I served my creation. My in-laws were astonished. They declared they'd never had such extraordinary carnitas. They were further amazed that the dish was made not by a Mexican but a gringo! And even my inner critic had to admit that the dish had indeed turned out very, very well.

The reason for this success was that I'd practiced the basic recipe many times. After I'd become expert in making it reliably and consistently, I began to experiment. I tried ingredients imported from osso bucco, a similar Italian recipe. I used my knowledge of physics and chemistry to improve the consistency of the dish, cooking the meat evenly rather than from the outside in. When it came time to make carnitas for my in-laws, I could not only make an expert version of the basic recipe, I could improvise in ways that made it even better.

The same is true of any skill. You can improvise in ballet, but it's wise to learn the pirouette first. You can modify automobile engines to get better fuel economy and performance, but unless you first learn the basics of how they work, your uninformed hacking and sawing will make the engine perform worse not better. For the same reasons, it's worth learning EFT's Basic Recipe thoroughly, to the point where you can apply it expertly, before you start improvising. You'll usually get good results from the simple form of EFT, and phenomenal results from the full range of techniques encompassed in Clinical EFT.

Once you are so skilled that you're able to pull any one of the 48 techniques out of your toolkit at a moment's notice to deal with a particular problem, you are likely to find yourself innovating. At that point, you're building on a solid foundation of knowledge and practice, like my experiments in making carnitas. You'll find that you can accomplish far more with EFT than you could in the early stages of understanding. For superficial problems, superficial knowledge of EFT is usually effective. Once you go to deeper layers of the psyche and encounter intractable problems, you're going to need every one of those 48 tools.

Not a Panacea

EFT reduces the stress component of disorders, whether they're psychological disorders such as anxiety and depression, physical disorders such as pain and inflammation, or performance problems such as fear of public speaking. This indicates a wide range of problems with which EFT can help. EFT is not a panacea, however. It does not work on all conditions, and it is better with some than with others. While the 86% success rate in the PTSD study quoted previously is impressive, that still means that 14% of the veterans were not helped by EFT (Church et al., 2013). Why is that?

EFT works on the emotional component of traumatic memories, whether they're childhood memories or adult memories. But how do you work with events of which you or a client has no memory? This includes memories that are so traumatic that you've dissociated, or "forgotten" about them. It also includes events that happened so early in your childhood, perhaps at the age of 1 or 2, that they occurred prior to your brain developing the ability to record memories. Another example is birth trauma or womb trauma. EFT has some specialized techniques for use in these cases, but even expert practitioners often find them very difficult to address.

Another limitation of EFT is problems that are purely physical and that have no emotional component. There's usually some emotional component of even a purely physical issue such as a bone fracture. The person with the fracture might feel angry about the event that produced the fracture, dissatisfied with their hospital treatment, frustrated that their body is healing slowly, and a range of other emotions. Yet the fracture itself is a purely physical injury, and EFT is likely to be less effective than for a problem that is primarily emotional.

There are many more cases of failure than success in the use of EFT for tinnitus, for instance. Tinnitus is a ringing in the ears, often due to nerve damage associated with loud sounds. The physical stimulus of loud noise produces the physical phenomenon of damaged auditory nerves, and there may be little emotional component to the ailment. EFT practitioner and physician Dr. David Lake also says that addictions are very hard to treat successfully whether by EFT or any other method (Lake, 2013).

In *Soul Medicine,* a book I authored with Harvard-trained neurosurgeon Norman Shealy, MD, PhD, we caution against any therapy, conventional or alternative, that makes broad and sweeping claims of efficacy (Shealy & Church, 2008). This applies equally well to EFT. In fact, EFT practitioners may be at more risk of making over-enthusiastic and inflated claims than practitioners of other therapies. You'll probably have excellent results the very first time you try EFT, and the first few times you try EFT. These early successes can be beguiling. They can lead you to the erroneous belief that EFT will be equally effective for every person and every problem. This is simply not the case.

As you gain experience, you'll run up against intractable problems in your life and in the lives of your clients. Despite EFT and all your other skills, you won't be able to solve them. This is part of the human condition. Even though studies show excellent results from EFT in most cases, they never show 100% success with 100% of cases. It's wise to approach any healing event with humility and a sense of wonder. If healing occurs, we can be humbly grateful. It can stoke our sense of wonder at the preciousness of life and the miracle of healing itself. If healing does not occur, we can hold ourselves and others in love and compassion regardless of the result.

The Dark Side of EFT

A dark side of EFT involves the lure of the ego. When a moderately successful life coach or psychotherapist learns EFT, they suddenly find themselves witnessing breakthrough results in their clients. It's very tempting to attribute these breakthroughs to one's own skills and abilities rather than the therapeutic methods being used. The ego sees the improvements and crows, "It must be me! I'm a super-coach or a super-therapist! Look what I've done!" The history of EFT and other energy psychology techniques is full of examples of gifted individuals who've been swallowed alive by their egos.

It's important to realize that your success may be due to the method, not to your special gifts. Research shows that when EFT is offered by a variety of well-trained practitioners, they all achieve similar results (Palmer-Hoffman & Brooks, 2011; Church & Brooks, 2010). Those you help may be very grateful to you, compliment you, and believe you're special. It's wise to stay humble and attribute your results to the technique and to the mysterious grace of the healing process. It's also essential to request supervision from experienced practitioners when you're in doubt about a course of action, and to receive feedback from people who may disagree with you. These potential pitfalls and problems with EFT practice are the reason that ethics training is a requirement for becoming a certified practitioner.

How to Use This Book

The next chapter explains the science behind EFT. It will show you that the seemingly miraculous results you may observe are solidly grounded in scientific evidence. The following chapter describes EFT's

Basic Recipe, which takes you through all the steps involved in applying EFT. It's quick and easy to learn. Read those two chapters and start using EFT yourself. Then read the other chapters for more techniques and case histories. Interspersed are a few of the approximately 5,000 case histories available at EFT Universe. They will give you a sense of how practitioners, as well as newcomers, have used EFT for a wide variety of problems. These will give you a tiny glimpse of EFT's broad potential. By the time you finish this book, you'll have learned all 48 Clinical EFT techniques and be well equipped with the basics. At the end, you'll find some recommendations for the next steps you can take in furthering your healing process.

The Science
Behind EFT

When you first watch an EFT session, or use EFT yourself, you might be surprised at how fast things change. Sometimes the changes are so profound and quick they seem to be miraculous. It's taken many years for science to be able to explain these rapid changes, but fortunately, there's now a solid framework of evidence showing what's happening in the body and mind during the process. This chapter summarizes that evidence, and shows the life-changing potential emerging from EFT research.

How EFT Is Able to Address Such a Wide Variety of Problems

A 23-year-old woman volunteered for an EFT demonstration on the first day of an EFT Level 1 class. She had an open, childlike face, but there was an air of great sadness about her. She told the group that she had suffered from rheumatoid arthritis since she was a child. She had been treated in various ways, including hydrocortisone injections into her knees starting at the age of 2. The symptoms had abated somewhat by the time she was 18, but then returned in full force 3 years later. When asked in the class for the current location of the pain, she reported pain in three locations: her right ankle, her left knee, and her left elbow. She was asked to rate the intensity of the pain using a scale from 0 to 10, with 0 representing no pain, and 10 representing the greatest pain possible. The pain in her elbow was 3, her knee 8, and her ankle 5, and was always present, day and night.

I asked her what was happening in her emotional life around the age of 2, when the symptoms began. In a low, hesitant voice, she said that her mother and father often had fights. She began to cry uncontrollably. We began to do EFT for "the big fight" she had witnessed, for the raised voices of her parents, for the fear she felt when they fought, and for how unsafe she felt when growing up.

Her suffering was so evident that many people in the room began to cry. Yet after about 15 minutes of EFT tapping on various aspects of her parents fighting, she reported a reduction in pain to 1 in her elbow, 5 in her knee, and 3 in her ankle. On the second day of the class, she reported no pain in her elbow and her ankle, though there was still some pain in her knee. She said that she didn't feel it was safe to let go of all the pain yet, and she was encouraged to let it go at her own pace, and not force the process. That second day, her appearance had also changed noticeably. She smiled, and participated lightheartedly in the group, in contrast to the heavy sense of oppression she'd exhibited the day before.

Drug treatments for rheumatoid arthritis are described in the medical literature, but emotional treatments are not. The website of the legendary Mayo Clinic, one of the most influential hospital systems in the United States, begins its web page on the condition with the definitive statement: "Rheumatoid arthritis has no cure." (Mayo Clinic, 2013). How can EFT have an effect so quickly on a problem that has not been solved by all the technology available to modern medicine? How can it resolve a physical symptom, like the woman's arthritis, when the EFT session did not even target physical pain? In the case just described, EFT worked on only the emotional issue, yet when that reduced in intensity, the physical problem went away too.

The answer to this question that is so central to EFT can be found in the insights that science has gained in the past two decades into the way our brains and bodies work.

When you have a traumatic experience as a child, for example, a bully at school knocks you down and you hit your head on a hard surface, you form an unpleasant association in your mind between the event and the pain. Part of our brain has the job of keeping us safe and is constantly scanning the horizon for threats to our well-being. It compares cues from the environment we are in right now with the banks of previous unpleasant experiences stored in memory. When it finds a match, it alerts us to a potential problem. If the bully had light blue eyes and blond hair, you might feel uneasy in the presence of people with similar coloring, without knowing why, as the brain goes on high alert when the possibility of a threat comes within the range of your perception.

The Brain's Ability to Detect Threats

The part of the brain that deals with threats is called the *limbic system* or midbrain, because it is located between the frontal lobes, which are responsible for conscious thought, and the hindbrain, which handles routine tasks like food digestion and blood circulation. The limbic system encodes negative experiences with an emotional charge. In effect, it attaches an emotional tag to a class of memories, the way a shopkeeper might attach a red label to all the items on sale. The red tag distinguishes important items from unimportant ones. It draws special attention to any item with that color tag. Our attention is heightened whenever we see a red tag. These emotional tags are attached to certain memories by the limbic system to warn us of potential danger. So if as a child you had your hand bitten by a dog, you feel a surge of emotional intensity when you see another dog later on, as the limbic system does its job, comparing the new sensory input of a different dog with the negative tag of the pain associated with the previous experience of a dog.

This machinery is very appropriate for physical threats, keeping us away from heights, from poisonous animals and plants, and from other dangerous situations. For the human species, this threat-assessment machinery has worked brilliantly for millennia. When our ancestors saw a tiger in the jungle, they took appropriate action: fight or flight. The human fight-or-flight response kicks in very rapidly in response to a perceived threat, and gets the body ready for life-or-death action. Because survival is the most fundamental need of a species, there is nothing slow, restrained, or casual about the way our bodies respond. We have a set of genes called the immediate early genes or IEGs that click on the moment we perceive a threat (Rossi, 2002). These genes contain the genetic code for stress hormones such as cortisol and adrenaline (also known as epinephrine).

Our adrenal glands pump out large quantities of these hormones *less than 3 seconds* after we recognize a threat; that's how quickly the IEGs are turned on. Stimuli that affect genes are called "epigenetic" signals; they signal the body to turn the appropriate genes on or off. The hormonal part of the stress-response system is referred to in traditional biology textbooks as the HPA axis, short for hypothalamus-pituitary-adrenal axis. These three organs are central to the function of the endocrine system of ductless glands that produce hormones. The stress response is triggered by the hypothalamus, part of the limbic system that recognizes stimuli that have red "high-emotion" tags attached to them. The hypothalamus passes that message to the pituitary, using "messenger molecules," molecules that signal other parts of the body to perform specific functions. The pituitary, sometimes called the "master endocrine gland," then signals other glands such as the adrenal glands.

A surge of adrenaline rapidly flows through the body. Our hearts race, signaled by histamine molecules. The blood vessels in our digestive tract, reproductive system, and all nonessential systems constrict, forcing blood to flow out to our peripheral muscles, making them ready for action. Our immune system shuts down, and the process of cell regeneration (facilitated by cortisol's hormonal cousin, called DHEA or dehydroepiandrosterone) comes to a halt.

Our liver dumps glucose sugar into our bloodstream, so that our cells will have an abundant supply of energy. Our pupils dilate, and blood drains out of the frontal lobes of our brains, because we don't need the ability to perform calculus when there's a tiger in the vicinity; we need to be able to see well and to run fast.

Our nervous system goes into overdrive, dominated by the part called the *sympathetic nervous system,* which handles emergencies. All our physiological resources are redeployed to meet the threat. It is this rapid response that allowed our ancestors to survive; those with slow fight-or-flight reflexes were the ones that were eaten, while those with fast reflexes lived to breed, and produce us. So we're the pinnacle of 570 million years spent perfecting this lightning-fast fight-or-flight response.

The problem is that modern adult human beings live in a world with very few threats to their physical survival. When was the last time you saw a tiger? This whole magnificent threat-assessment machinery sits at the core of our brains, always turned on, but with few actual objective physical threats to act on. So it occupies itself with imaginary ones: fears, worries, anxieties, resentments, projections, imaginings. When you think of an imaginary tiger, your body responds with a fight-or-flight response, much as though there were a real tiger in the room.

Brain Waves: Beta, Alpha, Theta, and Delta

The line between reality and imagination is even blurrier for children, especially those under the age of 6. The predominant brain waves at that age are slow rhythms, called delta and theta waves (Lipton, 2008). In adults, these brain waves are associated with the subconscious, with superlearning, with hypnosis, with trance, with energy healing, with profound creativity, and with sleep and dreaming (Fehmi & Robbins, 2010; Wise, 2002).

The brain waves associated with conscious deliberative thought processes, alpha and beta, don't start to predominate in the human brain till after the age of 6. Before then, we're in a mental state in which reality and imagination blend freely. We're in something like a hypnotic trance that facilitates superlearning. Think about children who have an imaginary friend, estimated to be about 65% of all children, for an example of the way fact and fancy blend freely in a child's mind. Think about the stories children tell, in which they mix fantasy and actual events, with little apparent ability to distinguish the difference, or interest in doing so. Think about how easily they can invent games of "Let's pretend."

This superlearning trance was fantastically useful to primal human children. In the first few years of life, they absorbed astonishingly large amount of information. This information included languages, social cues, survival behaviors, and tribal rituals. All these helped them to survive. They went from helpless infants, unable to even walk, to seasoned evolutionary competitors in just a few years. By the age of 5, a Paleolothic child might learn more skills than had accrued in the entire evolutionary history of another intelligent species like dogs. The child would have learned to communicate complex concepts to others through language, to anticipate the weather, to plant seeds and harvest crops, to make fire, to store food against emergencies, to barter, and a thousand other behaviors that aid in survival. The superlearning trance of human children gave our species an evolutionary edge.

Yet there's a dark side to the picture. Traumatic life experiences at that age can be experienced by children as threats to their survival. If Mommy is a raging angry person and Daddy is a crazy alcoholic, and they often scream at each other, the child frequently has the fight-or-flight machinery of the sympathetic nervous system activated. A child does not have the cognitive ability yet (those alpha and beta brain waves) to assess the threat consciously and say, "Well, Mommy might be yelling, but she probably is not actually going to kill me."

The child's cortisol rises, IEGs snap into action, and the sympathetic nervous system goes on high alert. A little boy may run and hide, a manifestation of flight, when a parent is raging. That memory is encoded in his limbic system. Now that same person is 40 years old, but when confronted by a similar situation, the limbic system automatically looks for a similar red tag. When a boss or spouse is yelling, it says, "Aha, this sounds like Mom, so I better hide." The man might fall silent, or withdraw emotionally.

How many men do you know who withdraw emotionally when a woman gets upset? The woman might then get more upset at the lack of emotional contact, which then prompts the man to withdraw further, in a dysfunctional relationship dance. In this way, neurological and hormonal responses that evolution gave us, that were perfectly adapted to life on the savannah 100,000 years ago, cause great grief and misery to us today. These traumas are stored in the brain and the body, sabotaging our happiness, and setting us up for misery in a world in which the tigers in our minds far outnumber the ones in the zoos.

Exposure, Cognitive Change, and Conditioned Responses

EFT works very simply and scientifically. It has us face and remember a negative emotional experience, a method referred to in psychology as "exposure." We then pair that remembered trauma with a new cognitive input, reframing the memory with a statement of self-acceptance: "I deeply and completely accept myself." While we hold these two items in mind, the traumatic exposure and the cognitive reframe, EFT then has us tap on our bodies. The tapping points used in EFT correspond to points used in acupuncture, and they release stress.

Tapping also soothes the body, introducing a non-traumatic physical stimulus, and interrupting the emotional triggering we've created through the traumatic memory. This pairing of a troublesome memory with a soothing physical stimulus often breaks the power of that memory, reducing its emotional intensity. In the language of behavioral psychology, we had a *conditioned response* of upset (a red tag) encoded to correspond to that memory. By thinking of the memory often and getting upset, we've established a strongly *conditioned feedback loop*.

Tapping signals the body that we're safe, and so the conditioned loop is broken. Afterward, the nervous system no longer associates the memory with stress. The speed with which EFT can drain the emotional intensity of even long-held memories is quite startling to people who have not witnessed it before.

One example occurred in front of a large psychology conference at which I was giving a keynote address. A 45-year-old therapist volunteered for an EFT session. She had pain in her neck and was unable to turn her head to the right. She said she had suffered from this condition since she was 9 years old, after being involved in a car accident. The car was being driven by her older sister, who was not yet of legal driving age. The woman described how she had worked on this problem for years, using all her psychotherapy skills, but with only limited success.

She did EFT as she described the minutes before the car crash, the crash itself, and the aftermath. After the crash, she and her sister were taken to the nearest house, where she sat, blood streaming down her face from a scalp wound, waiting for her aunt to collect her. She described the fear she felt waiting for her aunt, and the moment just before the crash, when she realized that their car was going to collide with an oncoming car. Even though she worked on all those aspects and several others, her pain did not subside, however, and her neck showed no improvement.

Suddenly, she gasped and said, "I've just remembered a detail I'd forgotten. I always knew my sister was driving illegally because she was underage. But I just recalled that, that day, *I dared her* to drive the car." She was flooded by a sense of guilt for her part in causing the accident, and she then used EFT on those feelings. When we checked in on her neck pain, it was down to a 0. And she turned her head all the way to the right, the first time she had been able to do so since the accident.

Notice how this therapist used exposure, remembering all the details of the accident, and how new cognitive awareness (her daring her sister) opened up, allowing her to find peace and self-acceptance. There are hundreds of stories in the EFT archive in which people report similar results (www.EFTUniverse.com).

Even when the feedback loop of pain or emotional trauma has been reinforced for years, EFT is often able to break it very quickly. When this happens, the neural bundles that have been transmitting the pain and muscle limitation messages appear to be deactivated, and the brain's threat-assessment machinery calms down. When people are hooked up to an EEG (electroencephalogram) machine, and then asked to recall a traumatic memory, the brain waves associated with the fear response are activated. When they do the kind of acupoint tapping used in EFT, their brain state changes to one of calm.

When they are then asked to remember the traumatic incident months later, while again hooked up to an EEG machine, their brain waves still remain calm. Measuring the brain's electromagnetic energy field with an EEG gives us a fascinating picture of what's happening to the brain under stress. There are several studies which use EEG to measure these changes in brain waves (see Swingle, 2010; Lambrou, Pratt, & Chevalier, 2003; Swingle, Pulos & Swingle, 2004; Diepold & Goldstein, 2008).

Electromagnetic Energy and Acupoints

In the 18th and 19th centuries, inquiring scientists began to invent instruments capable of detecting these electromagnetic fields (Shealy & Church, 2013). In 1903, a Dutch physician named Willem Einthoven measured the field of the human heart, which has the strongest electromagnetic field of any organ; and in 1924, he received the Nobel Prize for his work. In 1929, Hans Berger measured the electromagnetic field of the brain, and progressive refinements in instrumentation mean that today the electrical and magnetic fields of even single cells can be measured. Using the body's energy fields for diagnosis and treatment has led to such medical advances as the MRI (magnetic resonance imaging), ECG (electrocardiogram), and MEG (magnetoencephalogram). Electromagnetic fields are also used to treat many conditions. PEMS (pulsed electromagnetic stimulation) machines have been used with great success for depression, as well as physical symptoms ranging from migraine headaches to Parkinson's tremors.

The use of energy fields in medicine has been accompanied by great controversy. In the period between Einthoven's discovery and his Nobel Prize, the influential Flexner Report was published in 1910 in the United States. This report became the basis of the medical system we have today. It rejected approaches other than allopathic medicine, such as homeopathy. It condemned electromagnetism in medicine as "irregular science." Yet the evidence of the importance of energy fields in human biology continued to grow, from experiments conducted by Russian scientist Alexander Gurwitsch in the 1920s showing that light energy is emitted by living organisms, to studies by Robert Becker in the 1960s demonstrating that microcurrents can stimulate the healing of bone fractures, to the 1992 discovery of magnetic magnetite crystals in brain cells in the human limbic system (Oschman, 2003).

The observation that some kind of energy is involved in biological processes is not new. Chinese acupuncture diagrams dating from around 2,500 years ago show the energy flows that the doctors of that time used as a guide for inserting needles. Fast forward to today; several recent studies have shown that the stimulation of acupoints (acupuncture points) sends signals to the brain, espcially the limic system and other structures involved in the fear response (Hui et al., 2005; Fang et al., 2009; Napadow et al., 2007). Various scientific bodies, from the WHO (World Health Organization) to America's NIH (National Institutes of Health), have compiled a growing list of physical symptoms for which acupuncture has shown itself to be effective. Energy is central to healing, whether it is the electromagnetic energy flows mapped by the fMRI (functional MRI) and EEG machines prevalent in Western medicine today, or the acupoint meridians used for healing by the ancient physicians of Eastern medicine.

This body of knowledge is pertinent to EFT. The stimulation of acupoints has been shown in MRI studies to regulate the fear response in the brain. EFT studies performed over the last decade have shown that EFT relieves stress in its many manifestations, psychological and physical (reviewed by Feinstein, 2012). These studies have begun to identify conditions that EFT is best able to treat, and also the underlying physiological mechanisms at work in such rapid healing. As medical costs in Western countries soar, governments and organizations are increasingly insisting on "evidence-based" practices, treatments that can demonstrate convincingly that they work. EFT has established an impressive base of research results for a number of mental health problems such as PTSD, anxiety, phobias, and depression, as well as showing promise for physical conditions such as pain, cravings, obesity, traumatic brain injury (TBI) and fibromyalgia.

Evidence-Based Practice

Before we describe the essentials of how to do EFT yourself, here's a quick tour of the scientific evidence showing that EFT works. The studies outlined here were published in peer-reviewed journals. When a psychology or medical journal is described as "peer-reviewed," it means that it uses a committee of reviewers, usually doctors, statisticians, and psychologists, to scrutinize every word and number in a study before publication, and point out any weaknesses or errors, to ensure that only high-quality research is published.

We're summarizing this research here in *The EFT Manual* so that you have a sense of how grounded EFT is in good science, and so that, as you go forward with your exploration of EFT, you can do so with the confidence that rigorous, evidence-based methods have been used to establish the validity of EFT. For a more complete picture, including the abstracts of each study, full copies of many of them, and updates as new research is published, you can visit www.Research.EFTUniverse. com.

The first study of EFT published in a peer-reviewed journal was done by a research team led by Steve Wells, an Australian psychotherapist (Wells, Polglase, Andrews, Carrington, & Baker, 2003). It was a randomized controlled trial (RCT) of people with phobias. RCTs are regarded as the Gold Standard of research, because they control for all of the factors that can skew the results of a study and provide misleading results. Wells and his colleagues identified people with high phobic responses to small creatures such as bats, spiders, and snakes. They tested the aversion of study participants with a behavioral approach test (BAT), which measured how close to the feared creature the subject was capable of walking. They also used other measures of phobic response. To control for the placebo effect, the second group received an intervention known to be effective on anxiety, called diaphragmatic breathing (DB). The researchers found that after half an hour of treatment, the EFT group could walk much closer to the feared small creature than those in the DB group. When they retested some of the subjects 3 to 6 months later, most of the improvement had been maintained.

The Wells study was later replicated by psychology professor Dr. Harvey Baker of Queens University in New York, and his colleague Linda Siegel, who introduced additional rigor into the measurements by testing the degree of expectancy participants had that the treatment would help them (Baker & Siegel, 2010). Both groups in the Baker and Siegel study had the same degree of expectancy, so the results of the Wells study could not be explained by the placebo effect. The Wells study was also replicated by Maria Salas, Jack Rowe, PhD, and Audrey Brooks, PhD, of the University of Arizona at Tucson (Salas, Brooks, & Rowe, 2011). In this second replication, other phobias such as fear of heights were also tested, showing that the effects of EFT in reducing phobias aren't limited just to the fear of small living creatures.

While studies are important, replications are equally so. Until an independent research team has confirmed the findings of the first study, there is always a possibility of error. That's why the APA standards require two RCTs.

Several randomized controlled trials of EFT for PTSD have been conducted. One of these was conducted by a research team that I was privileged to lead (Church et al., 2013). The investigators included therapist Crystal Hawk; Audrey Brooks; Olli Toukolehto, MD, of Walter Reed Army Medical Center; Phyllis Stein, PhD, of the University of Washington Medical School; and Maria Wren of the Veterans Administration Newington Connecticut campus.

In this study, 59 war veterans were randomized into either an EFT group or a wait list. The wait list group received treatment as usual from their primary care provider (usually a VA hospital) while the other group received treatment as usual plus EFT. The EFT intervention took the form of six sessions delivered by life coaches or therapists who helped the veterans tap on their combat memories. While the wait list group did not improve over time, the PTSD symptoms of the EFT group plunged drastically, by 64%.

This study was designed based on the findings of an earlier pilot study, which also used six sessions, and found that EFT was very effective at lowering PTSD symptoms in veterans (Church, Geronilla, & Dinter, 2009). A third study of EFT for PTSD followed a group of veterans and their family members who went through a 5-day EFT intensive (Church, 2010b). Their PTSD levels also declined precipitously; one said afterward, "I got my life back again." Their experience is the subject of a documentary film, *Operation Emotional Freedom.* An independent research team at a hospital in Britain's National Health Service (NHS) also evaluated EFT for PTSD (Karatzias et al., 2011). They compared EFT to EMDR (Eye Movement Desensitization and Reprocessing), another effective treatment for PTSD. They found that both therapies were effective in four sessions. Another research team compared EFT to cognitive behavior therapy (CBT) in a group of female trauma survivors in the Congo (Nemiro, 2013). They found EFT to be as effective as CBT.

There are many moving stories of veterans who've been helped by EFT in the book *EFT for PTSD* (Church, 2014d), as well as insights from those who've helped them heal. Here's a story about "Don," a 61-year-old Vietnam veteran who has been diagnosed with Parkinson's disease. He and his EFT practitioner, who tells the story, worked together for a total of six EFT session hours, as part of the National Institute for Integrative Healthcare study of veterans with PTSD.

Lifting the Weight of PTSD
By Ingrid Dinter

Since returning from Vietnam, "Don" did not have one night of uninterrupted sleep. He usually went to bed between 9:30 p.m. and 10:30 p.m., and got up between 8:15 a.m. and 10:00 a.m., feeling fatigued. In this 10–12 hour time period that he spent in bed, he was woken up by horrific nightmares at least twice per night. He never slept more than 1–2 hours at a stretch, and never more than 4–5 hours total—for 40 years…

Our first session took only 20 minutes, as this was all that Don could handle that day. Before we started with EFT, he said his thoughts were like bumper cars, bouncing all over, but the tapping helped him relax and release the tension in his mind. It also stopped the tremors and shaking that are symptoms of Parkinson's disease. We tapped on finding peace with the war and peace with Vietnam. After this brief session, his sleep already greatly improved: He now slept 6–7 hours, woke up twice briefly, and felt rested instead of fatigued.

In our second session we worked through the traumatic memory of having shot someone's arm off 2 weeks before he returned home from Vietnam. His sadness and guilt for the Vietnam soldier was overwhelming and had followed him for 40 years. The Vietnamese had raised his weapon in front of him, and Don wasn't sure if he wanted to give up or shoot at him, so he shot first. This happened 2 weeks before he was supposed to return home. We released the sadness and guilt using the gentle EFT techniques: Tearless Trauma, Sneaking Up on the Problem, and the Movie Technique, and tapped on deserving forgiveness.

In his e-mail the morning after the session, Don reported: "Sleep is improving, no nightmares last night. My overall energy has been on an upswing. My hands still shake, but not as much, I've been tapping on the shakes and it seems to help. I think what we've worked on is quite amazing."

The third session dealt with a very traumatic event. His best friend, who usually walked to the left of Don, this time took his right side while scanning the jungle. When he got shot, Don felt that his friend had caught the bullet for him and never forgave himself for this. It didn't matter that he received a bronze star for the dangerous rescue efforts that he made to save his friend's life, Don felt that this was undeserved as he couldn't save him, and after all these years still cried about the loss and guilt. The images of turning his friend, whom he loved like a brother, over, and seeing his head exploded, haunted him daily.

After using EFT on this memory, he realized that if he had caught the bullet, and his friend survived, he would have forgotten and released him a long time ago. He would never expect or want him to feel the way he felt himself. This realization allowed him to finally find peace, love, and forgiveness.

In his e-mail he wrote: "Thank you for today's session, I feel much more at ease. I slept for 2 full hours after the session, a fairly sound sleep, I couldn't believe that it was for 2 hours, it seemed like only minutes. Thank you again for all your help."

Two days later, Don had an intense dream relating to the death of his father, who had killed himself while driving drunk when Don was 18. So we worked through his trauma, releasing pain and guilt he had carried for more than four decades.

Sleep: By now, he was going to bed between 9:45 and 10:15, sleeping 7–8 hours, waking up briefly once or twice in between, but no more nightmares. He just rolled over, and went back to sleep. He woke up fairly refreshed between 7:30 and 8:15 a.m. What an improvement for someone who had usually two serious nightmares each night and never got more than 4–5 hours!

In our fifth tapping session 3 days later, Don talked a lot about the improvements in his sleep and overall well-being. Then we tapped for the stress and feelings of lack of control resulting from the construction of his new home and people not doing what they were supposed to do. No more war memories came up for him! Reviewing his progress 2 weeks later, Don said, "I still think about Vietnam but it doesn't seem to bother me."

After 60 days, we did another session, and one more war memory came up: He had to identify comrades that had been killed and found in the jungle several days earlier. After tapping on all the aspects of what he saw and smelled and the disgust and nausea that he felt, he took a deep breath and stated: "Now the bad spirits are gone." He had felt as if these dead men had always been with him, somehow, weighing him down and taking his breath away. Now he reported that he felt as if a huge weight had been lifted off him, and he could breathe and think clearly.

Don's voice has a very different sound now. It is clearer, lighter, and faster. There is less roughness and he laughs more. It is truly nice to hear the hope and confidence in his voice. His sleep has improved from getting 4–5 hours per night in a 10-hour time period, interrupted by an average of two nightmares, to getting an average of 7–8 hours with no nightmares, waking up refreshed.

Between the first session and his 30- and 60-day follow-ups, Don's scores for depression, anxiety, hostility, and other psychological issues dropped gradually from 122 to 77. His PTSD score dropped from 65 to 34 after session 5, and remained there through the 30- and 60-day follow-ups.

He continues to tap on his Parkinson's symptoms to keep the shaking under control. His wife has noticed that he seems happier and relaxed. He feels comfortable socializing now, and is a true believer in EFT.

* * *

EFT can be effective for PTSD in other groups of people too. A study of EFT was undertaken with adolescent boys (Church, Piña, Reategui, & Brooks, 2012). The participants were residents in a group home to which they had been sent by a judge because they were being abused at home. One group received a single session of EFT in which they tapped on their most painful childhood memories, while those randomized into the control group did not receive treatment. When they were followed up a month later, the boys who'd received EFT reported 91% less emotional triggering, and they had all normalized on the Impact of Event Scale (IES; Horowitz, Wilner, & Alvarez, 1979), the questionnaire used to assess traumatic memories.

EFT has also been studied for its value in overcoming anxiety. In a trial comparing EFT and WHEE (another form of energy psychology) to cognitive behavior therapy (CBT) for test anxiety in college students, both EFT and WHEE were found to work much faster than CBT (Benor, Ledger, Toussaint, Hett, & Zaccaro, 2009). Another study randomized high school students into either an EFT or a second group that received progressive muscular relaxation, which is effective in alleviating anxiety (Sezgin & Özcan, 2009). The group that received EFT had a much greater drop, with test anxiety reducing by 37%. EFT has also been studied in a randomized controlled trial for its effect on public speaking anxiety; participants overcame their fears and, compared to a control group, reported increased confidence after EFT (Jones, Thornton, & Andrews, 2011).

One of the most intriguing studies of EFT was done by Gunilla Brattberg, MD, a professor at Lund University in Sweden (Brattberg, 2008). She studied patients afflicted with the painful and debilitating symptoms of fibromyalgia, but their whole course of EFT treatment occurred online! They enrolled in an 8-week Internet course, and used EFT on themselves, after which they reported a 29% improvement in depressive symptoms, as well as a 22% drop in pain. As you read *The EFT Manual* and visit the EFT website, remember the fibromyalgia study. Even tapping along with an online course can help, and during EFT training you will learn a technique called "Borrowing Benefits," in which you'll find that just watching other people do EFT onscreen, or onstage, while tapping along yourself at the same time can make a difference.

Another study at the University of Santo Tomas in Manila, the Philippines, took a group of adolescent college students with moderate to severe depression and gave them four 90-minute group EFT classes (Church, de Asis, & Brooks, 2012). Their depressive symptoms dropped an astonishing 72%. The study of the 59 war veterans discussed previously found that as their PTSD decreased, their anxiety, depression, and pain reduced significantly as well (Church et al., 2013).

People in pain have also improved in several other EFT studies. These are open trials, in which the participants' symptoms are compared before and after treatment. There is no control group, so open trials are regarded as a lower standard of proof than RCTs. For instance, pain levels would be measured in the same subjects before and after EFT, but without a placebo group or wait list to control against. Nonetheless, open trials provide us with valuable information; a person who has a big reduction in pain is not too worried about the fact that his or her pain (or depression or anxiety) is only being compared to how painful the injury was before treatment.

One study examined the effects of Borrowing Benefits EFT in a group of 216 health care workers (Church & Brooks, 2010). These were doctors, nurses, chiropractors, psychologists, alternative medicine practitioners, and those in similar professions. It found that their anxiety and depression improved significantly after a workshop in which they did Borrowing Benefits for 2 hours. Their pain dropped by 68%, and their cravings for such addictive substances as chocolate, alcohol, drugs, cigarettes, and coffee dropped by 83%. When they were followed up 3 months later, most of their improvements had remained stable, and those that had used EFT more frequently since the workshop had greater improvement than those who did not.

This study, performed by Audrey Brooks and myself, was modeled on the first open trial, which was conducted on the participants at an EFT workshop by Jack Rowe, PhD, who was then a professor at Texas A&M University (Rowe, 2005). He carefully measured psychological problems like anxiety and depression in 102 participants before and after the workshop, as well as at two follow-up points. He found that across the whole range of psychological problems, participants improved.

Together, these studies refute one of the early criticisms of EFT. Critics maintained that while EFT might work when Gary Craig delivered it, the results were due to some unique gift that only he possessed. In the Borrowing Benefits studies, however, no statistically significant difference was found between the people that received EFT from me and those receiving it from Gary Craig. In a follow-up study, no difference in results was found betwen various EFT expert practitioners, indicating that the results were due to Clinical EFT itself and not some individual's peculiar talent (Palmer-Hoffman & Brooks, 2011).

A pilot study examined Borrowing Benefits in a group of 38 self-identified addicts, and also found that the breadth and depth of their psychological problems improved significantly (Church & Brooks, 2013). In all these studies, the benefits were consistent regardless of which trained EFT practitioner led the workshop, further demonstrating that it was EFT creating the psychological improvements, and not a particular instructor.

Another devastating condition with which EFT might help is traumatic brain injury (TBI). An estimated 100,000 U.S. veterans who served in Iraq or Afghanistan are thought to have TBI. Symptoms such as dizziness, balance problems, and severe headaches are characteristic of TBI. The research team studying PTSD in veterans was not expecting to find a change in TBI but was merely collecting data on the severity of the TBI symptoms that accompany PTSD. To their surprise, as PTSD reduced after six sessions of EFT, the average reduction in TBI symptoms was 41% (Church & Palmer-Hoffman, 2014). EFT has been used for a number of serious diseases, and a common experience is that, when the emotional roots of a problem are addressed, the physical symptoms can lessen or even disappear completely.

EFT has also shown itself to be helpful with weight loss. In an RCT conducted by Peta Stapleton and her colleagues at Griffith University in Australia, subjects showed a significant reduction in food cravings, just like the health care workers in the open trial (Stapleton, Sheldon, & Porter, 2012). Over the following year, this led to their losing an average of 11.1 pounds. Weight loss after a program ends is rare; the average dieter regains all or part of the weight (Curioni & Lourenco, 2005). This is infrequent with EFT; a study of an online EFT program found that participants lost an addition 3 pounds in the 6 months after the program ended (Church & Wilde, 2013).The lessons learned in this study and similar programs are summarized in the book *EFT for Weight Loss* (Church, 2013d).

EFT and Performance

EFT isn't just for sick people; it can help healthy people too. In a study of elite athletes, a 15-minute EFT treatment clearing out the athletes' anxieties worked wonders on their sports performance (Church, 2008). This RCT was organized by EFT sports coach Greg Warburton, and took place at Oregon State University, with Greg and I testing the men's and women's basketball teams. After testing the athletes for the number of free throws they could successfully score, and how high they could jump, one group got EFT, while the other got a placebo treatment. Afterward, the EFT group performed 38% better at free throws than the control group. Pat Ahearne, Australian League Pitcher of the Year, says, "I am so amazed with the effectiveness of EFT that I've made it as important a part of my baseball routine as throwing or running or lifting weights. I have more consistency, better command of my pitches, and I accomplish more in big games with less effort. Using EFT, I found the mental edge that raises an athlete from average to elite." Seth Joyner, former Arizona Cardinals linebacker, said, "Golf is a game of how you react mentally. One bad shot or hole can ruin a round. EFT has improved how I think on the course, my calmness and my concentration." As the Oregon State basketball players showed, EFT can help even peak performers improve their results. Using EFT in this way is described in the book *EFT for Sports Performance* (Howard, 2014).

One other question that researchers ask about EFT or any other treatment is, "Do the results hold over time?" In all the studies of EFT that included a follow-up, at least some of the gains that participants had experienced after treatment remained steady (Feinstein, 2012). In some studies, such as the PTSD veterans study, 86% of veterans were still below the clinical PTSD threshold after 6 months; in another study, the veterans had maintained their gains even after a year.

Mechanisms of Action

These studies, whether they're open trials or RCTs, are a type of research called "outcome studies" because they study the outcome of an intervention. They answer the research question, "What happened as the outcome of treatment?" Another kind of scientific inquiry asks, *"How and why* did that happen? *What occurred in the body* to produce that outcome?" These studies, which look "under the hood" to find out how the engine works, usually take place years or even decades later than outcome studies. A new treatment such as EFT is typically discovered in practice, then has its effects measured in outcome studies, and finally has the "how and why" questions answered later on.

A number of scientific papers have been published in peer-reviewed journals that describe what happens in the body's nervous system, hormonal system, and genes in order to produce such rapid and dramatic change (reviewed by Feinstein, 2012). They show, among other findings, that *pressure* on acupoints is as effective as the insertion of acupuncture needles, that acupuncture sends fear-dampening signals directly to the limbic system, and that acupoint stimulation is an effective treatment for PTSD, depression, anxiety, pain, and other ailments. You'll find an updated research bibliography listing all these articles at www.Research.EFTUniverse.com.

With some colleagues and a large group of dedicated EFT volunteers, I designed a study that peered into the body's biochemistry (Church, Yount, & Brooks, 2012). We compared a group that received a session of EFT coaching against a second group that received a conventional talk therapy session. The study compared both to a third group randomized into getting no treatment at all, but just resting quietly in the waiting room of a clinic. Besides testing their levels of anxiety, depression, and other psychological problems, this RCT also measured subjects' levels of the signature stress hormone cortisol. When you and I are in fight-or-flight mode, and feeling stressed, our bodies produce more cortisol, and when we relax, our cortisol levels start to drop. Cortisol is also regarded as the main aging hormone, and the main weight gain hormone. When people are under prolonged stress, they make more cortisol, and their cells age and die more quickly. They also deposit more fat around the waistline, as all that blood glucose mobilized for the fight-or-flight response is stored in the fat cells around the liver.

Our research team reasoned that if psychological symptoms such as anxiety and depression were dropping, cortisol should be dropping as well. So we measured cortisol just before the participants began their treatment sessions, and again half an hour after they finished. By that time, the psychological relief of therapy might be measured in the form of lower cortisol.

We found that cortisol did indeed drop in all three groups, but the surprise was just how much more it dropped in the EFT group. The participants who received talk therapy had a 14% reduction in cortisol, and those just sitting quietly in a healing environment had a similar drop. Those who received an EFT session dropped even further, with cortisol falling by 24%. Symptoms of depression, anxiety, and other psychological problems dropped more than twice as much in the EFT group as in the other two groups. A significant correlation was found between reductions in mental health symptoms and cortisol; the two were linked.

Cortisol also correlates with changes in those rapid-fire IEG stress genes and the sympathetic nervous system, which means that after EFT, the whole stress response in the body got the message to "stand down" and restore function to the immune system and all the other systems from which our physiological resources are drained when we're under stress.

Counterconditioning

The word "stress" was coined by the German physician Hans Selye in the 1920s. He noticed that many symptoms were common to most of the patients in the hospitals he visited, and he used the term "stress" for this collection of dysfunctions. His Russian contemporary Ivan Pavlov became famous for his demonstrations of the conditioned response. Pavlov would feed dogs when a bell rang. Later, when the bell was rung without food being present, the dogs salivated anyway. They had learned to associate the sound of a bell with food, and the association produced the physiological response of salivation even when no food was present. In the language of behavioral psychology, the dogs had been taught a "conditioned response." American behavioral psychologist B. F. Skinner realized that these large behaviors could be broken down into small elements.

Meanwhile, in the 1950s, South African psychiatrist Joseph Wolpe experimented with "counterconditioning" in which a traumatic memory would be paired with an innocuous stimulus, leading to a gradual reduction in trauma. He called this "reciprocal inhibition." Wolpe and many subsequent therapists used "exposure," which means that a traumatic event is held in memory. While the client exposes him or herself to the stressful memory, therapeutic measures are taken to provide a new, nonthreatening stimulus that does not activate the fight-or-flight response.

In the 1970s, a new school of psychology, cognitive therapy, became ascendant over the behavioral school. Cognitive therapy and cognitive behavior therapy (CBT) are the forms of psychotherapy practiced predominantly today. Cognitive therapy focuses on changing "cognitions," the concepts about self and the world that we carry in our heads. We might, for instance, believe that the problems at our job are caused by the management, that the government is responsible for the country's problems, or that our relationship partner is the source of all the difficulties in the relationship. Since our cognition is that the problem is "out there," we feel little power to affect events. When our cognition shifts, and we recognize our role in maintaining the situation, we develop the power to change it.

A classic case cited by a cognitive behavior therapist is that of "Mr. A," a computer programmer (Craske & Barlow, 1993). He "requested treatment for panic disorder with agoraphobia. He had been symptomatic for at least 5 years. His condition had deteriorated to the point where he was largely housebound, although he was able to drive about half a mile to his workplace, where he worked in a cubicle and had little social contact. When Mr. A considered driving to the city to see an old friend or to a mall near his home, he would have thoughts such as 'I can't do it...I'll faint or I'll have a heart attack...I'll panic and lose control...I'll have a wreck and kill everyone in my path.' As might be expected, he had intense anxiety and autonomic arousal associated with these thoughts. His behavioral response was to avoid driving anywhere other than work and to avoid going anywhere there might be crowds. Each time he avoided these activities, his basic fears were reinforced, and eventually his symptoms became deeply ingrained." The therapist used CBT techniques to challenge the client's cognitions, and helped him develop new thoughts that counterconditioned his fear.

Neural Plasticity

Together, CBT and exposure therapies have established a long and successful track record in the treatment of emotional trauma. Not only do we feel different when emotional trauma is released, but our brains rewire themselves around the new cognitions. As late as the 1980s, the prevailing view in the field of biology was that the human brain grew till about the age of 17, and was then fully grown, and static, thereafter. In the 1990s, experiments began to demonstrate that the neural pathways in our brains are in constant flux, and grow in response to stimuli, just as our muscles grow when we lift weights at the gym, or our genes are turned on by epigenetic signals (Kandel, 1999). The brain region most involved in memory and learning, the hippocampus, is enlarged, for instance, in the brains of London taxicab drivers. They have to master the complex tangle of streets in the ancient city, and so their brains grow new neurons in order to accomplish this memory-intensive task (Maguire, Frackowiak, & Frith, 1997).

In 2000, Eric Kandel, MD, won the Nobel Prize in medicine for showing that *within just 1 hour of repeated stimulation, the number of connections in a neural bundle can double.* That's like doubling of the amount of electrical cable used in the wiring of your house, and it's remarkable that the body can create so much new wiring so quickly.

The opposite also occurs. If we don't use a neural pathway, it begins to shrink. Based on how we're using our brains, they are being rewired hour by hour and day by day, a phenomenon called "neural plasticity." That's a great term, because it conjures up a vision of a brain that is like putty, being shaped by the thoughts, feelings, and experiences being processed through it. People who have gone through a large emotional trauma, such as veterans suffering from PTSD, show changes in their brains over time, as flashbacks and intrusive traumatic thoughts and other negative stimuli rewire their neural circuits (Vasterling & Brewin, 2005). The brains of schizophrenics also show changes over time, and the genes that help them handle fear can become permanently shut down by the epigenetic signals sent by their psychological disease (McGowan et al., 2009). So CBT, exposure therapy, EFT, and other treatments that help relieve psychological suffering can produce positive changes in the wiring of our neuroplastic brains, as counterconditioned memories are turned into hardwired neural bundles.

EFT's most fundamental procedure is called the Basic Recipe, and it's described in the next chapter. While the Basic Recipe is very short, it borrows elements from all these earlier discoveries. The verbal part of EFT involves *remembering a specific incident with a strong emotional charge,* and combining the recall with *an affirmative statement of self-acceptance.* The element of recall involves *exposure.* The exposure part of EFT is then paired with the affirmation in order to introduce *cognitive change* in the form of accepting the situation. This counterconditions the conditioned stress response that your body has to the memory of the traumatic event.

When the conditioned response has been successfully counterconditioned by EFT, you can still remember the stressful event. In fact, your memory might get even clearer. However, the memory no longer triggers a stress response in your body. After the calming experience of EFT has been associated with the memory, the memory is no longer tagged by the body as a cue to go into fight or flight. Instead, it has a neutral emotional tone. Once you break the conditioned response, you can think of the memory again without any emotional charge. The memory remains, but the emotional association is gone, and your cognitive experience of the memory shifts. EFT thus uses elements of both CBT and exposure therapy in its verbal components.

In 2007, the Institute of Medicine (IOM) published a landmark report (Institute of Medicine, 2007). The IOM is the medical arm of America's National Institutes of Health (NIH), the government body responsible for health care standards and research, conducted a review of which treatments were effective for PTSD by carefully examining all the scientific studies performed to date. It found that CBT and exposure therapy were the most effective treatments available. Though in 2007 no studies on EFT for PTSD were yet complete and available to IOM reviewers, subsequent reviews by government bodies will include them.

Dr. Callahan's First Experience

One of the best-known single-session case histories in the field of energy psychology was described by psychologist Roger Callahan and dates from the late 1970s (Callahan, 2013). A client he calls "Mary" had a longstanding phobia of water. Her parents reported that she had exhibited a marked phobic response to water since infancy. Now in her 40s, she was still frightened every time it rained. She could not take baths in a tub full of water. Though she lived near the ocean, the mere sight of it caused her so much anxiety that she never visited the beach. She had frequent nightmares of being engulfed by water. Callahan worked with Mary using conventional techniques for 18 months but made little progress. He had a swimming pool near his home office, which he used to test her phobic reaction. The best result he had been able to obtain was having her sit on the edge of the pool and dangle her legs in the water, though even this degree of proximity triggered marked anxiety.

Mary had told Callahan that when she thought of water, she had a sick feeling in the pit of her stomach. Callahan had recently learned about acupuncture points and meridians, and knew that the end point of the stomach meridian was located under the pupil of the eyes. During one session, "not expecting much of anything to happen,"

Callahan suggested she use her fingertips to tap under her eyes. She did so, and exclaimed that the feeling in her stomach had vanished. She leaped from her chair and ran to the pool. Her fear of water had vanished. The nightmares ceased, and when followed up almost 30 years later, Mary's water phobia had not reappeared.

This experience led Callahan to experiment with a variety of acupressure points for a variety of psychological conditions, publish his findings, and eventually develop the therapeutic method called Thought Field Therapy or TFT (Callahan, 1985).

Along with tapping, TFT incorporates elaborate diagnostic procedures using muscle testing, which has the therapist apply pressure to opne of the client's muscles. Muscle strength is tested before and after treatment, to determine if the muscle tests stronger or weaker. TFT also taps acupoints in a particular order depending on the diagnosis; Callahan calls these tapping sequences "algorithms" (Callahan, 2000).

EFT dispenses with muscle testing and the entire suite of diagnostic procedures central to TFT, and it taps only on specified points. As there are only 12 tapping points and it takes under 2 minutes to tap them all, the points tapped in all possible treatment algorithms can be addressed in a very brief time frame. This allows many more troubling emotional memories to be treated in a single session. It also allows EFT to be learned quickly, and self-applied. EFT's tapping is done while using exposure, an established technique for treating trauma, in combination with cognitive shift, the other technique found to be effective by the IOM review. EFT thus combines the powerful Eastern energy techniques of acupoint stimulation with the best Western approaches, embodied in cognitive and exposure therapies, to produce rapid psychological shifts.

EFT research is still in the early stages. When Dr. Callahan and then others discovered that deep-seated psychological problems could be cured with miraculous speed, there were few answers from science as to how this was possible. Epigenetics and neural plasticity had not yet been discovered. Acupuncture had been around for thousands of years. So these pioneers, looking for explanations, seized on energy, acupuncture meridians, and quantum physics. Gary Craig generalized even further, stating that "The cause of all negative emotions is a disruption in the body's energy system." He called this the Discovery Statement and gave it central importance in his explanation of how and why EFT works (Craig & Fowlie, 1995). These "magical" explanations seem quaint today now that we know the role of genetics, stress hormones, early childhood experiences, behavioral conditioning, and neural signaling in the experience of negative emotion. We now have explanations for EFT's rapid effects that are grounded in solid science.

It's not uncommon for innovations such as EFT to be observed first in the clinic, then in outcome studies, and finally in "hard science" experiments. The history of medicine is full of treatments that followed the same path. Doctors used aspirin for a century, observing that it worked, before they discovered *how* it worked. The same is true for quinine, and many other treatments. The development path for proving EFT is typical of a new approach, and as additional studies are conducted, we'll get a better and better understanding of the mechanisms by which EFT works its magic in the body.

Studies like the ones described in this chapter provide *objective* evidence that EFT works. As you learn more about EFT, and dive into doing it yourself, you will quickly have *subjective* experiences of just how startlingly fast your body can respond. As you recall traumatic events in your life, whether they happened in early childhood or an hour ago, you'll feel exactly what it feels like to have an electromagnetic energy shift in your body. You'll feel your stress level receding as your levels of adrenaline and cortisol drop, and your sympathetic nervous system calms down. You'll quickly understand that you don't have to be afraid of dealing with your past emotional wounds. You now have a tool that allows you to release that stuck energy and your old biological patterns. It gives you the gift of emotional freedom.

How to Do EFT:
The Basic Recipe

Over the past decade, EFT has been the focus of a great deal of research. This has resulted in more than 20 clinical trials, in which EFT has been demonstrated to reduce a wide variety of symptoms. These include pain, skin rashes, fibromyalgia, depression, anxiety, and post-traumatic stress disorder (PTSD). Most of these studies have used the standardized form of EFT found in *The EFT Manual*. In this chapter, my goal is to show you how to unlock EFT's healing benefits from whatever physical or psychological problems you're facing. I have a passionate interest in relieving human suffering. When you study EFT, you quickly realize how much suffering can be alleviated with the help of this extraordinary healing tool. I'd like to place the full power of that tool in your hands, so that you can live the happiest, healthiest, and most abundant life possible.

If you go on YouTube or do a Google search, you will find thousands of websites and videos about EFT. The quality of the EFT information you'll find through these sources varies widely, however. Certified practitioners trained in EFT provide a small portion of the information. Most of it consists of personal testimonials by untrained enthusiasts. It's great that EFT works to some degree for virtually anyone. To get the most out of EFT and unlock its full potential, however, it's essential that you learn the form of EFT that's been proven in so many clinical trials. We call this Clinical EFT.

Every year in EFT Universe workshops, we get many people who tell us variations of the same story: "I saw a video on YouTube, tapped along, and got amazing results the first few times. Then it seemed to stop working." The reason for this is that a superficial application of EFT can indeed work wonders. To unleash the full power of EFT, however, requires learning the standardized form we call Clinical EFT, which has been validated, over and over again, by high-quality research, and is taught systematically, step by step, by top experts, in EFT workshops.

Why is EFT able to affect so many problems, both psychological and physical? The reason for its effectiveness is that it reduces stress, and stress is a component of many problems. In EFT research on pain, for instance, we find that pain decreases by an average of 68% with EFT. That's a two thirds drop, and seems very impressive. Now ask yourself, if EFT can produce a two-thirds drop in pain, why can't it produce a 100% drop? I pondered this question myself, and I asked many therapists and doctors for their theories as to why this might be so.

The consensus is that the two thirds of pain reduced by EFT is due largely to emotional causes, while the remaining one third of the pain has a physical derivation. A man I'll call "John" volunteered for a demonstration at an EFT introductory evening at which I presented. He was on crutches, and told us he had a broken leg as a result of a car accident. On a scale of 0 to 10, with 0 being no pain, and 10 being maximum pain, he rated his pain as an 8. The accident had occurred two weeks earlier. My logical scientific brain didn't think EFT would work for John, because his pain was purely physical. I tapped with him anyway. At the end of our session, which lasted less than 15 minutes, his pain was down to a 2. I hadn't tapped on the actual pain with John at all, but rather on all the emotional components of the auto accident.

There were many such components. His wife had urged him to drive to an event, but he didn't want to go. He had resentment toward his wife. That's emotional. He was angry at the driver of the other car. That's emotional. He was mad at himself for abandoning his own needs by driving to an event he didn't want to attend. That's emotional. He was upset that now, as an adult, he was reenacting the abandonment he experienced by his mother when he was a child. That's emotional. He was still hurt by an incident that occurred when he was five years old, when his mother was supposed to pick him up from a friend's birthday party and forgot because she was socializing with her friends and drinking. That's emotional.

Do you see the pattern here? We're working on a host of problems that are emotional, yet interwoven with the pain. The physical pain is overlaid with a matrix of emotional issues, like self-neglect, abandonment, anger, and frustration, which are part of the entire fabric of John's life.

The story has a happy ending. After we'd tapped on each of these emotional components of John's pain, the physical pain in his broken leg went down to a 2. That pain rating revealed the extent of the physical component of John's problem. It was a 2. The other six points were emotional.

The same is true for the person who's afraid of public speaking, who has a spider phobia, who's suffering from a physical ailment, who's feeling trapped in his job, who's unhappy with her husband, who's in conflict with those around him. All of these problems have a large component of unfinished emotional business from the past. When you neutralize the underlying emotional issues with EFT, what remains is the real problem, which is often far smaller than you imagine.

Though I present at few conferences nowadays because of other demands on my time, I used to present at about thirty medical and psychological conferences each year, speaking about research and teaching EFT. I presented to thousands of medical professionals during that period. One of my favorite sayings was "Don't medicalize emotional problems. And don't emotionalize medical problems." When I would say this to a roomful of physicians, they would nod their heads in unison. The medical profession as a whole is very aware of the emotional component of disease.

If you have a real medical problem, you need good medical care. No ifs, ands, or buts. If you have an emotional problem, you need EFT. Most problems are a mixture of both. That's why I urge you to work on the emotional component with EFT and other safe and noninvasive behavioral methods, and to get the best possible medical care for the physical component of your problem. Talk to your doctor about this; virtually every physician will be supportive of you bolstering your medical treatment with emotional catharsis.

When you feel better emotionally, a host of positive changes also occur in your energy system. When you feel worse, your energy system follows. Several researchers have hooked people up to electroencephalographs (EEGs), and taken EEG readings of the electrical energy in their brains before and after EFT. These studies show that when subjects are asked to recall a traumatic event, their patterns of brain-wave activity change. The brain-wave frequencies associated with stress, and activation of the fight-or-flight response, dominate their EEG readings. After successful treatment, the brain waves shown on their EEG readings are those that characterize relaxation.

Other research has shown similar results from acupuncture. The theory behind acupuncture is that our body's energy flows in twelve channels called meridians. When that energy is blocked, physical or psychological distress occurs. The use of acupuncture needles, or acupressure with the fingertips, is believed to release those energy blocks. EFT has you tap with your fingertips on the end points of those meridians; that's why it's sometimes called "emotional acupuncture." When your energy is balanced and flowing, whether it's the brain-wave energy picked up by the EEG or the meridian energy described in acupuncture, you feel better. That's another reason why EFT works well for many different kinds of problem.

EFT is rooted in sound science, and this chapter is devoted to showing you how to do Clinical EFT yourself. It will introduce you to the basic concepts that amplify the power of EFT, and steer you clear of the most common pitfalls that prevent people from making progress with EFT. The basics of EFT are easy to use and quick to learn. We call this EFT's "Basic Recipe." The second half of this chapter shows you how to apply the Basic Recipe for maximum effect. It introduces you to all of the concepts key to Clinical EFT.

Testing

EFT doesn't just hope to be effective. We test our results constantly, to determine if the course we're taking is truly making us feel better. The basic scale we use for testing was developed by a famous psychiatrist called Joseph Wolpe in the 1950s, and measures our degree of discomfort on a scale of 0 through 10. Zero indicates no discomfort, and 10 is the maximum possible distress. This scale works equally well for psychological problems such as anxiety and physical problems such as pain.

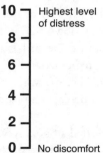

SUD scale (intensity meter)

Dr. Wolpe called this rating SUD or Subjective Units of Discomfort. It's also sometimes called Subjective Units of Distress. You feel your problem, and give it a number on the SUD scale. It's vital to rate your SUD level as it is *right now,* not imagine what it might have been at the time in the past when the traumatic event occurred. If you can't quickly identify a number, just take your best guess, and go from there.

I recommend you write down your initial SUD number. It's also worth noting *where in your body* the information on your SUD level is coming from. If you're working on a physical pain such as a headache, where in your head is the ache centered? If you're working on a traumatic emotional event, perhaps a car accident, where in your body is your reference point for your emotional distress? Do you feel it in your belly, your heart, your forehead? Write down the location on which your SUD is based.

A variation of the numeric scale is a visual scale. For example, if you're working with a child who does not yet know how to count, you can ask the child to spread his or her hands apart to indicate how big the problem is. Wide-open arms means big, and hands close together means small.

Whatever means you use to test, each round of EFT tapping usually begins with this type of assessment of the size of the problem. This allows us to determine whether or not our approach is working. After we've tested and written down our SUD level and body location, we move on to EFT's Basic Recipe. It has this name to indicate that EFT consists of certain ingredients, and if you want to be successful, you need to include them, just the way you need to include all the ingredients in a recipe for chocolate chip cookies if you want your end product to be tasty.

Many years ago I published a book by Wally Amos. Wally is better known as "Famous Amos" for his brand of chocolate chip cookies. One day I asked Wally, "Where did you get your recipe?" I thought he was going to tell me how he'd experimented with hundreds of variations to find the best possible combination of ingredients. I imagined Wally like Thomas Edison in his laboratory, obsessively combining pinches of this and smidgeons of that, year after year, in order to perfect the flavor of his cookies, the way Edison tried thousands of combinations before discovering the incandescent light bulb.

Wally's offhand response was, "I used the recipe on the back of a pack of Toll House chocolate chips." Toll House is one of the most popular brands, selling millions of packages each year, and the simple recipe is available to everyone. I was astonished, and laughed at how different the reality was from my imaginary picture of Wally as Edison. Yet the message is simple: Don't reinvent the wheel. If it works, it works. Toll House is so popular because their recipe works. Clinical EFT produces such good results because the Basic Recipe works. While a master chef might be experienced enough to produce exquisite variations, a beginner can bake excellent cookies, and get consistently great results, just by following the basic recipe. This chapter is designed to provide you with that simple yet reliable level of knowledge.

EFT's Basic Recipe omits a procedure that was part of the earliest forms of EFT, called the 9 Gamut Procedure. Though the 9 Gamut Procedure has great value for certain conditions, it isn't always necessary, so we leave it out. The version of EFT that includes it is called the Full Basic Recipe (see Appendix A of *The EFT Manual*).

The Setup Statement

The Setup Statement systematically "sets up" the problem you want to work on. Think about arranging dominoes in a line in the game of creating a chain reaction. Before you start the game, you set them up. The object of the game is to knock them down, just the way EFT expects to knock down your SUD level, but to start with, you set up the pieces of the problem.

The Setup Statement has its roots in two schools of psychology. One is called cognitive therapy, and the other is called exposure therapy. Cognitive therapy considers the large realm of your cognitions— your thoughts, beliefs, ways of relating to others, and the mental frames through which you perceive the world and your experiences.

Exposure therapy is a successful branch of psychotherapy that vividly exposes you to your negative experiences. Rather than avoiding them, you're confronted by them, with the goal of breaking your conditioned fear response to the event.

We won't go deeper into these two forms of therapy now, but you'll later see how EFT's Setup Statement draws from cognitive and exposure approaches to form a powerful combination with acupressure or tapping.

Psychological Reversal

The term Psychological Reversal is taken from energy therapies. It refers to the concept that when your energies are blocked or reversed, you develop symptoms. If you put the batteries into a flashlight backward, with the positive end where the negative should be, the light won't shine. The human body also has a polarity (see illustration). A reversal of normal polarity will block the flow of energy through the body. In acupuncture, the goal of treatment is to remove obstructions, and to allow the free flow of energy through the 12 meridians. If reversal occurs, it impedes the healing process.

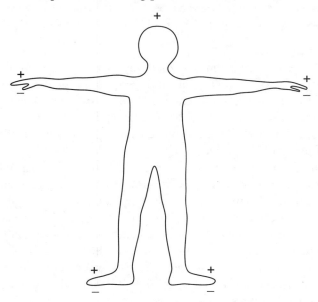

The human body's electrical polarity (adapted from
ACEP Certification Program Manual, 2006)

The way Psychological Reversal shows up in EFT and other energy therapies is as a failure to make progress in resolving the problem. It's especially prevalent in chronic diseases, addictions, and conditions that resist healing. If you run into a person who's desperate to recover, yet who has had no success even with a wide variety of different therapies, the chances are good that you're dealing with Psychological Reversal. One of the first steps of EFT's Basic Recipe is to correct for Psychological Reversal. It only takes a few seconds, so we include this step whether or not Psychological Reversal is present.

EFT's Setup includes stating an affirmation with those elements drawn from cognitive and exposure therapies, while at the same time correcting for Psychological Reversal.

Affirmation

The exposure part of the Setup Statement involves remembering the problem. You expose your mind repeatedly to the memory of the trauma. This is the opposite of what we normally do; we usually want an emotional trauma to fade away. We might engage in behaviors like dissociation or avoidance so that we don't have to deal with unpleasant memories.

As you gain confidence with EFT, you'll find yourself becoming fearless when it comes to exposure. You'll discover you don't have to remain afraid of old traumatic memories; you have a tool that allows you to reduce their emotional intensity in minutes or even seconds. The usual pattern of running away from a problem is reversed. You feel confident running toward it, knowing that you'll quickly feel better.

The EFT Setup Statement is this: *Even though I have (name of problem), I deeply and completely accept myself.*

You insert the name of the problem in the exposure half of the Setup Statement. Examples might be:

Even though I had that dreadful car crash, I deeply and completely accept myself.

Even though I have this migraine headache, I deeply and completely accept myself.

Even though I have this fear of heights, I deeply and completely accept myself.

Even though I have this pain in my knees, I deeply and completely accept myself.

Even though I had my buddy die in my arms in Iraq, I deeply and completely accept myself.

Even though I have this huge craving for whiskey, I deeply and completely accept myself.

Even though I have this fear of spiders, I deeply and completely accept myself.

Even though I have this urge to eat another cookie, I deeply and completely accept myself.

The list of variations is infinite. You can use this Setup Statement for anything that bothers you.

While exposure is represented by the first half of the Setup Statement, before the comma, cognitive work is done by the second half of the statement, the part that deals with self-acceptance. EFT doesn't try to induce you to positive thinking. You don't tell yourself that things will get better, or that you'll improve. You simply express the intention of accepting yourself just the way you are. You accept reality. Gestalt therapist Byron Katie wrote a book entitled *Loving What Is,* and that's exactly what EFT recommends you do.

The Serenity Prayer uses the same formula of acceptance, with the words, "God grant me the serenity to accept the things I cannot change; courage to change the things I can; and wisdom to know the difference." With EFT you don't try and think positively. You don't try and change your attitude or circumstances; you simply affirm that you accept them. This cognitive frame of accepting what is opens the path to change in a profound way. It's also quite difficult to do this in our culture, which bombards us with positive thinking. Positive thinking actually gets in the way of healing in many cases, while acceptance provides us with a reality-based starting point congruent with our experience. The great 20th-century therapist Carl Rogers, who introduced client-centered therapy, said that the paradox of transformation is that change begins by accepting conditions exactly the way they are.

I recommend that you use the Setup Statement in exactly this way at first, but as you gain confidence, you can experiment with different variations. The only requirement is that you include both a self-acceptance statement and exposure to the problem. For instance, you can invert the two halves of the formula, and put cognitive self-acceptance first, followed by exposure. Here are some examples:

I accept myself fully and completely, even with this miserable headache.

I deeply love myself, even though I have nightmares from that terrible car crash.

I hold myself in high esteem, even though I feel such pain from my divorce.

When you're doing EFT with children, you don't need an elaborate Setup Statement. You can have children use very simple self-acceptance phrases, like "I'm okay" or "I'm a great kid." Such a Setup Statement might look like this:

Even though Johnny hit me, I'm okay.
The teacher was mean to me, but I'm still an amazing kid.

You'll be surprised how quickly children respond to EFT. Their SUD levels usually drop so fast that adults have a difficult time accepting the shift. Although we haven't yet done the research to discover why children are so receptive to change, my hypothesis is that their behaviors haven't yet been cemented by years of conditioning. They've not yet woven a thick neural grid in their brains through repetitive thinking and behavior, so they can let go of negative emotions fast.

What do you do if your problem is self-acceptance itself? What if you believe you're unacceptable? What if you have low self-esteem, and the words "I deeply and completely accept myself" sound like a lie?

What EFT suggests you do in such a case is say the words anyway, even if you don't believe them. They will usually have some effect, even if at first you have difficulty with them. As you correct for Psychological Reversal in the way I will show you here, you will soon find yourself shifting from unbelief to belief that you are acceptable. You can say the affirmation aloud or silently. It carries more emotional energy if it is said emphatically or loudly, and imagined vividly.

Secondary Gain

While energy therapies use the term "psychological reversal" to indicate energy blocks to healing, there's an equivalent term drawn from psychology. That term is "secondary gain." It refers to the benefits of being sick. "Why would anyone want to be sick?" you might wonder. There are actually many reasons for keeping a mental or physical problem firmly in place.

Consider the case of a veteran with PTSD. He's suffering from flashbacks of scenes from Afghanistan where he witnessed death and suffering. He has nightmares, and never sleeps through the night. He's so disturbed that he cannot hold down a job or keep a relationship intact for long. Why would such a person not want to get better, considering the damage PTSD is doing to his life?

The reason might be that he's getting a disability check each month as a result of his condition. His income is dependent on having PTSD, and if he recovers, his main source of livelihood might disappear with it.

Another reason might be that he was deeply wounded by a divorce many years ago. He lost his house and children in the process. He's fearful of getting into another romantic relationship that is likely to end badly. PTSD gives him a reason to not try.

These are obvious examples of secondary gain. When we work with participants in EFT workshops, we uncover a wide variety of subtle reasons that stand in the way of healing. One woman had been trying to lose weight for five years and had failed at every diet she tried. Her secondary gain turned out to be freedom from unwanted attention by men.

Another woman, this time with fibromyalgia, discovered that her secret benefit from the disease was that she didn't have to visit relatives she didn't like. She had a ready excuse for avoiding social obligations. She also got sympathetic attention from her husband and children for her suffering. If she gave up her painful disease, she might lose a degree of affection from her family and have to resume seeing the relatives she detested.

Just like Psychological Reversal, secondary gain prevents us from making progress on our healing journey. Correcting for these hidden obstacles to success is one of the first elements in EFT's Basic Recipe.

How EFT Corrects for Psychological Reversal

The first tapping point we use in the EFT routine is called the Karate Chop point, because it's located on the fleshy outer portion of the hand, the part used in karate to deliver a blow. EFT has you tap the Karate Chop point with the tips of the other four fingers of the opposite hand.

The Karate Chop (KC) Point

Repeat your affirmation emphatically three times while tapping your Karate Chop point. You've now corrected for psychological reversal, and set up your energy system for the next part of EFT's Basic Recipe, the Sequence.

The Sequence

You now tap on meridian end points in sequence. Tap firmly, but not harshly, with the tips of your first two fingers, about seven times on each point. The exact number is not important; it can be a few more or less than seven. You can tap on either the right or left side of your body, with either your dominant or nondominant hand.

First tap on the meridian endpoints found on the face. These are: (1) at the start of the eyebrow, where it joins the bridge of the nose; (2) on the outside edge of the eye socket; (3) on the bony ridge of the eye socket under the pupil; (4) under the nose; and (5) between the lower lip and the chin.

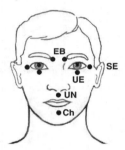

EB, SE, UE, UN and Ch Points

Then tap (6) on one of the collarbone points (see illustration). To locate this point, place a finger in the notch between your collarbones. Move your finger down about an inch and you'll feel a hollow in your breastbone. Now move it to the side about an inch and you'll find a deep hollow below your collarbone. You've now located the collarbone acupressure point.

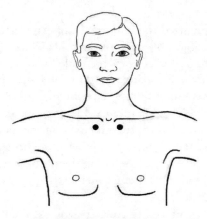

The Collarbone (CB) Points

About four inches below the armpit (for women, this is where a bra strap crosses), you'll find (7) the under the arm point.

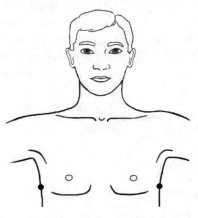

Under the Arm (UA) Points

The Reminder Phrase

Earlier, I emphasized the importance of exposure. Exposure therapy has been the subject of much research, which has shown that prolonged exposure to a problem, when coupled with techniques to calm the body, effectively treats traumatic stress. EFT incorporates exposure in the form of a Reminder Phrase. This is a brief phrase that keeps the problem at the front of your mind while you tap on the acupressure points. It keeps your energy system focused on the specific issue you're working on, rather than jumping to other thoughts and feelings. The aim of the Reminder Phrase is to bring the problem vividly into your experience, even though the emotionally triggering situation might not be present now.

For instance, if you have test anxiety, you use the Reminder Phrase to keep you focused on the fear, even though you aren't actually taking a test right now. That gives EFT an opportunity to shift the pattern in the absence of the real problem. You can also use EFT during an actual situation, such as when you're taking an actual test, but most of the time you're working on troublesome memories. The Reminder Phrase keeps you targeted on the problem. An example of a Reminder Phrase for test anxiety might be *"That test"* or *"The test I have to take tomorrow"* or *"That test I failed."* Other examples of Reminder Phrases are:

> *The bee sting*
> *Dad hit me*
> *Friend doesn't respect me*
> *Lawyer's office*
> *Sister told me I was fat*
> *Car crash*
> *This knee pain*

Tap each point while repeating your Reminder Phrase. Then tune in to the problem again, and get a second SUD rating. The chances are good that your SUD score will now be much lower than it was before. These instructions might seem complicated the first time you read them, but you'll soon find you're able to complete a round of EFT tapping from memory in one to two minutes.

Let's now summarize the steps of EFT's Basic Recipe.

1. Assess your SUD level.

2. Insert the name of your problem into the Setup Statement: *"Even though I have (this problem), I deeply and completely accept myself."*

3. Tap continuously on the Karate Chop point while repeating the Setup Statement three times.

4. While repeating the Reminder Phrase, tap about seven times on the other seven points.

5. Test your results with a second SUD rating.

Isn't that simple? You now have a tool that, in just a minute or two, can effectively neutralize the emotional sting of old memories, as well as help you get through bad current situations. After a few rounds of tapping, you'll find you've effortlessly memorized the Basic Recipe, and you'll find yourself using it often in your daily life.

If Your SUD Level Doesn't Come Down to 0

Sometimes a single round of tapping brings your SUD score to 0. Sometimes it only brings it down slightly. Your migraine might have been an 8, and after a round of EFT it's a 4. In these cases, we do EFT again. You can adjust your affirmation to acknowledge that a portion of the problem sill remains, for example, *"Even though I still have some of this migraine, I deeply and completely accept myself."* Hear are some further examples:

Even though I still feel some anger toward my friend for putting me down, I deeply and completely accept myself.

Even though I still have a little twinge of that knee pain, I deeply and completely accept myself.

Even though the beesting still smarts slightly, I deeply and completely accept myself.

Even though I'm still harboring some resentment toward my boss, I deeply and completely accept myself.

Even though I'm still somewhat frustrated with my daughter for breaking her agreement, I deeply and completely accept myself.

Even though I'm still upset when I think of being shipped to Iraq, I deeply and completely accept myself.

Adjust the Reminder Phrase accordingly, as in *"some anger still"* or *"remaining frustration"* or *"bit of pain"* or *"somewhat upset."*

EFT for You and Others

You can do EFT on yourself, as you've experienced during these practice rounds. You can also tap on others. Many therapists, life coaches, and other practitioners offer EFT professionally to clients. Personally I'm far more inclined to have clients tap on themselves during EFT sessions, even during the course of a therapy or coaching session. While the coach can tap on the client, having the client tap on themselves, along with some guidance by the coach, puts the power squarely in the hands of the client. The client is empowered by discovering that they are able to reduce their own emotional distress, and leaves the coaches office with a self-help tool at their fingertips any time they need it. In some jurisdictions, it is illegal or unethical for therapists to touch clients at all, and EFT when done only by the client is still effective in these cases.

The Importance of Targeting Specific Events

During EFT workshops, I sometimes write on the board:

The Three Most Important Things About EFT

Then, under that, I write:

Specific Events
Specific Events
Specific Events

It's my way of driving home the point that a focus on specific events is critical to success in EFT. In order to release old patterns of emotion and behavior, it's vital to identify and correct the specific events that gave rise to those problems. When you hear people say, "I tried EFT and it didn't work," the chances are good that they were tapping on generalities, instead of specifics.

An example of a generality is "self-esteem" or "depression" or "performance problems." These aren't specific events. Beneath these generalities is a collection of specific events. The person with low self-esteem might have been coloring a picture at the age of four when her mother walked in and criticized her for drawing outside the lines. She might have had another experience of a schoolteacher scolding her for playing with her hair during class in second grade, and a third experience of her first boyfriend deciding to ask another girl to the school dance. Together, those specific events contribute to the global pattern of low self-esteem. The way EFT works is that when the emotional trauma of those individual events is resolved, the whole pattern of low self-esteem can shift. If you tap on the big pattern, and omit the specific events, you're likely to have limited success.

When you think about how a big pattern like low self-esteem is established, this makes sense. It's built up out of many single events. Collectively, they form the whole pattern. The big pattern doesn't spring to life fully formed; it's built up gradually out of many similar experiences. The memories engraved in your brain are of individual events; one disappointing or traumatic memory at a time is encoded in your memory bank. When enough similar memories have accumulated, their commonalities combine to create a common theme like "poor self-esteem." Yet the theme originated as a series of specific events, and that's where EFT can be effectively applied.

You don't have to use EFT on every single event that contributed to the global theme. Usually, once a few of the most disturbing memories have lost their emotional impact, the whole pattern disappears. Memories that are similar lose their impact once the most vivid memories have been neutralized with EFT.

Tapping on global issues is the single most common mistake newcomers make with EFT. Using lists of tapping phrases from a website or a book, or tapping on generalities, is far less effective than tuning into the events that contributed to your global problem, and tapping on them. If you hear someone say, "EFT doesn't work," the chances are good they've been tapping globally rather than identifying specific events. Don't make this elementary mistake. List the events, one after the other, that stand out most vividly in your mind when you think about the global problem. Tap on each of them, and you'll usually find the global problem diminishing of its own accord. This is called the "generalization effect," and it's one of the key concepts in EFT.

Tapping on Aspects

EFT breaks traumatic events and other problems into smaller pieces called aspects. The reason for this is that the highest emotional charge is typically found in one small chunk of the event, rather than the entirety of the event. You might need to identify several different aspects, and tap on each of them, before the intensity of the whole event is reduced to a 0.

Here's an example of tapping on aspects, drawn from experience at an EFT workshop I taught. A woman in her late 30s volunteered as a subject. She'd had neck pain and limited range of motion since an automobile accident 6 years before. She could turn her head to the right most of the way but had only a few degrees of movement to the left. The accident had been a minor one, and why she still suffered 6 years later was something of a mystery to her.

I asked her to feel where in her body she felt the most intensity when recalling the accident, and she said it was in her upper chest. I then asked her about the first time she'd ever felt that way, and she said it was when she'd been involved in another auto accident at the age of 8. Her sister had been driving the car. We worked on each aspect of the early accident. The two girls had hit another car head on at low speed while driving around a bend on a country road. One emotionally triggering aspect was the moment she realized that a collision was unavoidable, and we tapped till that lost its force. We tapped on the sound of the crash, another aspect. She had been taken to a neighbor's house, bleeding from a cut on her head, and we tapped on that. We tapped on aspect after aspect. Still, her pain level didn't go down much, and her range of motion didn't improve.

Then she gasped and said, "I just remembered. My sister was only 15 years old. She was underage. That day, I dared her to drive the family car, and we totaled it." Her guilt turned out to be the aspect that held the most emotional charge, and after we tapped on that, her pain disappeared, and she regained full range of motion in her neck. If we'd tapped on the later accident, or failed to uncover all the aspects, we might have thought, "EFT doesn't work."

Aspects can be pains, physical sensations, emotions, images, sounds, tastes, odors, fragments of an event, or beliefs. Make sure you dig deep for all the emotional charge held in each aspect of an event before you move on to the next one. One way of doing this is to check each sensory channel, and ask, "What did you hear/see/taste/touch/smell?" For one person, the burned-rubber smell of skidding tires might be the most terrifying aspect of a car accident. For another, it might be the smell of blood. Yet another person might remember most vividly the sound of the crash or the screams. For another person, the maximum emotional charge might be held in the feeling of terror at the moment of realization that the crash is inevitable. The pain itself might be an aspect. Guilt, or any other emotion, can be an aspect. For traumatic events, it's necessary to tap on each aspect.

Thorough exploration of all the aspects will usually yield a complete neutralization of the memory. If there's still some emotional charge left, the chances are good that you've missed an aspect, so go back and find out what shards of trauma might still be stuck in place.

Finding Core Issues

One of my favorite sayings during EFT workshops is "The problem is never the problem." What I mean by this is that the problem we complain about today usually bothers us only because it resembles an earlier problem. For example, if your spouse being late disturbs you, you may discover by digging deep with EFT that the real reason this behavior triggers you is that your mother didn't meet your needs in early childhood. Your spouse's behavior in the present day resembles, to your brain, the neglect you experienced in early childhood, so you react accordingly. You put a lot of energy into trying to change your spouse when the present-day person is not the source of the problem.

On the EFT Universe website, we have published hundreds of stories in which someone was no longer triggered by a present problem after the emotional charge was removed from a similar childhood event. Nothing changed in the present day, yet the very problem that so vexed a person before now carries zero emotional charge. That's the magic that happens once we neutralize core issues with EFT. Rather than being content with using EFT on surface problems, it's worth developing the skills to find and resolve the core issues that are at the root of the problem.

Here are some questions you might ask in order to identify core issues:

- Does the problem that's bothering you remind you of any events in your childhood? Tune into your body and feel your feelings. Then travel back in time to the first time in your life you ever felt that same sensation.

- What's the worst similar experience you ever had?

- If you were writing your autobiography, what chapter would you prefer to delete, as though it had never happened to you?

If you can't remember a specific childhood event, simply make up a fictional event in your mind. This kind of guessing usually turns out to be right on target. You're assembling the imagined event out of components of real events, and the imaginary event usually leads back to actual events you can tap on. Even if it doesn't, and you tap on the fictional event, you will usually experience an obvious release of tension.

The Generalization Effect

The *generalization effect* is a phenomenon you'll notice as you make progress with EFT. As you resolve the emotional sting of specific events, other events with a similar emotional signature also decrease in intensity. I once worked with a man at an EFT workshop whose father had beaten him many times during his childhood. His SUD level on the beatings was a 10. I asked him to recall the worst beating he'd ever suffered. He told me that when he was 8 years old, his father had hit him so hard he had broken the boy's jaw. We tapped together on that terrible beating, and after working on all the aspects, his SUD dropped to a 0. I asked him for a SUD score on all the beatings, and his face softened. He said, "My dad got beat by his dad much worse than he beat me. My dad actually did a pretty good job considering how badly he was raised." My client's SUD level on all the beatings dropped considerably after we reduced the intensity of this one beating. That's an example of EFT's generalization effect. When you knock down an important domino, all the other dominos can fall.

This is very reassuring to clients who suffered from many instances of childhood abuse, the way my client at that workshop had suffered. You don't need to work through every single horrible incident. Often, simply collapsing the emotional intensity behind one incident is sufficient to collapse the intensity around similar incidents.

The reason our brains work this way is because of a group of neurons in the emotional center of the brain, the limbic system, called the hippocampus. The hippocampus has the job of comparing one event to the other. Suppose that, as a 5-year-old child in Catholic school, you get beaten by a nun. Forty years later, you can't figure out why you feel uneasy around women wearing outfits that are black and white. The reason for your adult aversion to a black-and-white combination is that the hippocampus associates the colors of the nun's habit with the pain of the beating.

This was a brilliant evolutionary innovation for your ancestors. Perhaps these early humans were attacked by a tiger hiding in the long grass. The tiger's stripes mimicked the patterns of the grass yet there was something different there. Learning to spot a pattern, judge the differences, and react with fear saved your alert ancestors. They gave birth to their children, who also learned, just a little bit better, how to respond to threats. After thousands of generations, you have a hippocampus at the center of your brain that is genetically engineered to evaluate every message flooding in from your senses, and pick out those associated with the possibility of danger. You see the woman wearing the black-and-white cocktail dress at a party, your hippocampus associates these colors with the nun who beat you, and you have an emotional response.

Yet the opposite is also true. Assume for a moment you're a man who is very shy when confronted with women at cocktail parties. He feels a rush of fear whenever he thinks about talking to an attractive woman dressed in black. He works with an EFT coach on his memories of getting beaten by the nun in Catholic school, and suddenly he finds himself able to talk easily to women at parties. Once the man's hippocampus breaks the connection between beatings and a black dress, it knows, for future reference, that the two phenomena are no longer connected.

This is the explanation the latest brain science gives us for the generalization effect. It's been noted in EFT for many years, and it's very comforting for those who've suffered many adverse experiences. You may need to tap on some of them, but you won't have to tap on all of them before the whole group is neutralized. Sometimes, like my client who was beaten repeatedly as a child, if you tap on a big one, the generalization effect reduces the emotional intensity of all similar experiences.

The Movie Technique and Tell the Story Technique

When you take an EFT workshop, the first key technique you learn is the Movie Technique. Why do we place such emphasis on the Movie Technique? The reason for this is that it combines many of the methods that are key to success with EFT.

The first thing the Movie Technique does is focus you on being specific. EFT is great at eliminating the emotional intensity you feel, as long as it's used on an actual concrete event ("John yelled at me in the meeting"), rather than a general statement ("My procrastination").

The Movie Technique has you identify a particular incident that has a big emotional charge for you, and systematically reduce that charge to 0. You picture the event in your mind's eye just as though it were a movie, and run through the movie scene by scene.

Whenever you reach a part of the movie that carries a big emotional charge, you stop and perform the EFT sequence. In this way, you reduce the intensity of each of the bad parts of the movie. EFT's related technique, Tell the Story, is done out loud, while the Movie Technique is typically done silently. You can use the Movie Technique with a client without them ever disclosing what the event was.

Try this with one of your own traumatic life events right now. Think of the event as though it were a scary movie. Make sure it's an event that lasts just a few minutes; if your movie lasts several hours or days, you've probably picked a general pattern. Try again, selecting a different event, till you have a movie that's just a few minutes long.

One example is a man whose general issue is "Distrust of Strangers." We trace it to a particular childhood incident that occurred when the man, whom we'll call John, was 7 years old. His parents moved to a new town, and John found himself walking to a new school through a rough neighborhood. He encountered a group of bullies at school but always managed to avoid them. One day, walking back from school, he saw the bullies walking toward him. He crossed the street, hoping to avoid their attention. He wasn't successful, and he saw them point at him, then change course to intercept him. He knew he was due for a beating. They taunted him and shoved him, and he fell into the gutter. His mouth hit the pavement, and he chipped a tooth. Other kids gathered round and laughed at him, and the bullies moved off. He picked himself up and walked the rest of the way home.

If you were to apply EFT to John's general pattern, "Distrust of Strangers," you'd be tapping generally—and ineffectually. When instead you focus on the specific event, you're honing in on the life events that gave rise to the general pattern. A collection of events like John's beating can combine to create the general pattern.

Now give your movie a title. John might call his movie "The Bullies."

Start thinking about the movie at a point before the traumatic part began. For John, that would be when he was walking home from school, unaware of the events in store for him.

Now run your movie through your mind till the end. The end of the movie is usually a place where the bad events come to an end. For John, this might be when he picked himself up off the ground, and resumed his walk home.

Now let's add EFT to your movie. Here's the way you do this:

1. Think of the title of your movie. Rate your degree of your emotional distress around just the title, not the movie itself. For instance, on the distress scale of 0 to 10 where 0 is no distress and 10 represents maximum distress, you might be an 8 when you think of the title "The Meeting." Write down your movie title, and your number.

2. Work the movie title into an EFT Setup Statement. It might sound something like this: "Even though [Insert Your Movie Title Here], I deeply and completely accept myself." Then tap on the EFT acupressure points, while repeating the Setup Statement three times. Your distress level will typically go down. You may have to do EFT several times on the title for it to reach a low number like 0 or 1 or 2.

3. Once the title reaches a low number, think of the "neutral point" before the bad events in the movie began to take place. For John, the neutral point was when he was walking home from school, before the bullies saw him. Once you've identified the neutral point of your own movie, start running the movie through your

mind, until you reach a point where the emotional intensity rises. In John's case, the first emotionally intense point was when he saw the bullies.

4. Stop at this point, and assess your intensity number. It might have risen from a 1 to a 7, for instance. Then perform a round of EFT on that first emotional crescendo. For John, it might be, "Even though I saw the bullies turn toward me, I deeply and completely accept myself." Use the same kind of statement for your own problem: "Even though [first emotional crescendo], I deeply and completely accept myself." Keep tapping till your number drops to 0 or near 0, perhaps a 1 or 2.

5. Now rewind your mental movie to the neutral point, and start running it in your mind again. Stop at the first emotional crescendo. If you sail right through the first one you tapped on, you know you've really and truly resolved that aspect of the memory with EFT. Go on to the next crescendo. For John, this might have been when they shoved him into the gutter. When you've found your second emotional crescendo, then repeat the process. Assess your intensity number, do EFT, and keep tapping till your number is low. Even if your number is only a 3 or 4, stop and do EFT again. Don't push through low-intensity emotional crescendos; since you have the gift of freedom at your fingertips, use it on each part of the movie.

6. Rewind to the neutral point again, and repeat the process.

7. When you can replay the whole movie in your mind, from the neutral point, to the end of the movie when your feelings are neutral again, you'll know you've resolved the whole event. You'll have dealt with all the aspects of the traumatic incident.

8. To truly test yourself, run through the movie, but exaggerate each sensory channel. Imagine the sights, sounds, smells, tastes, and other aspects of the movie as vividly as you possible can. If you've been running the movie silently in your mind, speak it out loud.

When you cannot possibly make yourself upset, you're sure to have resolved the lingering emotional impact of the event. The effect is usually permanent.

When you work through enough individual movies in this way, the whole general pattern often vanishes. Perhaps John had 40 events that contributed to his distrust of strangers. He might need to do the Movie Technique on all 40, but experience with EFT suggests that when you resolve just a few key events, perhaps 5 or 10 of them, the rest fade in intensity, and the general pattern itself is neutralized.

The Tell the Story Technique is similar to the Movie Technique; usually the Movie Technique is performed silently while Tell the Story is out loud. One great benefit of the Movie Technique done silently is that the client does not have to disclose the nature of the problem. An event might be too triggering, or too embarrassing, or too emotionally overwhelming, to be spoken out loud. That's no problem with the Movie Technique, which allows EFT to work its magic without the necessity of disclosure on the part of the client. The privacy offered by the Movie Technique makes it very useful for clients who would rather not talk openly about troubling events.

Constricted Breathing

Here's a way to demonstrate how EFT can affect you physically. You can try this yourself right now. It's also often practiced as an onstage demonstration at EFT workshops. You simply take three deep breaths, stretching your lungs as far as they can expand. On the third breath, rate the extent of the expansion of your lungs on a 0 to 10 scale, with 0 being as constricted as possible, and 10 being as expanded as possible. Now perform several rounds of EFT using Setup Statements such as:

> *Even though my breathing is constricted...*
> *Even though my lungs will only expand to an 8...*
> *Even though I have this physical problem that prevents me breathing deeply...*

Now take another deep breath and rate your level of expansion. Usually there's substantial improvement. Now focus on any emotional contributors to constricted breathing. Use questions like:

What life events can I associate with breathing problems?
Are there places in my life where I feel restricted?
If I simply guess at an emotional reason for my constricted breathing, what might it be?

Now tap on any issues surfaced by these questions. After your intensity is reduced, take another deep breath and rate how far your lungs are now expanding. Even if you were a 10 earlier, you might now find you're an 11 or 14.

The Personal Peace Procedure

The Personal Peace Procedure consists of listing every specific troublesome event in your life and systematically using EFT to tap away the emotional impact of these events. With due diligence, you knock over every negative domino on your emotional playing board and, in so doing, remove significant sources of both emotional and physical ailments. You experience personal peace, which improves your work and home relationships, your health, and every other area of your life.

Tapping on large numbers of events one by one might seem like a daunting task, but we'll show you in the next few paragraphs how you can accomplish it quickly and efficiently. Because of EFT's generalization effect, where tapping on one issue reduces the intensity of similar issues, you'll typically find the process going much faster than you imagined.

Removing the emotional charge from your specific events results in less and less internal conflict. Less internal conflict results, in turn, in greater personal peace and less suffering on all levels—physical, mental, emotional, and spiritual. For many people, the Personal Peace Procedure has led to the complete cessation of lifelong issues that other methods did not resolve. You'll find stories on the EFT Universe website written by people who describe relief from physical maladies like headaches, breathing difficulties, and digestive disorders. You'll read other stories of people who used EFT to help them deal with the stress associated with AIDS, multiple sclerosis, and cancer. Unresolved anger, traumas, guilt, or grief contributes to physical illness, and cannot be medicated away. EFT addresses these emotional contributors to physical disease.

Here's how to do the Personal Peace Procedure:

1. List every specific troublesome event in your life that you can remember. Write them down in a Personal Peace Procedure journal. "Troublesome" means it caused you some form of discomfort. If you listed fewer than 50 events, try harder to remember more. Many people find hundreds. Some bad events you recall may not seem to cause you any current discomfort. List them anyway. The fact that they came to mind suggests they may need resolution. As you list them, give each specific event a title, like it's a short movie, such as: Mom slapped me that time in the car; I stole my brother's baseball cap; I slipped and fell in front of everybody at the ice skating rink; My third-grade class ridiculed me when I gave that speech; Dad locked me in the toolshed overnight; Mrs. Simmons told me I was dumb.

2. When your list is finished, choose the biggest dominoes on your board, that is, the events that have the most emotional charge for you. Apply EFT to them, one at a time, until the SUD level for each event is 0. You might find yourself laughing about an event that used to bring you to tears; you might find a memory fading. Pay attention to any aspects that arise and treat them as separate dominoes, by tapping for each aspect separately. Make sure you tap on each event until it is resolved. If you find yourself unable to rate the intensity of a bad event on the 0-10 scale, you might be dissociating, or repressing a memory. One solution to this problem is to tap ten rounds of EFT on every aspect of the event you are able to recall. You might then find the event emerging into clearer focus but without the same high degree of emotional charge.

3. After you have removed the biggest dominoes, pick the next biggest, and work on down the line.

4. If you can, clear at least one of your specific events, preferably three, daily for 3 months. By taking only minutes per day, in 3 months you will have cleared 90 to 270 specific events. You will likely discover that your body feels better, that your threshold for getting upset is much lower, your relationships have improved, and many of your old issues have disappeared. If you revisit specific events you wrote down in your Personal Peace Procedure journal, you will likely discover that the former intensity has evaporated. Pay attention to improvements in your blood pressure, pulse, and respiratory capacity. EFT often produces subtle but measurable changes in your health, and you may miss them if you aren't looking for them.

5. After knocking down all your dominoes, you may feel so much better that you're tempted to alter the dosages of medications your doctor has prescribed. Never make any such changes without consulting with your physician. Your doctor is your partner in your healing journey. Tell your doctor that you're working on your emotional issues with EFT, since most health care professionals are acutely aware of the contribution that stress makes to disease.

The Personal Peace Procedure does not take the place of EFT training, nor does it take the place of assistance from a qualified EFT practitioner. It is an excellent supplement to EFT workshops and help from EFT practitioners. EFT's full range of resources is designed to work effectively together for the best healing results.

Is It Working Yet?

Sometimes EFT's benefits are blindingly obvious. In the introductory video on the home page of the EFT Universe website, you see a TV reporter with a lifelong fear of spiders receiving a tapping session. Afterward, in a dramatic turnaround, she's able to stroke a giant hairy tarantula spider she's holding in the palm of her hand.

Other times, EFT's effects are subtler and you have to pay close attention to spot them. A friend of mine who has had a lifelong fear of driving in high-speed traffic remarked to me recently that her old fear is completely gone. Over the past year, each time she felt anxious about driving, she pulled her car to the side of the road and tapped. It took many trips and much tapping, but subtle changes gradually took effect. Thanks to EFT she has emotional freedom and drives without fear. She also has another great benefit, in the form of a closer bond to her daughter and baby granddaughter. They live 2 hours drive away and, previously, her dread of traffic kept her from visiting them. Now she's able to make the drive with joyful anticipation of playing with her granddaughter.

If you seem not to be making progress on a particular problem despite using EFT, look for other positive changes that might be happening in your life. Stress affects every system in the body, and once you relieve it with EFT, you might find improvements in unexpected areas. For instance, when stressed, the capillaries in your digestive system constrict, impeding digestion. Many people with digestive problems report improvement after EFT. Stress also redistributes biological resources away from your reproductive system. You'll find many stories on EFT Universe of people whose sex lives improved dramatically as a by-product of healing emotional issues. Stress affects your muscular and circulatory systems; many people report that muscular aches and pains disappear after EFT, and their blood circulation improves. Just as stress is pervasive, relaxation is pervasive, and when we release our emotional bonds with EFT, the relaxing effects are felt all over the body. So perhaps your sore knee has only improved slightly, but you're sleeping better, having fewer respiratory problems, and getting along better with your coworkers.

Saying the Right Words

A common misconception is that you have to say just the right words while tapping in order for EFT to be effective. The truth is that focusing on the problem is more important than the exact words you're using. It's the exposure to the troubling issue that directs healing energy to the right place; the words are just a guide.

Many practitioners write down tapping scripts with lists of affirmations you can use. These can be useful. However, your own words are usually able to capture the full intensity of your emotions in a way that is not possible using other people's words. The way you form language is associated with the configuration of the neural network in your brain. You want the neural pathways along which stress signals travel to be very active while you tap. Using your own words is more likely to awaken that neural pathway fully than using even the most eloquent words suggested by someone else. By all means use tapping scripts if they're available, to nudge you in the right direction. At the same time, utilize the power of prolonged exposure by focusing your mind completely on your own experience. Your mind and body have a healing wisdom that usually directs healing power toward the place where it is most urgently required.

The Next Steps on Your EFT Journey

Now that you've entered the world of EFT, you'll find it to be a rich and supportive place. On the EFT Universe website, you'll find stories written by thousands of people, from all over the world, describing success with an enormous variety of problems. Locate success stories on your particular problem by using the site's drop-down menu, which lists issues alphabetically: Addictions, ADHD, Anxiety, Depression, and so on. Read these stories for insights on how to apply EFT to your particular case. They'll inspire you in your quest for full healing.

Our certified practitioners are a wonderful resource. They've gone through rigorous training in Clinical EFT and have honed their skills with many clients. Many of them work via telephone or videoconferencing, so if you don't find the perfect practitioner in your geographic area, you can still get expert help with remote sessions. While EFT is primarily a self-help tool and you can get great results alone, you'll find the insight that comes from an outside observer can often alert you to behavior patterns and solutions you can't find by yourself.

Take an EFT workshop. EFT Universe offers more than a 100 workshops each year, all over the world, and you're likely to find a Level 1 and 2 workshop close to you. You'll make friends, see expert demonstrations, and learn EFT systematically. Each workshop contains eight learning modules, and each module builds on the one before. Fifteen years' experience in training thousands of people in EFT has shown us exactly how people learn EFT competently and quickly, and provided the background knowledge to design these trainings. Read the many testimonials on the website to see how deeply transformational the EFT workshops are.

The EFT Universe newsletter is the medium that keeps the whole EFT world connected. Read the stories published there weekly to stay inspired and to learn about new uses for EFT. Write your own experiences and submit them to the newsletter. Post comments on the EFT Universe Facebook page, and comment on the blogs.

If you'd like to help others access the benefits you have gained from EFT, you might consider volunteering your services. There are dozens of ways to support EFT's growth and progress. You can join a tapping circle, or start one yourself. You can donate to EFT research and humanitarian efforts. You can offer tapping sessions to people who are suffering through one of EFT's humanitarian projects, like those that have reached thousands in Haiti, Rwanda, and elsewhere. You can let your friends know about EFT.

EFT has reached millions of people worldwide with its healing magic but is still in its infancy. By reading this book and practicing this work, you're joining a healing revolution that has the potential to radically reduce human suffering. Imagine if the benefits you've already experienced could be shared by every child, every sick person, every anxious or stressed person in the world. The trajectory of human history would be very different. I'm committed to helping create this shift however I can, and I invite you to join me and all the other people of goodwill in making this vision of a transformed future a reality.

How People Use EFT for the Five Major Life Areas: Relationships, Health, Work, Money, and Spirituality

Why suffer? Suffering is part of the human condition. Human beings get sick, and die. Yet there are two kinds of suffering: the inevitable and the unnecessary. A random accident like being hit by a bus might induce unavoidable pain and suffering. Yet other kinds of suffering, such as emotional distress, can be induced entirely by our thinking, or by replaying old negative experiences in our minds. If we stay in that rut, we continue to suffer. We can also make choices that pull us out of the rut, and eliminate our suffering. We can make choices that result in emotional freedom. Here's the story of "Lisa," who decided to tackle her issues head on with EFT; that choice resulted in a permanent lifting of her suffering.

Removing the Blocks to Love's Presence
By Fraeda Scholz

This article is about using EFT creatively to assist spiritual shifts in a series of five phone sessions I facilitated with a fellow EFT practitioner, we will call her "Lisa." Lisa and I met in 2007 and have traded EFT sessions fairly consistently since that time. The idea for this series of five sessions came from Lisa who wanted to use EFT to help her remove the blocks to "Love's Presence" inside her as part of her spiritual work, specifically related to a spiritual book and path she has been on for 3 years. Below are the essential details of the fifth phone session, which lasted about 80 minutes.

At the beginning of the session Lisa presented two main issues:

Issue 1: A family situation, ongoing for a long time, which could have a big impact on her life. She has tapped on this issue on her own as it has unfolded since 2006. The day before the session she met with some family members on a conference call and many feelings, thoughts, and judgments were stirred up in her and she quickly became "lost in them." Lisa's two main beliefs/judgments of herself that came out of the family situation were that she was both a "guilty perpetrator and sinner" and an "innocent victim of blame contaminated by family circumstances." Her SUD levels on these feelings were 5–8.

Issue 2: Lisa saw her reactiveness to the family issue as "a way that my ego mind caught me up in an old familiar web of anguish and anxiety. I became upset because my ego mind wanted to play with the event in order to drag me back into the seductive drama of my life story and keep me distracted from my spiritual connection to Love's Presence within myself."

Lisa chose these issues to enhance the depth of emotion, making the clearing process deeper and more complete by using extreme Setup Statements like "Even though I am a guilty, complicit, perpetrator sinner and a victim contaminated by the circumstances of my family, I deeply and completely love and accept myself." Throughout the session we used the entire basic EFT recipe, including the 9 Gamut sequence. We ended on a positive note, tapping on "This awe, this Love, this gratitude."

Lisa and I then sat together (although 500 miles apart) in silence for a little while, being present with the moment. We then checked her SUD levels, which had ranged from 5 to 8; all were now at a 0. The original judgments and beliefs about her family felt "totally irrelevant and absurd to me now. Simply silly egoic thoughts, signifying nothing, next to the powerful feeling of connection to Source."

After this session Lisa wrote the following testimonial about her experience:

"I felt a profound and dramatic shift into feeling/being that divine Love that I was longing for. I shifted over into deep and global mind states of surrender, peace, and communion with Loving Presence, in the eternal 'Now' moment. This shift was deeper and felt truer than my past experiences with Divine Presence. Fear dissolved. Worry vanished. I came to recognize the old familiar, habitual, and negative egoic mind chatter as just flimsily that—nothing more than mind chatter—instead of identifying with or getting lost in it. I now have confidence that I can return to those places, with the focus of EFT. There is less fear, less resistance, and more ease in clearing the seeming egoic obstacles that arise in my mind as I move forward in life day to day. I firmly believe that all disease begins in the mind, and that is where the true healing lies—in the mind."

For myself, as a result of the use of EFT and other energy psychology techniques, I often feel happy for "no reason." I often feel surrounded and pervaded by a subtle feeling of love and connection. This did not happen all at once, but it did happen relatively quickly once I really set my mind to using these techniques combined with other teachings and learning. EFT is an invaluable and very practical, "where the rubber meets the road," kind of tool on my personal spiritual path as well, which I am still on.

* * *

Imagine an alternative reality in which Lisa had not made the conscious decision to address her issues with EFT. She would have continued to suffer from her family situation and her reactions to it. By making the new choice, she eliminated her suffering. You might think that your suffering is intrinsic to your situation, and imposed upon you by outside circumstances and people. But much more than you suppose may be due to your thinking, infused by strong emotion. Tap away the emotion, release the hold those negative experiences have over your mind, and your whole experience of life can change. This is true even if the people and circumstances around you may stay the same.

EFT can be used in many situations that involve unnecessary suffering. It can lift the burden of suffering that would otherwise weigh down a person's life, and give that person a future free of that emotional baggage. I'd like to give you a sense of how and where people are using it, to spark an awareness in your mind of its value in your life, especially in the areas where suffering is optional. As you read these stories, and see how people like you and me apply EFT to different aspects of their lives, think about the places in your life that could use improvement, and how you can change some of the problematic situations in your life by tapping. As you'll see, even serious and long-standing problems often shift after EFT. Be inspired, and open your mind to the possibilities!

Families

EFT can make all the difference between whether a family is a place of suffering and emotional pain, or whether it's a haven of joy. Here are some examples of how EFT has helped parents, children, and married couples.

EFT Is Instrumental in Bringing a Couple Back Together
By Carey Mann

Peter came to me 2 weeks after his girlfriend broke up with him. He felt angry and confused as to why she left, as he thought that they would be together forever. He wasn't eating or sleeping and was obsessed with getting her back. He wasn't taking any responsibility for himself and his actions, however. We began tapping on statements like "I was the perfect partner" and "It's all her fault."

At this point I asked if these statements were true. Peter broke down, his anger shifting suddenly to sadness. I asked him to put his hand on his heart and focus on breathing in and out of the heart— breathing in whilst counting to 5 and breathing out whilst counting to

5 (a HeartMath technique). This quickly brought his level of intensity down from 9 out of 10 to a 4, and the feeling was in his heart.

I asked if the feeling had a shape or a color and, if so, what was it. Peter responded that it was like a small penknife.

Even though I have this small penknife in my heart...

We did a full round on "this penknife in my heart" and his level of intensity dropped to a 0 out of 10. I then asked him who put the knife there and he explained that he put it there a few minutes ago when he realized that he spent 4 years in a relationship, rarely ever telling her or showing her how much he loved her knowing that that was exactly what she had wanted and needed. So we tapped on statements like "Even though I didn't tell her how much I loved her…" and "Even though I didn't show her how much I loved her in the way that she needed…"

Peter then told me that his father didn't express his love through touch or speech and that he was repeating the patterns of his father. We tapped on "Even though my dad was visual and not kinesthetic and auditory…" and "Even though I'm repeating the patterns of my dad…"

I asked Peter to close his eyes and look at himself as a little boy. He said that the little boy looked sad. So I asked him to have a chat with the little boy and perhaps cuddle him and give him the type of love that he had yearned for when he was young. I also asked him if it was possible to bring his dad in to the picture and for all three of them to have a chat and find some resolution.

After several minutes he opened his eyes and smiled. He said that his dad said, "It's too late for me, but you can show and give love in ways that I never could."

We worked together for a further five sessions and Peter and his girlfriend are now back together, living their dream of a blissful and fully functional relationship, thanks to EFT.

* * *

Counselor Uses EFT to Improve Math Abilities
By Syandra Ingram

I am an elementary school guidance counselor on a PK-6th grade campus. In Texas, our public schools must give state standardized tests, the Texas Assessment of Knowledge and Skills (TAKS), in core subjects. Students must pass these tests in order to advance to the next grade. As you can imagine, as test time approaches, both teachers and students are highly stressed.

Last spring, the sixth-grade math tutor expressed concern about the students she was tutoring. With the TAKS test only 2 weeks away, the students just didn't seem to be making the progress they needed to make. I decided to try EFT.

I invited all 16 of the sixth-grade students in her tutoring groups to participate in an after school "TAKS Stress Reliever and Math Phobia Busting Academy," and sent home permission letters to their parents. Of the 16 students, 10 chose to participate. This group committed to meet after school for an hour each day. Due to Easter Break, we only had eight meetings.

In our sessions, we used EFT for issues relating to math and test-taking phobias, math difficulties, and stress and anxiety. I gave the students the freedom to be honest with me, and allowed them to tell me, without censorship, what they thought their problems with math were.

One of the girls said her problems with math began when she went to kindergarten where she was confronted with numbers for the first time. The other children seemed to know what numbers were and how to use them, and she didn't. She felt embarrassed, ashamed, and dumb...a feeling that persisted with her all the way through school.

After identifying each student's particular current and past problems surrounding math, we identified the 0–10 intensity for each concern, and selected a student to tap on. The rest of the students were to Borrow Benefits, tapping on themselves along with the student "on stage." The students were amazed that their own intensity levels kept falling even though they weren't the student being tapped on!

The students were enthusiastic participants and loved being the volunteer who was tapped on and being the volunteer who sometimes did the tapping on someone else. Students were given "tapping" home-work each night.

Final results? Nine of the 10 students who participated in the TAKS Academy passed the TAKS, and the 10th made significant improvement, although not enough to pass the test. Of the six students who chose not to participate, four passed and two failed. I think that's significant. Beyond that, though, the students who learned and used EFT developed a new self-confidence and self-empowerment. All of them said that they would continue to use EFT in the future.

After 10 years of being a school counselor and feeling like I was putting Band-Aids on major wounds, I finally, with EFT, have some-thing to offer these children that will not only help in the "here and now," but will also be something they can use for the rest of their lives to create the lives they deserve. These 10 students learned that they have the power to shape their own lives.

* * *

Tapping for the Aftermath of Domestic Violence
By Ann Peck

EFT tapping has been instrumental in my healing in so many ways. My history includes sexual, physical, and verbal abuse, among other things. While EFT has helped in healing the effects of past abuse, sadly, it cannot prevent abuse from happening. It does, however, give us something to use when and if abuse occurs.

Recently, I my former husband physically assaulted me. My chil-dren were present and my oldest got involved by jumping onto her father, telling him not to hurt her mom. She then called 911.

EFT to the rescue…

Upon getting to safety and while waiting for the police, I immediately began tapping. (I can't believe he did this—I'm really okay—It wasn't my fault—I didn't cause this to happen—Need to calm down—Kids need me.)

EFT calmed my emotions and pulled my scattered energies back into balance, allowing me to attend to my oldest child. She told me she was so scared and that she thought her dad was going to kill me. I asked her if we could tap together. She looked back at her dad and promptly refused. (Her dad is against tapping.)

I tapped as a surrogate for her and noticed her breathing began to even out and the crying and shaking stopped. (I tapped on "this precious child—this amazing strong child—this courageous child—feeling safe—breathing calmly.)

Later that evening I tapped with my youngest as we talked about what happened. By the time we were done, he was able to rest peacefully through the night. Life continues to give us many opportunities for tapping as we navigate our own individual healing. I cannot imagine my life without EFT.

* * *

EFT Improves Memory in Mother with Alzheimer's
By Debra Trojan

Here's an EFT success I've recently had with my 82-year-old mother who has Alzheimer's. She's been declining over a period of 5 years. She recognizes close family members but not friends. She can carry on a conversation as long as you keep it current. She's particularly deficient in her short-term memory. (After 5 minutes, she's forgotten what's she's done or said.)

She lives with my sister and her husband (Janet and Rudy). Whenever they go on a trip, she stays with me. She can never remember where they are when they go. So it's common for her to ask (very often) where they are.

A week ago, Janet and Rudy went to Texas to visit Janet's daughter Miranda. As expected, Mom started asking me where they were 5 minutes after settling in at my house. She continued to ask me where they were every few hours. Each time, I would tell her, "Janet and Rudy flew to Texas to visit Miranda and Josh and their baby Benjamin." After the fifth day (and after answering that question approximately 25 times), my frustration level was reaching a pinnacle. It's usually in times of frustration and desperation that I think of EFT. It occurred to me that if I tapped on her while I told her where they were, she might actually be able to remember it. (If only I had done this the first time she asked me.)

I had her repeat the phrase "Janet and Rudy flew to Texas to visit Miranda and Josh and their baby Benjamin" while I tapped on her. She was able to follow my lead on the 9 Gamut and really got into singing "Happy Birthday." I finished up with the sequence and waited 10 minutes before I popped the big question. You can imagine how excited I was when, after reflecting for a few seconds, she told me: "Janet and Rudy flew to Texas to visit Miranda and Josh and their baby Benjamin."

An hour later when my 16-year-old son came home from school, I couldn't wait for him to ask her the question and see his surprise. Sure enough, she delivered perfectly. Every couple of hours, I tested her. She would always think for a few seconds and then come out with it. It's been 4 days and she's still remembering. (I've asked her approximately 20 times in those 4 days.) Sometimes she has to think about it, but (so far) she's been able to remember.

* * *

These are just a few of the hundreds of stories in the EFT archives showing that people like you and me have dramatically changed the level of happiness in their families by using EFT. There is now an entire 12-week course called Tapping Deep Intimacy (www. TappingDeepIntimacy.com) that trains people in using EFT to rewrite their old relationship scripts and embrace new and happier behaviors. Family relationships is just one area of life in which tapping can help. There are many others, such as physical pain and disease symptoms. Here are some examples, some light, some about serious problems, of people using EFT to help them with such problems.

Pain and Physical Symptoms

The Bowling Ball in My Intestines

On the second morning of an EFT workshop, Howard, a physician attending the workshop, reported that he had a toothache. "I tried EFT on it last night and this morning, but it's still there," he said. I asked Howard how intense it was on a scale of 0 to 10. He said it was an 8.

I asked if there was anything that might be contributing to it emotionally. He was certain there was no emotional component, that it was "just a toothache." He was a doctor, after all, he should know!

It occurred to me to ask a metaphorical question. "Howard, what are you chewing on, emotionally?"

He said that he had been ruminating on his relationship with his longtime partner in his medical practice. His partner had made some investments that had turned out to be very successful and were pulling his attention away from his customary devotion to his patients.

I inquired Howard how his own investments were doing, and he said, "I've lost most of my savings in the real estate bust."

I asked him to think about his investment portfolio and give me a SUD level. The intensity was a 7. I asked, "How do you know it's a 7?" and he said, "Because I feel like there's a bowling ball stuck in my intestines."

I requested that he think about the first time in his life he could remember that physical sensation of a bowling ball down there. He said, "I was 6 years old. I was playing in the hallway of the apartment building where we lived, and a stranger appeared. He pulled down the zipper of his pants and exposed himself to me. I ran away and hid in the basement of the building."

We did some tapping around the memory of the flasher, but his bowling ball SUD did not go down below a 4, so we used the Movie Technique to review each one of the "emotional crescendos" of the incident. They were all at a 0. I realized there must be additional aspects to the event that we had not yet addressed, so I asked him what happened right after the incident.

Howard recounted that after he left the basement, he went and told his mother what had happened. She said, "You're always getting yourself into trouble." He felt she was blaming him, and this led to a feeling that his misfortunes were always his fault, that he was never good enough. I tested his SUD level around his mother's response, and it was a 10. Suddenly, he gasped and said, "I guess I am more angry at my mother for not protecting me than I am at the man!"

We tapped on that memory till it went down to 0, and because time was short, we tapped on a lot of general statements such as "My feelings don't count. I don't deserve to be protected. Other people are okay, I'm not." I sometimes use generalities when we need to "sneak away" from an incident due to a lack of time. I asked Howard to tell me about the bowling ball in his gut, and he said that it had evaporated into dew. His SUD rating regarding his medical practice partner was also now a 0. So I asked what number his toothache was, and his eyes opened wide. "I can hardly feel it! Maybe a 1 or a 2."

* * *

Howard's story provides us with a good demonstration of the link between emotions and physical symptoms. There might be a real dental problem to take care of, which is the "1 or 2" remaining SUD. It's then vital to seek appropriate medical care. Releasing the emotional issues along with getting competent medical help means, however, that you address the problem from both ends, rather than medicalizing the emotional component of a symptom.

Tapping for Cervical Cancer Pain
By Krysti Wesley

I had the most incredible result with a woman who has had cervical cancer. She came to me for treatment, as she was having no relief from the specialist for her pain. When she arrived, she was obviously in a lot of discomfort.

She was in incredible pain when she went to the toilet, and could not sit comfortably on a chair. I checked her SUD [0–10 intensity] and she said she was a 20! We first used the statement "Even though I have pain in my uterus..."

There didn't seem to be much change, so we changed the statement to "Even though I have pain in my vagina..." and, bingo, she dropped down to a 5 in the first round.

By round three she was pain free and the pain had disappeared from her face. There was a lightness to her whole energy.

The next day she reported to me that she had experienced some nausea and stomach cramps several hours later, which lasted for about an hour. That was about 6 weeks ago and there has been no reoccurrence of the pain since. There are other aspects she is working on as to why the cancer occurred...but she is very happy.

I have been looking for an easier, faster therapy for my clients and this in conjunction with my other work is fantastic.

* * *

EFT Eliminates Searing Burn Pain
By Rebecca Snyder

I have been an enthusiastic EFTer for a couple of years now, and I am so grateful for this amazing tool. I've had some amazing successes on myself and others, but I wanted to share the latest right now, because it comes under the category of "EFT First Aid."

Last night I was making dinner for a group of friends and, amid conversation, I took a pan out of a 400-degree oven and set it on the stovetop. I turned to answer a question, and without thinking, grabbed the handle of the pan without a mitt. OUCH!

I immediately turned to the sink, and while I ran cold water over the burned left hand, started tapping with my right. I didn't use a Setup Statement, because the pain was intense and immediate. I tapped first on this searing pain. The tap water in Georgia this time of year is never really cold, so it didn't seem to be doing much good. I continued tapping while I got a few ice cubes, and held them for about 5 minutes.

During this whole time, the conversation continued around me, my friends unaware that I had anything wrong with me. (They're used to seeing me tap frequently, and since I didn't make a big fuss about the burn, they paid no attention.) I wasn't really getting a lot of relief from the tapping I was doing, and I think it was because I was distracted by the conversation. So I left the room and went to tap in concentration.

I switched from "This pain" to how stupid I felt for having grabbed a 400-degree pan right after taking it out of the oven. The pain began to diminish from a level of intensity of 10 out of 10 to perhaps a 7 out of 10. I continued to tap on the stupidity…and again got stuck.

So I switched to a Setup of "Even though I did something stupid, I forgive myself, and ask my body's vast wisdom to heal the damage I did," then did the abbreviated basic recipe, alternating points with "I forgive my stupidity" and "My body's healing wisdom." The pain went to 0 everywhere but the palm, where the most severe burn was, and that was maybe at a 2 out of 10.

I started thinking about how bad it would be for me to try to work (I'm a hairstylist) with blisters on my hand, so I tapped a few rounds on "Even though burns always blister, and it would be impossible for me to do hair with blisters on my hand, I know my body can heal without blistering and allow the healing to pass that stage."

The pain was at 0 everywhere on my hand, and the skin in the burned areas became sort of "leathery." I put some healing oil on it, and went to have dinner with my friends. All in all, I tapped for about 20 minutes. I was able to enjoy my company for the rest of the evening, even to playing pool for an hour!

This morning, there's only a slight pinkness on my palm, and no pain whatsoever.

* * *

The use of EFT for pain and physical symptoms leads naturally to the question: "How about EFT being used by doctors and hospitals?" Increasingly, because of the large research base EFT enjoys, EFT is finding its way into medical settings and psychotherapy offices. Here are some examples of what that looks like.

The Health Care System

At an integrative medicine conference at which I presented several times, a physician came up to me. He runs a large private clinic in Chicago, supervising teams of doctors, nurses, and support staff. He expressed his gratitude for having learned EFT from me 2 years before. He said they'd implemented EFT at his facility, and described how and when they used EFT.

Because of the financial pressure on doctors, they typically spend only a few minutes with each patient. The average visit is only 13 minutes (Gottschalk & Flocke, 2005). Visits at the Chicago clinic were no exception, and that time frame doesn't allow for an EFT session.

The intake session at this physician's facility, however, was an exception. The clinic scheduled 3½ hours for these. Patients filled out a variety of forms, and were given a battery of tests by the physicians' assistants. The Chicago doctor used this long intake process to administer a thorough EFT session, as well as completing the rest of the process.

What he found is that many of the problems with which patients came to him simply vanished after EFT. For instance, their levels of physical pain were reduced. The part of pain due to emotional upset went away. That left the actual medical part of pain to be treated by appropriate medical means. In the Health Care Workers study, which a colleague and I conducted, an average of 68% of pain disappeared after a 30-minute EFT session (Church & Brooks, 2010). What remained was about one third of the pain.

This portion of the pain was most likely tied to medical causes, and amenable to medical treatment. The Chicago clinic was then able to treat that pain with medical means after first eliminating the emotional part of pain. They could prescribe medication levels appropriate to the physical part of pain, instead of engaging in futile attempts to medicate the two thirds of the pain that was tied to emotions. Setting these priorities is a way in which EFT helps both patients and doctors in clinics and hospitals.

Emergencies

A study examined the use of EFT for symptoms of traumatic stress following automobile accidents (Swingle, Pulos, & Swingle, 2004). This research team used EEG machines to measure the brain waves of participants, and also collected their SUD scores. These declined from an average of 8.3 before treatment to an average of 2.5, and those that received the most benefit from EFT had significant improvements in the brain-wave frequencies associated with stress. This type of improvement is also found in many stories, like the following report by Linda Compton who used EFT right after stepping on a bee. After Linda's story is an account by a mother who used EFT for her son's foot injury, and noticed a rapid recovery.

Step on a Bee, Use EFT
By Linda Compton

Last Sunday, at a fair in San Rafael, California, the sun was blazing and I took my shoes off to walk in the grass. I felt a piercing in my foot, raised it up, and found that I had stepped on a bee. I brushed it away, but the stinger was still in my foot.

I have never felt that kind of pain located so centrally in one spot. The pain was so bad I couldn't even cry. Then I remembered that I am an EFT practitioner. I started at a pain level of 10, did three rounds, and the pain went down to a 3. At that point, I could stand for a doctor to look at my foot. Even though I have done EFT for 6 or 7 years with clients and for myself, I am still amazed at the power of it.

* * *

EFT for Child's Foot Injury Reduces Swelling in Minutes
By Angela Seaman

I began doing EFT on myself, my friends, and my son about 6 months ago and have had wonderful success. However, I had what I consider an amazing experience 2 evenings ago at home with my son.

My 8-year-old-son, Joseph, was bouncing on my bed showing me some "cool new moves" when all of a sudden he fell onto the bed and twisted his foot. He immediately began to cry. I looked at his foot and there was a large bump a couple of inches up from his big toe. His toe was swollen, as was the area around his ankle.

When I asked him to move his foot, he was unable to do so without a lot of pain and tears. I immediately began to do EFT on him. (He repeated the Setup and Reminder phrases while I tapped the Basic Recipe and the 9 Gamut series.) Amazingly enough, after each round, the swelling in all areas of his foot had gone down! I was and am still flabbergasted at how amazing EFT is! After approximately six to seven rounds, the bump was barely visible, there was no other swelling, and he was able to walk on the foot again!

Frankly, when this occurred, I thought I would have to keep him home from school the next day and perhaps have to take him to see a doctor. When he woke up the next morning, he was running around as usual with no aftereffects!

* * *

These stories are drawn from TraumaTap.com, a website for people using EFT for first aid. The site contains many other stories, showing how EFT is used to counter the immediate trauma of accidents and emergencies. People write about how EFT has helped with abrasions, bites, bruises, burns, choking, cuts, nosebleeds, nausea, poisoning, scrapes, sprains, and stings. It's surprising just how many emergency situations have been improved by an alert friend or parent pulling out their tapping finger and providing immediate help to the person affected.

Weight Loss

With one third of people in developed countries overweight, and another one third obese, weight loss is a concern for two thirds of the population. It's likely to affect you or people in your circle. EFT has been used successfully for weight loss by thousands of people. Though many diets and eating programs can produce weight loss, the evidence shows that most dieters later gain back all the weight they lost, and more. After all that deprivation and discipline, they wind up in worse shape than they were at the start. That's discouraging, to say the least.

Studies show that EFT is one of the few approaches that results not only in weight loss, but also in continued weight loss after the program ends (Stapleton, Sheldon, & Porter, 2012; Church & Wilde, 2013). That's because EFT reduces food cravings, and permanently changes behavior (Church & Brooks, 2010). You don't just get a temporary effect from an EFT weight loss program, you get emotional freedom from the compulsions and cravings that resulted in you being overweight in the first place.

There are a number of EFT weight loss programs. One of them, a six-week online program called Skinny Genes, has been the subject of scientific research (Church & Wilde, 2013). The study found that participants lost an average of 12 pounds in the course of the program. But what was even more encouraging is that they continued to lose weight after the program ended: an average of 3 pounds in the next 6 months. Another EFT program created by Bond University professor Peta Stapleton, PhD, found that participants lose an average of 11.1 pounds in the year after the program ends. I don't know of any approach other than EFT that results in continuing weight loss instead of the usual pattern of weight regain. Here are two examples of emotional eating drawn from actual live Skinny Genes coaching calls I offered. You'll see from these moving true stories that these people could not have overcome their cravings using any other method.

The Chocolate Dream Pie

"Sarah" had worked on herself using many self-help methods, and had succeeded in most areas of her life, including eating. But there was one food undermining her diet. She could not shake her craving for a dessert called Chocolate Dream Pie, no matter how hard she tried. Sarah had a wrapper in front of her during the call, and estimated her craving for the treat as a 10 out of 10. I asked her about a childhood event involving pie, and she described an incident when she was 10 years old. She and her parents went to visit her brother, who was mentally disabled and confined to an institution. He had never developed the ability to speak. During the visit, Sarah sat with him and felt close to him regardless. Afterward, her parents took her to a restaurant, and everyone had dinner, including pie. No one said anything about the boy, even though they all felt sad. I asked what kind of pie they ate that night, and it was chocolate cream pie. We tapped on this event till Sarah's sadness shifted, and she began to feel gratitude for the time she'd had with her brother. She then reassessed her craving for Chocolate Dream Pie, and it was now a 0! Her craving for the food was really all about the emotions the family had not expressed—the sadness, the regret, the sense of loss. She was displacing those emotions onto food. When the emotions were tapped away, her craving simply disappeared.

* * *

Cinnamon Rolls

"Lottie" craved many sugary treats, but chief among them were cinnamon rolls. As she described the smell and texture of cinnamon rolls on the coaching call, she was so graphic that my mouth began to water! Her craving for them was 10 out of 10 in that moment. We tapped on several events in Lottie's childhood, but a dominant one involved her great-aunt Carla. There wasn't much love in her life, but

Carla had been the person Lottie felt loved her the most. And guess what was Carla's signature dish? Cinnamon rolls! Now, 40 years later, Lottie still associated cinnamon rolls with love. We tapped on the taste, smell, and texture of the rolls, and on being able to feel love without needing to eat. Her craving for cinnamon rolls dropped to a 0, and she said, "Now I can really feel the love that I had with Carla." We'd broken for good her brain's association between love and cinnamon rolls.

* * *

Both Sarah's and Lottie's cases are examples of emotional eating. They could have tried every diet and weight loss plan under the sun but still been unsuccessful, because their problem wasn't that they didn't know what to eat and not eat. Most dieters know more about nutrition and weight loss than the experts! That still doesn't help them gain traction over their habits. Skinny Genes is the one and only program that focuses squarely on emotional eating. Once you've discovered and tapped on the roots of the problem in this way, you'll eliminate self-sabotage, and you'll find everything else you're doing to lose weight is much easier. That's why, whatever else you're doing, you must have Skinny Genes to be successful.

Work

EFT deserves a place at the center of your work life. Why? It can solve problems like lateness, procrastination, blame, excuse making, lack of motivation, and all the other impediments to productivity and creativity at work. One of the biggest drags on the economy is absenteeism, people away from work for various reasons. Yet surprisingly, experts estimate that even more economic activity is lost to "presenteeism." This is the term they use for people whose physical bodies are at the workplace, but whose minds and hearts are elsewhere. They've shown up for work, but they're so distracted they may as well not be present. They show up in a head count, but not in a mind count. Do you know people like that?

Many factors produce subpar performance at work. Personal conflicts between members can hamstring a team's productivity. Public disagreements can jangle the nerves of a whole office, leading to distraction and impaired performance. Harsh, ineffective, or insensitive leadership can leave a whole organization functioning in fear. Worries about children, spouses, and money can be imported into the workplace from outside, crippling productivity. Few workplaces are playgrounds of joy and creativity. According to a recent Gallup report, seven out of 10 workers say they are "not engaged" or "actively disengaged" at work (Gallup, 2013). This is estimated to cost the U.S. economy as much as $550 billion in lost economic activity each year.

EFT can help with all these problems. Let's hear from some dedicated tappers who have transformed their work performance with EFT.

The Man Who Was Afraid to Imagine Success
By Aileen Nobles

I believe James is an example of something that happens to a lot of people. The reasons we choose to not excel are different, but living without believing we can realize our potential is doing ourselves a disservice. We are so much more than we sometimes think we are, and EFT can dissolve the barriers quicker than anything else I have come across.

James was a bright, educated man stuck in mediocrity. Everything he did was the middle of the road. He had tried for years to imagine himself being more successful in his career as a lawyer, yet still he didn't have as many clients as he wanted, and financially he was always just keeping his head above water. Lately, he had been feeling quite hopeless and depressed.

James also had a talent for painting, with some success, yet when offered the opportunity to have a show in a gallery, he became scared and never followed through.

James was the eldest child of alcoholic parents. He was by far the brightest. As a child, he encouraged his brothers and tried to help them, but they felt he was teaching and preaching, and it caused fighting and anger. His parents expected him to keep the peace at home, and blamed him when the brothers fell behind in their schoolwork.

Many times he was told, "You're too big for your boots, thinking you're so much better than your brothers. At school it was much the same; if he excelled, his friends became jealous and began to ostracize him. He remembered being so miserable one night after the usual fighting with his brothers and verbal abuse from his inebriated parents that he thought about suicide. He felt alone, unsupported, and scared. He made a conscious choice that he wanted to fit in and be like everyone else. He wanted to be accepted and appreciated, and to feel safe. He fell into mediocrity.

We tapped on many of the beliefs he'd acquired such as, "Even if part of me says it's not safe to be successful, I would love to love and accept myself anyway" and "Even though I'm no good, I don't deserve to be successful." At this point, James was feeling that a lot of the stuckness had shifted.

He then tapped on the side of his hand, closed his eyes, and imagined himself being successful. It was uncomfortable, but it was the first time he had been able to imagine good changes. We tapped more on phrases like "As an adult I am safe now and ready to shine," "I don't have to have a ceiling anymore," and "My art work is my joy and gift to others, and I am ready to get it out there."

Now James was actually excited about visualizing his future. What a different person walked out of my office that day! James was the featured artist at a couple of galleries last year and is on his way up. He says he feels like a new man...the real James stood up, thanks to EFT.

* * *

Workplace Session Addresses Grief and Pain
By Yair Halfon

"Tom" works at a desk near mine, and has a variety of problems. A few years back, he lost his baby son at the age of 1 year old. I sensed that his grief had never been resolved, and might be the underlying cause of most of his issues. I offered to help and he agreed, a few weeks later, after I had used EFT successfully with a mutual friend of ours.

We went to a private meeting room and I asked Tom about his issues. He had a sciatic nerve problem, which was quite severe, causing pain in his right leg. He could hardly feel his leg and it was so painful that he struggled to tie his shoelaces in the morning. His SUD level was 8 out of 10. He also suffered from neck pain and a twitch around his eye.

I started working with him on the trauma of losing his child by identifying the most troubling memories. He said that the most traumatic memory was the burial ceremony. We did EFT on that using the "Tell the Story" Technique, and brought it down to 0 in a few rounds. Then we did a few rounds on when his son was in the hospital before he died, and getting weaker by the day. This also went down to 0.

When I tested the intensity of the memories with him, it seemed, at least at that moment, that he didn't have any emotional charge.

I then checked with him on his leg pain problem. He said it had gone down to a 5 out of 10, but also it had moved from all over his leg to now only in his foot area. He also reported that he had started feeling his leg now. We did a couple of rounds on those issues, and they went down to 1 out of 10. I left it at that, since we were in the middle of our workday, and he wanted to target other issues too.

We then worked on the neck. In a few rounds it went from 6 to 0. We then focused on the twitch in his eye, and this also went to 0 in a couple of rounds. The whole session took about 1 hour and 20 minutes.

The next day, I asked him how he felt. He said that his eyes and neck were still 0, and the sciatic nerve issue causing him pain his leg had been reduced by 90%.

* * *

Money and Abundance

When we offer live EFT workshops, one of the modules is designed to surface all the objections to success lurking in the minds of participants. We group these by topic, and the area in which we find people have the most barriers is that of money. Yet it doesn't have to be that way! Money can be a joyful experience in every way. Receiving money can spark positive emotions like gratitude and happiness. Spending money can awaken thankfulness for the services being received, and the privilege of having the money to buy them. Saving money can engender emotions like satisfaction and a sense of security. Making money can feel like great fun.

This is not the experience of most people, I've found. Money is often laden with fear. People who need money often live with a sense of lack, insecurity, and fear. If you're one of them, you probably imagine that those with millions of dollars in their bank accounts don't have those worries. You'd be wrong! In my experience, many people who have more money than they can spend in a lifetime worry just as much. They worry about losing money, about their investments going bad, about economic uncertainty. Whether money is plentiful or scarce, we have a habit of projecting many of our unhappy emotions onto it.

EFT can help you establish a healthy relationship with money. After tapping on your fears and early experiences, you can enjoy having it, spending it, saving it, and investing it. When paired with emotional freedom, money can be a happy part of your life. Here are some people who used EFT to change their attitude toward money, and their level of prosperity.

Studies have shown that the most successful stock traders are those who avoid emotional swings. In this account from psychologist Steve Wells and his client James, they share how James cleared his blocks to successful trading.

Clearing Inner Blocks to Successful Stock Trades
By Steve Wells and James

I am very pleased to send you this post from one of my clients, "James," which outlines how he used EFT to achieve massive success in the share market. What makes sending this even more pleasing for me is that James is married to Kathy whose experiences in using EFT to remake her life were outlined in a post I sent previously. Kathy and James have had a beautiful little boy together and are truly living their dream, their very own version of success. And a large part of that success has come about due to the considerable work they have done both separately and together using EFT.

James and I continued to work together using EFT and, recently, we discussed the success he was having and his desire to share with others what has worked for him. The result is the following post on EFT and the Markets, which outlines how James used EFT to bolster and boost his trading success. Here is part of the post by James:

> I was aware of my issues like perfectionism and self-acceptance through my long-term study of self-development and psychology. (I believe that success in the markets is 100% within yourself.) But what I realised was that whilst I had conceptualized all my inner ughhs, I needed to de-energise them. So I went back over my life and tapped on all my hurtful memories. I found lots of residual "stuff" to de-energise.
>
> I did a few more sessions with Steve, mostly on the "have to" and "letting go" parts of my psychobabble. I discussed with Steve that my tapping wasn't by the book, that I made it up as I went. He said: "Tap on 'have to.'" But it was the way he said it, and all the things he didn't say that made the penny drop for me. I went home and tapped without inhibition—life's been so sweet since then.
>
> When I feel that my blocks are removed, I tap whilst visualizing what I want. Then when I get to the last tapping point, I take a long breath, summarize all my tapping, and

wish all the negativity away to the heavens. I usually use both arms to motion my psychobabble to the ethers. This nuance started when I found that tapping outside at nighttime was highly liberating for me. This act of sending off my ughh is the most important part of tapping for me. For me, it feels very neat and wholesome.

I finally and completely trusted myself. I then entered the most amazing life zone. Money from the markets was falling on my head; e.g., I made 400% on one account in 3 months from an hour a week. Not from one lucky trade, but from consistently being in tune with the markets; great trading is effortless, without struggle. And EFT wasn't just working for me in the markets. I would lose something and then find myself walking to it and picking it up unconsciously. My timing in life was uncanny—I was in the most splendid state of being. My inner self no longer took the world personally. I kept noticing one of the quotes stuck on my desk: "It is what it is."

The markets are a boundary-less abstraction, where traditional models of success don't work. The financial industry thinks they have the markets all figured out, with all their fads, big words, herd mentality, and elaborate explanations of why the market did this or that. Whenever I hear "The market went down because investors are taking profits," I smile because I know that if the markets could talk, they would never say that. As do a very small percentage of other market participants who make the vast majority of money in the markets. Why do so few make so much? I believe it is because they have found their true selves in the markets. And the best way to do that is to look within; it's all within. This is why EFT is the icing on my cake.

P.S.: I've overcome 8 years of clinical depression and about 30 years of anxiety and self-doubt. And, like Charles Barkley, the majority of people told me what I couldn't do. The 1% who supported me are now my closest family and friends.

* * *

Manifesting Money with EFT

By Annette Vaillancourt

I estimate that EFT has helped me manifest approximately $70,000 in the last 3 years.

A couple of years ago, soon after I learned EFT, I decided to make a list of affirmations that at the time I doubted I would ever believe. Being the geek that I am, I made an audio recording of the affirmations on my computer and burned them onto a CD, so that I could listen to them in my car. I decided to use the EFT tapping points as I was stating each affirmation aloud. I figured that would clear up any "tail-enders" and speed up my belief of the new affirmations.

Well, not only did I start to believe each affirmation in a short amount of time (and without daily practice), but also those beliefs started to manifest! My favorite was "Large sums of money come to be quickly and easily." In the meantime, I had been wanting to save about $3,000 to buy into a mutual fund for my retirement. It was going to take me several months to set aside that kind of money. To my surprise and delight, I got a call from my brother who informed me that I was going to be receiving two checks from the proceeds of the sale of my mother's house. I had grown up in a blue-collar family and never expected any kind of inheritance, so this was a total shock. Guess what the total was...$3,000!

Then about 6 weeks later, I received another unexpected check from a health insurance refund for about $1,100.

Then in January 2008, I got a call from one of my website clients who asked, "How much can I pay you to work on my website every day?" Why? Because in a 10-day period, he'd written $50,000 worth of business from the site. As he said, "Every time you work on the site (to optimize it), I make money." I had to think about it. Two weeks later, he called again to ask if I wanted to do this and he suggested the following dollar figure, "How about $100,000?" Right then and there I decided to go to an attorney and have a contract drawn up. By the time I'd finished that, his wife had convinced him to drop the offer down to $50,000. Shucks, right?

In late 2009, I also manifested an unexpected $16,000, which allowed me to sell my house and buy the condo of my dreams.

Currently, I am running an EFT tapping group for small business owners and entrepreneurs. The day after that group meets, I always get an influx of new business. So do my group members.

* * *

Aren't those inspiring stories? Don't they open up a fresh horizon in your mind of what your relationship with money might look like after you tap on your issues? Please don't assume that your fears and limitations spring from money itself. Money is simply the trigger that evokes those feelings. When you tap them away, you'll see money very differently.

Spiritual and Moral Development

EFT can help with spiritual and moral problems. Many people find it difficult to create time in their lives for a daily spiritual practice. You might know it's good for you to have a time of prayer, contemplation, or meditation. With all the other demands of your life, you have trouble setting that time aside. EFT can help dissolve some of the blocks that originate in your mind or in your schedule, and support your spiritual practice. Here are a couple of practical examples of this use of EFT.

Uncluttered Mind and a Feeling of Calm
By Colin Carter

Over many years I have learned numerous techniques for meditating. It has never been permanently successful because:

A. It takes up too much time.

B. I can't seem to stop my mind from chatting too much.

C. It's boring.

D. The results were not strong enough to be committed to it.

What I have discovered is a very effective EFT alternative to traditional ways of meditating or relaxing. I sit in a quiet place, I close my eyes, and I welcome every thought that comes into my mind.

If the thought is not obviously happy in any way, I consider it a "problem" to be treated with EFT (without the 9 Gamut). Many times I wonder if the thought is a "problem," but I accept it as such and I might start EFT with: "Even though I have some concern about…"

It's amazing how many little things have some effect on our day-to-day stress levels!

I then wait for the next thought and apply the technique. What I find after about 10 minutes is that I suddenly become aware of myself, where I am and what is going on around me. My thoughts seem to be very distant and "cloudy."

For some minutes I experience an uncluttered mind and feeling of calm. I don't force it to continue—I just open my eyes and continue with other tasks. I just know I have cleaned out a lot of subtle emotional feelings, which individually don't seem a problem, but collectively are causing some degree of "stress."

It's great to do just before bedtime. It just shows how EFT applies not only to specific issues, but also can be applied as an overall technique for achieving calm in our lives.

* * *

Spirituality, Stress, and Thoughts of an Affair
By Aileen Nobles

"Harry" is a successful publisher with a great deal of stress. He had been unable to get more than a few hours sleep for years due to anxiety and a negative voice in his head that he couldn't turn off. As I tuned in to him, I saw a very spiritual man in a great deal of conflict. We talked about his desire to run away from his present life, to live in a monastic way. I asked him what had been going on in his life around the time his insomnia started. A couple of major issues came up.

Harry is a man with his own strong moral sense. Although married, he had fallen in love with a colleague and was grappling over thoughts of having an affair. Even though he never did have the affair, he was eaten up with guilt. He had also given this woman a large amount of money to produce a television show, and 4 years later he had not seen the show produced, and his own financial situation was suffering. His nighttime was filled with guilt and worry about his life and finances. We started tapping, and tapped on all of his worries, such as, "Even though I thought about having an affair…" and "Even though I didn't live up to my own moral standard in my head…" We continued in this vein for a while until he really found the whole situation amusing, even though he is a very serious man. Next we worked with his angst over giving this woman so much money for a television project.

Harry reported the following week that his sleep patterns had been two steps forward and one step back. Considering his penchant for focusing on the worst, I thought that we had had a major breakthrough.

In the following session, I combined EFT with meditation. I have found this to be extremely effective with clients who are open and ready, and it can be used on most situations after the intensity of specific issues have been collapsed. After using this, Harry reported joyfully that he was sleeping well most nights, and was able to be in a more relaxed state during the day.

* * *

Deeper Meditation, and a Prostate Bonus
By Jonas Slonaker

Part of my regimen for staying healthy and free of cancer or other disease is meditation along with prayer, taking good care of myself, and, of course, tapping!

I had prostate cancer 9 years ago and my latest PSA was 0.4. It doesn't go much lower than that. I feel very grateful for EFT.

Concerning my daily meditation, I have discovered that using EFT helps me to reach a deep meditative state much quicker. Here's how it works.

When I meditate, I sit until my mind is quiet, until I am in the "Power of Now," as Eckhart Tolle puts it. Most of the time, my mind quiets down in a short period of time, but sometimes it dredges up conflicts, resentments, worries, etc. When that happens, I often use EFT on the issue at hand and am able to release it.

Now and then, my mind will pop with multiple rapid-fire issues. When that happens, I put my finger to my mouth and make the shhh sound. I continue to shhh while I tap on the EFT points and my mind becomes quiet and I enter into a deep meditative state; I am infused with and surrounded by bright white light.

* * *

As you've read these moving and inspiring stories of personal growth and change, I'm sure your mind has been working away in the background, imagining how you can apply EFT in your own life. You've pictured circumstances in your life that you'd love to see change, and imagined how they might be improved by tapping.

As these case histories show, EFT can be applied to every walk of life. Once you tap away the stress you experience, even if your circumstances don't change, you feel better. That frees up your mental and emotional resources to invent new solutions to old problems. Even though your life is exactly the same now as when you began to read this chapter, your mind is now filled with new possibilities. Those possibilities, when applied to unsatisfactory areas of your life, will change your own internal experience. As your subjective experience changes, you'll find your outer objective circumstances naturally changing. Change your mind by opening it to fresh potential, and change your heart by embracing emotional freedom, and you take a bold and essential step toward changing your life. That change can be for the better, and be radical and discontinuous, setting you up for a future that is dramatically different from your past.

Resources

- 9 Gamut Procedure: 9Gamut.EFTUniverse.com
- Borrowing Benefits: BorrowingBenefits.EFTUniverse.com
- Money Stories: MoneyStories.EFTUniverse.com
- Money Online Course: MoneyCourse.EFTUniverse.com
- Movie Technique: MovieTechnique.EFTUniverse.com
- Relationship Stories: RelationshipStories.EFTUniverse.com
- Skinny Genes Online Weight Loss Course: SkinnyGenesFit.com
- Spirituality Stories: SpiritualityStories.EFTUniverse.com
- Tail-enders: TailEnders.EFTUniverse.com
- Tapping Deep Intimacy Online Relationship Skills Course: TappingDeepIntimacy.com
- "Tell the Story" Technique: TelltheStory.EFTUniverse.com
- Work Stories: WorkStories.EFTUniverse.com

Common Questions, Comments, and Problems

I've trained thousands of people in EFT over the years in various formats. These range from small in-depth training workshops to brief demonstrations following keynote speeches at large conferences to Internet radio and television shows. I've fielded many questions during that time, and these are some of the most common ones asked.

How do I find the right words?

One of the most common worries of newcomers to EFT is that they'll select the wrong words for the Setup Statement. How can you be sure you've phrased it correctly, especially if you're in a situation where you don't have the instructions in front of you?

The answer to this question is to start tapping the Karate Chop point and say the first thing that pops into your head. It's more important to tap than it is to formulate the Setup Statement perfectly. You say the Setup three times, and you can change it on the second or third rounds if a more descriptive phrase occurs to you.

Keep it simple. If you've hurt your thumb, and you're tapping for that, you can simply say, "My thumb hurts." If you've been emotionally triggered by a bad experience, you can say, "This bad experience." If you're feeling annoyed, you can say, "Even though I'm feeling annoyed" while you tap. Start tapping, say any words that keep you focused on the problem, whether they're the perfect words or not, and complete a round or two of EFT. You don't need to go into elaborate explanations of why you feel the way you do, such as, "I'm annoyed at Sally. She told me to mind my own business, and she's always saying things like that. She's such a pain that I don't know why I ever talk to her…" and so on. Just keep it simple: "I'm annoyed at Sally."

With experience, you'll find yourself easily selecting the words that have the most emotional impact, but at the beginning, it's fine to use any words that come to mind. What's important is to stay focused on the problem and tap, and avoid getting into mental considerations about the relative merits of this or that Setup Statement.

Do I need to tap on the exact points?

No. You can tap near the points, or even far away from the points, and still get some effect. At the beginning, just tap, without worrying too much about whether or not you're on the exact points.

Researchers have asked the question of whether using acupuncture needles on sham points that are not real acupuncture points is as effective as needling the points themselves. Their research results are ambiguous, with some studies showing equal effects from sham and real points, while others show the real points having a larger effect (Harris, Zubieta, Scott, Napadow, Gracely, & Clauw, 2009). If you can imagine a line between the full effect of stimulating the points and no effect, stimulating the wrong points may lie somewhere in the middle. It might be better than no acupuncture at all, and less effective than using the precise points.

When you next have an EFT tapping point diagram available, note the location of the points and practice tapping on those exact spots. When you practice EFT using the instructions in this book, you can find the exact points by looking at the diagrams and then in a mirror. Most of the points have tiny indentations in the bone and cartilage right below the skin, and you can find them with your fingertips. It's worth doing that a few times, so that you get into the habit of tapping on the actual acupuncture points rather than nearby places on the skin.

When you need EFT in real life and don't have a diagram available, however, just tap on the locations as you best remember them.

Is it essential that I tap every point?

No. If you forget a point, skip it and tap the next point.

With practice, you'll quickly memorize all the points, and tap them all. At the beginning, it's fine to skip a point or two. Even experienced practitioners sometimes forget to tap a point if they become completely focused on a client. You'll be doing many rounds of EFT, and you'll catch the missing point later on.

What if I don't feel a change in my SUD scores?

Sometimes you'll do EFT on a problem, but when you test your SUD levels before and after, they stay the same. You don't feel your emotions or your body change.

That's okay. There are many reasons why your SUD score might not change. You might need to tune in to the problem more strongly. Part of your psyche might be reluctant to confront the problem. Changes might be happening on a level too subtle for you to notice. You might be dehydrated. Your mind might be convinced that EFT can't work that fast, so it dismisses or minimizes real change. You might be tapping on an associated problem, skirting the real problem. You might be tapping on a surface issue, not yet having discovered a deeper issue that's the real problem. Some issues, like compulsions and addictions, have many layers that can take a long time to reveal themselves. You might need the help of a practitioner or a workshop to address this particular issue. There are thousands of reasons why your SUD score might not go down.

If you finish a round of EFT and your SUD score hasn't dropped at all, don't be discouraged. Pick up the work later on, and you might find new insights and better progress. You might also discover that when you think about the problem a day or two later, your SUD score is now lower. EFT might have had a delayed effect. When your SUD doesn't drop for a particular issue, don't assume that EFT hasn't worked or will never work. Sometimes it works in the background, or has a delayed effect.

What if I can't figure out my SUD?

You might have memories of events that were painful, but when you try and assign them a SUD score, your mind goes blank, or you don't feel any strong feelings. There are several approaches you can use in such cases.

One is just to invent a SUD score. Perhaps a bully beat you up in second grade in school, and you know it was a horrible experience, but you can't figure out what your SUD number is. You can simply imagine a score, making it relative to other experiences in your life. If a happy memory is a 0 and the worst experience of your life is a 10, give the beating a number that seems logical even if you can't come up with a SUD number based on your feelings.

Another is to tap without identifying a SUD score. You can formulate a Setup Statement and perform a whole round of EFT without any SUD rating at the beginning or end. Afterward, think of the problem and ask yourself, "Do I feel better now?" If you do, that's an indication EFT has worked, even though you never assigned the problem a numerical score.

SUD is a useful way to assess progress, but like any other part of the EFT routine, if it hangs you up, drop it and tap anyway. Don't let the inability to come up with a SUD score serve as a bock to starting a round of EFT.

Do I measure my SUD level right now or at the time of the event?

Now. You might remember a traumatic event like a car crash and recall that your SUD level was a 10 at the moment of impact. Perhaps that was 7 years ago, and your SUD level when you now recall the event is a 5. Use your SUD level now, not your SUD level at the time of the event. The reason for this is that EFT works on your nervous system in present time. When you recall the crash and give it a SUD rating of 5, that indicates that the part of your neural network carrying the signals associated with the trauma is active. That's the neural activity we target with EFT.

Some events may have been a 10 when they happened, but you've integrated them into your life story and they're now 0, completely neutral. You're at peace when you think of them, even though they were tragic at the time. Others may still be a 10 when you recall them decades later. Using your current SUD level allows you to focus on events that carry a lasting emotional charge.

This focus on the present level of distress, not the past level, also allows us to test the results we're getting with EFT. If your SUD level around the accident goes down to a 1, you know you've discharged four fifths, or 80%, of the emotional intensity now associated with the accident. If instead you had tried to use your SUD level at the time of the accident, you'd then be comparing a SUD level in the distant past with one now, which would not give you an accurate barometer of progress.

What if my SUD level doesn't go down to 0?

There are many reasons why a SUD level might not drop to a 0, and this is not a problem with EFT.

One case is when you achieve slight progress. Perhaps your SUD rating goes from 9 to 7, or from 5 to 1, but won't go down to 0, despite many rounds of EFT. Even a drop from 10 to 6 is a 40% drop, which represents enormous progress. Sometimes that's enough.

If you're working on a long-standing issue, it's possible for your SUD level to drop to a 0, but a drop even of 10% or 20% indicates a significant reduction in your degree of emotional suffering. That's the goal of EFT. A reduction in suffering is good, even when we can't completely eliminate that suffering.

Another reason your SUD level might not go to 0 is that EFT often has a delayed effect. You might have pain from a bone fracture, for instance, and tapping brings it from an 8 to a 3, but it won't go down further, even after you've tapped several times. You might find it's a 0 or a 1 the day after.

Emotional problems often respond the same way. You might find that you've gone from an 8 to a 2 around some bad childhood event, but your intensity isn't going lower. The next day, try thinking of the event again and assessing your SUD score. You'll often find it's now 0.

If you're working with other people, ask them about their SUD levels frequently during a session. If their SUD levels don't go to 0 for every issue, that's fine. Some issues are easy and go to 0 after just one round of tapping. Others might drop gradually over time. Some might be very difficult, and drop only slightly even after years of tapping. Whatever a client tells you, whatever your own body tells you, trust and accept it.

Another reason why a SUD level doesn't go down to 0 is that it might take time for the reality of change to sink into our bodies and brains. I've often tapped with people and seen their pain or upset go away based on the expression on their faces or their body language. I witness clearly that they're at or near a 0. But then when I ask them for a SUD score, I can see the wheels turning in their heads. Their minds are saying, "Wait a moment! Where's that pain? I can't find it? Where did it go? It can't really be gone." They might get confused or panicked, as the mind searches for pain that's no longer there. The mind is baffled by this sudden absence, and can't explain it. These individuals might give you a SUD above 0 simply because their minds can't believe the pain could vanish so fast.

That's okay. It can take us a while to adjust, especially if a long-standing problem simply vanishes. A big chunk of our inner story might be tied up with that problem, and its sudden absence produces a hole. It can take the mind a while to adjust to the absence of the problem. That's a common reason why people report a high SUD even when it's a 0.

If you believe that a client's SUD is lower than the client's last number, you can gently ask, "Are you sure it's that number?" Sometimes, when you ask a second time, the client tunes in, and realizes the number has gone down further than first believed.

That might not happen, the SUD rating stays high, and that's okay too. In every case, you accept what your clients say, and give them time to adjust. Love and patience provide fertile ground for healing, and a good practitioner accepts the pace of healing just the way it is.

What if I can't remember a specific event?

You might feel bad emotionally or physically and be unable to tie it to any specific event. There are several options in these cases. One is to create an imaginary event in your mind. Perhaps your parents fought when you were a child, and you can't remember the specifics of even one of those fights.

If you use your imagination to fill in the blanks, and just create a likely scenario in your mind, you have a starting point for your EFT session.

This method is usually very effective. The reason it works so well is that the elements of the imaginary situation are being retrieved from our own memory banks. They might be fictional, but the only reason you can imagine them at all is that they resemble an actual event you once saw or heard. To create any imaginary event, you have to draw from reality. So while your fictional event might not have actually happened, it has a high affinity for literal events.

You can also start tapping without an event. You might have an uneasy emotional feeling, for instance. Though it's helpful to trace that uneasiness to an event, you might not be able to remember one, no matter how hard you try. In that case, simply tap on the uneasy feeling.

Interesting directions for an EFT session often appear when you experiment with tapping on the inability to remember an event. You incorporate this situation into your Setup Statement, for example, "Even though I can't remember a specific event, I deeply and completely accept myself." I've done this many times with clients, and found that it often sparks the recall of an event. Tapping seems to lower the barriers to remembering events, and tapping on accepting the inability to recall them removes the pressure to come up with one. That act of relaxation then opens the doors of memory, and specific events pop out.

What if I have many similar traumatic events in my history?

Start with one of them. You can use a particularly troubling one, or go to the other end of the spectrum and tap first on one of the least triggering events.

Imagine working with a client who, as a child, was beaten repeatedly by her mother. She has many beatings, perhaps hundreds, all contributing to her emotional distress. Which one should you pick?

You can ask her if one beating stands out in her memory, and tap on that particular beating. You can also work with the worst beating, if the client is willing and able to handle the emotions that come up. A client might very well not want to remember the worst beating. In that case, you can work on the least severe beating, and tap only on that. If the client is able to dispose of the emotional trauma of that mild beating and go to a low SUD number, they may gain the confidence to tap on more beatings and worse beatings.

Another possibility is to tap on the first beating. You might ask, "What's the first time you remember your mother hitting you." The chances are good that the first in a series of bad memories was a particular shock to the child, violating her expectations of safety and love from a parent.

Because of EFT's generalization effect, when you tap on a particular beating and then tap on a few other particular beatings, it's likely that the emotional charge around all beatings will diminish. Our brains make associations between similar events, and when we process the distress around one, our brains may remove the emotional charge around others too.

Whether you tap on a big event or a small one, a recent event or the first one, don't be deterred from tapping just because you have a frighteningly large number of similar events. Collectively, they may look too big to handle, but you'll typically find that once you tap on a few of them, your SUD score goes down for the whole collection.

What if an event is too big or scary for me to deal with?

Most of us have events in our lives that are too horrible or frightening to contemplate. We can't imagine talking about them, let alone tapping on them.

Don't force yourself to tap on any event for which you are not ready. Tap first on events that you feel are manageable. Gain confidence and experience, and you'll increase your skills. Then you can tackle bigger problems.

Clinical EFT also includes a set of skills called the Gentle Techniques. These are specially designed to deal with overwhelming emotional trauma, and there's an extended section on them in this manual. After you learn these, you'll become more sophisticated in your ability to use EFT for big or scary events.

Can EFT work if my problem has existed for many years?

Yes. You'll be surprised how effective EFT can be even if you've had a problem your whole life. Many clients with lifetime problems believe that EFT won't work because nothing else has. It's very moving to witness clients find release from an issue that has plagued them for many years.

You'll find many stories of EFT working for pain that's been afflicting a person for decades, or clearing emotional baggage that's been weighing someone down for years, or changing a core belief that's kept someone limited their whole life. Long-standing problems don't always disappear as if by magic, but they do sometimes, and the fact that a problem has endured for a very long time is no barrier to now using EFT to work on it.

What if I have physical as well as psychological problems?

Many people use EFT for physical issues like pain and disease symptoms. These are often compounded by psychological issues. For instance, a person might have pain after breaking his or her arm 2 weeks ago. That fracture, and that pain, is a physical problem.

Yet it might also be a psychological problem. Perhaps he broke his arm playing football. He might be angry at the person who knocked him over, or at the referee, or at the doctors at the hospital. People with symptoms are often fearful that they won't heal, worried that the pain won't stop, and angry at themselves for getting into the situation. These psychological problems interact with, and compound, the physical problem.

You can use EFT at both ends of the spectrum. You could tap on the football player's pain. You could also ask him about the circumstances surrounding the injury. Who does he blame? Why is he angry? Who were the people and what were the conditions involved in the event? You can tap on all the negative emotions associated with the physical problem.

It's always worth exploring the psychological aspects of physical problems, even if the problem seems purely physical. You can ask, "If there were an emotional element to this physical problem, what would it be?" This and similar questions often uncover a whole collection of emotional issues associated with the physical problem.

It's also worth exploring the physical parts of psychological problems. If someone is angry, ask, "Where do you feel that anger in your body?" Often the person will report a particular physical location. There may be pain, tension, or other physical sensations at that site. You can tap on both the emotion, and also the body sensations. Perhaps the angry person feels a thick black bar of tension embedded in her shoulders. You can work this physical description into a Setup Statement like "Even though I have this thick black bar embedded in my shoulders, I deeply and completely accept myself." Many clients will make additional progress by tuning in to their bodies as well as tuning in to their emotions.

Do the positive effects last?

Generally, yes. In all the studies that have included a follow-up assessment, the effects of EFT last over time (Feinstein, 2012a). That's true whether the problem was posttraumatic stress disorder (PTSD), phobias, depression, or anxiety. Once people reduced their psychological trauma with EFT, they tended to remain at that reduced level. In the Health Care Workers study, we also compared those who did more EFT with those who did less (Church & Brooks, 2010). We found that those who did more EFT after their initial one-day workshop had a better long-term result than those who did less.

While you might get immediate relief from EFT, you're strongly encouraged to continue using it long-term. Sometimes our immediate problem goes away after we tap, and we then don't do any more tapping. Although that positive experience is a good thing in and of itself, it's better to regard it as a pointer toward the direction we should take for the rest of our lives. We can work on many more issues, and release stress whenever and wherever it affects us.

It's interesting to note how some clients stop tapping once their immediate problem is solved. In the Health Care Workers study, about a third of participants didn't use EFT again after the workshop. Another third used it a few times over the next 6 months. Only a few became regular tappers.

To me this represents a missed opportunity. Why release only a small portion of your suffering and live with the rest? Yet you'll find many clients are quite content with having the immediate problem solved, and don't continue to use EFT. You might want them to heal further, but it's up to them to make that choice. You can certainly encourage people to clear more of their emotional distress after their first positive experiences, but many won't respond. As practitioners, we love and validate people where they are, and know that when the time comes for the next step on their healing journey, help will be available to them.

How do I know if a loved one has or I have a mental health diagnosis such as depression or PTSD?

You can find lists of symptoms on authoritative websites such as that of the National Institute for Mental Health (NIMH.gov) and the American Psychological Association (APA.org). Diagnosing mental health conditions is the province of licensed professionals, and you're not going to be able to know for sure until a person has been formally diagnosed by such a professional.

If you suspect a loved one has one of these serious psychological problems, encourage that person to visit a mental health practitioner for a diagnosis.

For individuals diagnosed with a serious mental health disorder, we recommend using EFT only in conjunction with proper medical care. EFT isn't ever a substitute for proper medical or mental heath care. It's for use in addition to proper care. In my experience, mental health professionals are supportive of EFT under these circumstances.

When should I work with an EFT practitioner?

There are several circumstances under which you might consider working with a certified EFT practitioner. An obvious one is when you aren't making progress working alone.

You'll find you can easily solve some problems by using EFT on yourself. On others, you'll find you make little or no progress. In these cases, the advice of an experienced practitioner is valuable.

You might also consider working with a practitioner who specializes in your condition. Most practitioners develop specialties. They have clusters of clients with common problems, such as sports performance, PTSD, self-esteem, or obesity. Some have specialized training in the form of a credential such as Certified EFT Weight Loss Coach or Certified Psychological Trauma Coach. Such a practitioner will bring a wealth of experience to your situation, and you're likely to make much faster progress than you'll make alone.

You can often make faster progress learning the subtleties of EFT by working with one or more practitioners. Each one has a different style, and you'll start to notice varying tricks and techniques. You'll learn which of these work best for you, and incorporate them into your process of learning EFT. This gives you a wider spectrum of techniques and perspectives than you're going to develop doing EFT all by yourself.

Having a practitioner can contribute to your psychological and physical support system, even if you don't see them very often. Just talking to them once in a while might give you the boost you need to overcome a particular problem. Knowing there's a practitioner who is there in case you need them can provide security. After a few sessions, your practitioner will get to know you, and your patterns, and can be a powerful ally on your healing journey.

A practitioner can also provide accountability. We often break promises that we make to ourselves. We make a pledge we'll go to the gym and work out 3 days a week. Then when the alarm clock sounds in the morning, we turn it off and catch an extra hour's sleep instead. Having an external person to whom you make yourself accountable can help you meet your goals. If you've told your practitioner you're going to the gym three times a week and are e-mailing your practitioner at the end of each week, you're much more likely to stick to your commitments. An accountability partner provides us with an external reference point to keep us on track with our goals. If you feel resistance to going to the gym coming up, you can tap with your practitioner on that resistance. Your practitioner can help you identify secondary gain that might lie beneath self-sabotaging behaviors as well as keeping you accountable.

Many practitioners work over the phone, or via video conferencing services such as Skype. This makes it easy and convenient to do an EFT session without leaving home or work. Other times, however, a session in the office might be more powerful than a phone session. You might try in-person sessions with a practitioner in your geographic area, and see if you make faster progress this way. In a study of veterans with PTSD, those who received in-person sessions had a significantly greater reduction in symptoms than those receiving phone sessions (Hartung & Stein, 2012). While remote sessions were still useful, an in-person session provided the practitioner with many therapeutic cues that could help get to the heart of an issue.

How do I find a practitioner?

There are several ways to find a practitioner, and many different types of EFT practitioners. There is a free resource called the EFT Community Map. This allows any practitioner, anywhere in the world, to enter their information free of charge. You can locate practitioners who are geographically near you using the EFT Community Map (CommunityMap.EFTUniverse.com).

There is no screening of these practitioners for competence. Some may be highly competent and well trained; others may have watched a 10-minute EFT video on YouTube and then hung out a shingle as a practitioner. It's essential to examine the credentials of a practitioner before entrusting your psychological or physical health to their keeping.

The practitioners listed at Practitioners.EFTUniverse.com are certified in Clinical EFT. Clinical EFT is the method that has been validated in over 20 clinical trials, and has a large evidence base showing that it works. These practitioners have taken academic classroom training in all 48 Clinical EFT techniques, had their competence assessed by a written exam, submitted case histories to demonstrate their abilities in offering EFT, and complete continuing education (CE) classes every 3 years.

There's no guarantee, however, that a particular practitioner is a good fit for you just because they've put so much time and energy into getting certified. That's why most practitioners offer a free session. I recommend you sample the services of several practitioners and then choose one with whom you get particularly good results. Think of this as a long-term relationship you're establishing to support your health and well-being, and give it commensurate importance. Your EFT practitioner is a vital part of your personal support system and your health team, and should be cultivated as a key healing relationship.

How do I know if a practitioner is competent?

Certified Clinical EFT practitioners pass through several layers of training to determine if they're competent. This includes a written exam, the presentation of case histories to a mentoring consultant who gives them feedback, and many classroom hours. Only those who have gone through this process are listed in the practitioner database on EFT Universe (Practitioners.EFTUniverse.com). There are also several other organizations other than EFT Universe that certify practitioners, and each has different standards.

Check out practitioners with your head first, and then with your heart. A practitioner will usually have a website and provide information about their credentials there. Read these, and assess how credible they seem. You can ask a practitioner questions about his or her training and experience. Also see what certifications and training the practitioner has accumulated in methods other than EFT, and which other continuing education/ continuing medical education (CE/CME) courses they've taken, since these are often a guide to how dedicated a practitioner is to improving their skills over time.

Once you've used your brain to assess whether or not a practitioner has the external trappings of confidence, use your instincts. A sample session will tell you a lot about whether you and a practitioner are a good fit. You'll usually feel good once you've found a practitioner who's right for you.

How do I explain EFT to friends, family, and colleagues?

My preference is to demonstrate EFT rather than explain it. A single 5-minute session is usually more effective at convincing people than reading a 500-page book. Once they feel it in their bodies, their minds usually come along for the ride. I keep my explanations brief, even when talking to medical professionals such as doctors, psychiatrists, and nurses.

EFT can be briefly summarized as:

- A relaxation technique.

- Simple physical exercises to reduce stress.

- A scientifically validated method for addressing anxiety and depression.

- A fast way of shifting the fight-or-flight response.

- Acupressure such as is used in massage methods like Shiatsu.

- A body-based stress reduction system.

- Acupuncture without needles.

- A quick method for reducing cortisol and stress hormones.

- A way to regulate the nervous system.

- Like qigong and tai chi, exercises to balance the body's energy system.

In time and with practice, you'll find your own brief "elevator speech" that allows you to explain EFT fast so you can get people tapping. Once you've given them their first experience, little more explanation is necessary.

Can I tap on a family member?

Yes, as long as you've asked permission, just as you need permission from an adult who is not a family member. In the case of a child, you need permission from the child's caregiver, usually the mother or father.

EFT is a wonderful resource for families. You'll find yourself wanting to use it with your parents, your children, and your spouse, as well as cousins and uncles, nephews and nieces. Many types of problem that would otherwise interfere with goodwill and love within a family are solved by EFT. This ranges from arguments and disagreements to physical scrapes and bumps.

If, for instance, your child has an injury, you might tap the points on their body immediately. The same applies to an emotional upset. When upset, the child is unlikely to be able to focus on the points, and the most expeditious way to relieve their suffering may be to tap on them. Children are usually very much in touch with their feelings, and so you don't usually need many words. Tapping on or with a child who is crying is usually effective without words till at least the teenage years. From the teen years on, work with a child as you would with an adult.

My preference is to see both adults and children learn EFT and use it themselves, rather than relying on someone else to tap on them. So when using EFT with a family member for the first time, it's wise to focus on teaching it to them as a self-help technique, rather than you becoming the family's resident tapper. There are many stories by people who've used it successfully with family members at RelationshipStories. EFTUniverse.com.

What if I begin, or someone I'm working with begins, to cry uncontrollably?

This is a scary situation for a newcomer to EFT, or a novice practitioner. You're working with a friend or client on a small emotional issue, and they get in touch with a big emotional issue. They're overwhelmed by the intensity of the emotion, and begin crying as though they'll never stop.

I was working with a therapist once on the issue of her annoyance with her boyfriend. Every Wednesday night, he left her to attend a book reading group. He'd had this hobby and been a member of the group since before their relationship began, and it was one of the joys of his life. Yet she felt annoyed that he'd make the choice to be with other people rather than with her on a regular weekly basis. She was tapping on her annoyance, but rather than going down, her SUD level kept going up, and she began to cry uncontrollably.

She got in touch with a memory she didn't want to think about. From birth, she had huge challenges with her family. Her mother was depressed, and spent time in and out of mental institutions. Her father was overwhelmed trying to take care of his wife, as well as her and her brother.

Then, when she was 2 years old, her mother committed suicide. That morning, her father was getting her and her brother ready for school, and the three of them were in the kitchen. They heard a loud sound and her father said to the two children, "Stay here," while he rushed from the room. Despite his instructions the two children ran after him, and they found their mother in a pool of blood where she'd shot herself.

This was the memory that had surfaced when the therapist thought about her boyfriend. She'd worked on this memory using talk therapy many times before, but during the EFT session it brought up a flood of emotion. She cried as though she were never going to stop. We tapped for about half an hour on all the different aspects of the experience, and eventually her tears abated.

It also became apparent that the current annoyance, her boyfriend leaving for the reading group, was only an issue because it recapitulated her abandonment by her mother (suicide) and her father (overwhelm). While we believe our feelings are caused by others, the way she believed hers were caused by her boyfriend, they're usually not caused by the current person or situation at all, and instead have their roots in very early childhood. We're triggered by a current event, like the book group, only because it resembles some early experience. We tap on the book group, but underneath might lurk a huge loss, like her mother's suicide. When you start tapping on the small loss of the boyfriend leaving the house on Wednesday night, the overwhelming emotion encapsulated in the big loss comes to the surface. You might try and keep an EFT session focused on modest and manageable goals, but emotions are unpredictable. Open a door just a crack, and you might find you've unwittingly opened Pandora's box.

When you're in the heat of the moment, the experience of overwhelming emotion might seem endless. You or the client might feel as though it will never end. Yet eventually it will. Emotions are fluid, and even the most intense of experiences has a start, a middle, and an end. At the start, the degree of feeling might be small. In the middle, it's large, and its difficult to believe that this will pass, but eventually it will have an end.

So the answer to the question of what you do when you encounter overwhelming emotion is this: Just keep tapping. The emotions, and the tears, will flow, but eventually the cycle will come to an end.

Whatever you do, *don't stop tapping*. I've often seen people in EFT practice groups get so caught up in a client's tragic story that they forget to tap. The client keeps talking and crying, and the listener gets so enmeshed in the emotion that both of them forget to tap. So it's vital that you remember to tap, no matter how big the emotion. Talking without tapping may simply be reliving the experience without emotional release or catharsis. Add tapping, and the emotion is being processed and released, not just relived. The next time the memory is recalled, it might be accompanied by much less emotion.

Though most clients cry in response to overwhelming emotion, others (especially men) may express it differently. They might become silent and withdrawn, shake, or feel acute physical pain. Whatever the manifestation of intense emotion, just keep tapping, and remember that the process has a beginning, middle, and end.

Can I combine tapping with my regular psychotherapy?

Yes. If you're currently seeing a psychotherapist and you're also learning EFT, the two work well together. We often hear reports of people making much faster progress in therapy after adding EFT.

If you've just learned EFT and you've been seeing a therapist, you might feel so elated at the changes you notice in yourself that you're tempted to abandon your course of therapy. The therapy has been part of your mental health support system, however, so rather than make an abrupt change, consider taking things slowly. Talk to your therapist about the improvements, and get their perspective on your condition. Most courses of therapy have a natural end point at which the client feels they have made progress on the issue that brought them into the therapist's office. Marking that end point with your therapist is a more graceful way to conclude the process than an abrupt end. As future challenges arise in your life, you may well need your therapist again, as well as EFT.

Should I tell my doctor I'm doing EFT?

Yes. I have lectured to thousands of medical professionals such as doctors, nurses, and psychiatrists, and I have generally found them to be interested, curious, and respectful when it comes to EFT. Your primary care physician needs to know about all the complementary and alternative medicine approaches you are using, including EFT. It's important to tell your doctor about a Chinese herb you're taking or a dietary supplement you're experimenting with, because some of these can interact unfavorably with drugs your doctor might prescribe. It's also important to tell your doctor about EFT and other approaches you might be using for stress management, weight loss, or psychological health.

If your doctor wants to know more about EFT, it's useful to reference the research pages at Research.EFTUniverse.com. This will give your doctor a sense of the strong research base that underlies Clinical EFT.

How does EFT work with medical prescriptions?

EFT can work well with medical prescriptions in several ways. One I use myself is to tap when I'm taking a prescribed medication, imagining that this pill is going to do me the maximum amount of good. Tapping while affirming my highest good engages my belief system, and I get the placebo effect working on my behalf. EFT may be able to enhance the positive effects of a medication in this way.

You can also tap for your body accepting a medication easily. Some prescription drugs have severe side effects, and EFT can mitigate these. This has been done by cancer patients receiving chemotherapy, for instance. Several have reported that when they imagine the chemotherapy cocktail clearing out the cancer in their bodies, while tapping, they don't experience the side effects that most other patients endure.

Another example is the drug Xanax. Research shows that the drug helps one person in six, which sounds good. However, one person in three experiences negative side effects (Whitaker, 2011). The net effect of these two numbers is that twice as many people experience harm (3) as benefit (6). If you're able to reduce the side effects of Xanax or any other drug, then you're able to get the benefits without the side effects.

Research has not shown that combining EFT with prescription drugs poses a risk. One study of hospital patients monitored their prescription drug use during their EFT treatment; no adverse reactions were reported (Karatzias et al., 2011). Similarly, veterans with PTSD had their prescriptions noted before and after EFT (Church et al., 2013). Their prescription drug use did not go up or down during the 6 weeks of the study and, again, they did not report any adverse events.

Finally, by reducing stress, EFT makes it easier for your doctor to prescribe drugs for you appropriately. Recall the Health Care Workers Study, which showed that two thirds of physical pain vanished after a brief EFT session (Church & Brooks, 2010). The remaining one third might well require medication. Your doctor is likely to appreciate that you've taken care of the two thirds of your pain that's emotional using EFT rather than trying to suppress the symptoms temporarily through high levels of medication. This also signals to your doctor that you're a responsible patient taking responsibility for your own well-being.

If I feel better after using EFT, should I reduce my dose of medication?

Only after consultation with your physician. There are few absolutes in the health world, but this concept comes close to being one of them. Your doctor has prescribed a certain dose of a medication based on his or her rigorous training, extensive experience, and the results of clinical trials, so it is essential that you follow the dosage instructions carefully. If you're feeling better after EFT, consult your physician about your dose. Your doctor might want to taper it down gradually, see you frequently to monitor your progress, or counsel you to maintain your dose for a certain period of time. Don't modify your dose unless in consultation with your physician.

Can EFT be harmful?

My experience is that EFT, at worst, produces no effect. There are rare cases in which people tap and absolutely nothing happens, then or later. In many thousands of cases, I haven't yet encountered a single one in which EFT has harmed someone. The same applies to acupuncture, which is generally considered safe.

The primary danger with EFT is overconfidence. You'll find that many problems that bothered you before are suddenly gone. This makes it tempting to believe that EFT will be equally effective on every problem.

That's not usually the case. There are many problems that require good medical care, expert mental health care, spiritual counseling, or professional life coaching in order to make progress. There may be some issues in your life that don't improve, despite EFT and everything else you try.

One danger of overconfidence is an inflated ego. If you're a practitioner, such as a life coach or psychotherapist, and you begin using EFT, you're likely to see much better results in your clients. This can lead to an unwarranted belief in your own powers. It's tempting to ascribe the results to your personal brilliance, not to EFT.

The world of spiritual development and transformational teaching, as well as EFT, is full of cautionary examples of great practitioners and teachers who have fallen victim to the siren song of the ego. They attract large groups of admiring followers who reinforce the ego of the leader. The leader takes the adulation of these followers as proof that they're specially gifted, and the ego puffs itself up even further. Power corrupts, and the more influence a leader has, the greater the temptation and possibility of corruption.

The main potential for harm with EFT lies in your own ego, and the egos of others who have been seduced by the results EFT has produced for people around them. I don't believe EFT itself is harmful, but there have been several unfortunate cases of prominent practitioners blinded by ego engaging in behavior that is harmful to others.

Watch these tendencies in yourself. Maintain a daily spiritual practice such as meditation, and remain humble. Abide by the Golden Rule. Ask yourself, "Is the way I am about to act or speak to this other person the way I would like this other person to act or speak to me?" Maintain high ethical standards. When in doubt about a course of action, talk to a wise and well-informed supervisor. Always be open to feedback from those around you, even if it's bad news. It's important to listen carefully to criticism, whether or not it's accurate. You can often find benefit even in uninformed criticism. If you remain spiritually and ethically aware, you can moderate the pull of the ego, and you're much less likely to engage in harmful thinking or action.

Are there cases where EFT should not be used?

I don't believe it hurts to try EFT, but I have encountered rare cases for which EFT was not the appropriate path to take.

For example, a participant at one particular 4-day workshop seemed to be helped by EFT. She'd start out every practice session weeping as she thought of her emotional problems. Her starting SUD level was usually a 10. She'd then usually go down to a 2 or 3 by the end of the session.

The next session, however, she'd be back up to a 10. This went on for all 4 days of the workshop. I worked with her privately, and I came to the conclusion that she did not have a strong enough set of positive beliefs and experiences in her mind to support her healing. She'd been weepy and overwhelmed most of her life, and had a very poor self-image. Psychologically, there wasn't a lot of positive material to work with. So while EFT could help delete negative emotion, there wasn't any positive emotion available to emerge at the end of the process.

I recommended she work using another method with a licensed mental health professional to build her inner psychospiritual resources first, before trying EFT again. Six months later, I asked one of my team members to follow up with her. When they contacted her, she reported that she'd begun working with a good psychotherapist, using methods other than EFT, and made great progress. She was very grateful that I'd recommended a path that was productive for her, rather than insisting that EFT was the answer to her every problem.

So the primary set of clients with which to consider using methods other than EFT, or using EFT in conjunction with other methods, are individuals who have limited inner resources. If they have no positive beliefs or self-concepts to support them, they may need to develop those resources first.

Though the standard approach in EFT is to identify negative life events and tap on them, there are exceptions to this rule. One is when a client needs to build up a sense of self first. You can use other psychotherapeutic and spiritual methods to do this, and you can also tap on positive cognitions. Examples of these are: "I am lovable. I am competent. I have inner strength. The world is a safe place. I am a good person. My life can turn out well." Tapping for the positive is usually not the most productive way to use EFT, but in such cases, it may be the place to start.

Why does EFT focus on negative problems rather than positive thinking?

This frequently puzzles newcomers. EFT practitioners keep asking about negative life events to tap on. They ask you about problems that have occurred in your recent past, in your work, your family, your marriage, your finances, your health. They dig deep into your childhood for negative events that happened early in life. What about the power of positive thinking? Why don't we tap on positive affirmations as well as negative feelings and life events?

There are several good reasons that EFT takes this approach. The first one is that our culture emphasizes positive thinking, and does not emphasize fully processing negative emotions. From an early age, we receive messages like "Big boys don't cry" and "This too shall pass." We're encouraged to look on the bright side of life, to find the silver lining behind every cloud.

As a result, we rarely mourn our losses, or grieve adequately. Children are urged to stop crying and cheer up, rather than receiving a respectful hearing as they grieve pets, relatives, and friends that they've lost. After decades of this, most of us have a large backlog of unprocessed emotional trauma. EFT sessions are often the first real opportunity we've had to catch up on this backlog of grief and loss. If you go to the positive side too quickly, you short-circuit the natural process of letting go, grieving, and moving on.

As with every rule, there are exceptions, but one of the biggest mistakes novice or poorly trained practitioners make is going positive. What you'll notice is that once you've really and truly processed your negative emotions, you'll naturally move to the positive pole without any prompting or urging. If you're working with a client, you'll find the client will choose when the grieving process is complete, and tell you when they're ready to go positive. Leading them in a positive direction before this point actually aborts the grieving process, delaying their progress and ensuring that they have to come back to their negative feelings in the future in order to heal. You can't easily go wrong focusing on the negative with EFT, but you can easily deprive yourself or a client of an opportunity to heal by going positive. That's why EFT has you focus relentlessly on the negative. When it's time to go positive, you'll naturally shift to that perspective, with the healing process complete.

Why is drinking water during a session helpful?

Your body is 70% water, and water is an electrolyte that conducts electricity. Water is essential for the biochemical processes by which your cells signal each other. Many people are dehydrated without knowing it, because we're rarely trained to drink enough water. We've become accustomed to being dehydrated, and may mistake our body's signals of thirst for hunger, anxiety, or compulsive behavior. It's a good idea to drink water before and during an EFT session, to make sure that you and your client stay well hydrated.

During the experience of strong emotion, your sympathetic nervous system becomes active. It shifts resources toward body systems required for fight or flight, such as blood circulation and your muscles. It shifts resources away from nonessential systems like immunity and digestion. That's why your mouth goes dry when you're under stress. Remember that intense job interview during which your salivary glands dried up? Or when you proposed marriage to your spouse? Or when you had to make that public speech, you were very nervous, and your mouth went completely dry? Those are symptoms of the fight-or-flight response.

The simple antidote is to have water handy during each EFT session, and take frequent sips. This helps reassure your body that it's being taken care of, even though you're processing strong emotion.

How do I find other EFT users with the same problem as mine?

Connecting with other tappers is a great idea. You can find support, encouragement, insight, and the answers to questions that might perplex you. On the whole, the tapping community is helpful and supportive.

There are many ways to connect with other tappers. These include:

Tapping Circles. These are groups of tappers who meet regularly to talk and tap together. The gatherings may be weekly or monthly. Some circles have a fee while others are free. A couple are virtual. You can find a list of them at TappingCircles.EFTUniverse.com, which also provides time-tested instructions for how to start your own local tapping circle.

Meetups and Hangouts. You can find EFT groups through social networking sites such as Meetup.com and Google Hangouts. There are several EFT Facebook groups. You can also make local tapping friends by advertising in the "activity partners" classified section of sites such as Craigslist.org.

Online Forums. You'll find many free discussion groups where you can post messages and interact with other tappers. There are specialized forums for weight loss, business, families, and many other topics (Forums.EFTUniverse.com).

The Tapping Insiders Club. This is a paid resource with many excellent articles and the opportunity to discuss them with other members of the EFT community. You can find it at TIC.EFTUniverse.com.

Search. Among the thousands of stories in the EFT Universe archives, you can easily find people who've used EFT for problems similar to yours using the Search and Advanced Search features. Many of these stories include links to the writer's website, and their e-mail address, allowing you to make personal contact.

Just Get Started

Whatever your questions are, don't let them stop you from jumping in to EFT. The saddest outcome is for you to continue suffering because you have the tools to end that suffering but don't use them. Perhaps your mind goes blank when you try and formulate a Setup Statement. That's fine. Just tap each of the points in turn anyway, and say any words that come to mind.

Perhaps you're embarrassed about tapping in front of your children or spouse, but you're extremely upset. Tap anyway. It's more important that you take care of yourself, and relieve your pent-up emotions, than that you worry about what other people will think of you.

Perhaps you have a child in pain and are afraid that your inexperience with EFT makes you unqualified to tap with them. Jump in and try it. You can't go too far off track, and you won't gain experience until you release those worries and risk messing up. Even the most experienced EFT practitioner started somewhere and, at that beginning, was as puzzled and incapable as you are at the start of your healing journey.

Our minds can invent 10,000 reasons why we shouldn't do EFT on the problem in front of us. Ignore them, and dive into tapping anyway. Your mind can become a labyrinth of arguments and counter-arguments, tying itself in logical knots and preventing you from taking action. It's more important to launch yourself into your journey of practicing EFT than it is to first answer every objection and qualification to practice.

You'll find you quickly gain confidence and expertise as you use the tools in this book, and soon you'll be surprising yourself at how quickly you've learned. Only as you use EFT and witness it work in many different situations, often with startling results, will you gain experience and confidence. Whether your question was addressed in this chapter's FAQ list or not, you'll find the answers emerging when you understand EFT from the inside out, by having applied it in many situations many times. Tap first, and ask questions later!

Resources

- EFT Community Map: CommunityMap.EFTUniverse.com

- Forums: Forums.EFTUniverse.com

- Practitioners: Practitioners.EFTUniverse.com

- Relationship Stories: RelationshipStories.EFTUniverse.com

- Research: Research.EFTUniverse.com

- Tapping Circles: TappingCircles.EFTUniverse.com

- Tapping Insiders Club: TIC.EFTUniverse.com

The Gentle Techniques

There are many situations in which psychological trauma is overwhelming. EFT's Basic Recipe requires you or your client to focus on a specific event. What do you do when the event is laden with fear, and you don't want to remember it? What about the case of a memory filled with terror and pain, one that you've been pushing from your mind for years or even decades, and cannot bear to think about? How can you apply EFT in such cases? Here are some examples of people who might be unable to do EFT without a gentler or more gradual approach:

• A male veteran in his 70s who committed atrocities against civilians in wartime. His actions occurred long ago and are not known to anyone except him. He's never talked to anyone about what he did, and he is so riddled by guilt that he dissociates, pushing the memories out of his conscious mind. Yet he still has involuntary flashbacks, nightmares, and intrusive thoughts about the people he injured and killed. His SUD score is 10 at the mere thought of talking about these events.

• A 22-year-old woman who, as a child, was ritually abused by her aunt and uncle who raised her. She recently underwent a course of psychotherapy in which memories of the abuse surfaced. She also suffers from unexplained symptoms like migraine headaches, irregular periods, and has been diagnosed with rheumatoid arthritis.

• A woman, 33, whose husband and children were killed in a car crash. She was the driver, and escaped unharmed. Whenever she gets close to thinking about it, she begins to shake and cry uncontrollably.

• A woman in her mid 30s who is disabled by chronic pain. Medical tests are unable to find anything wrong with her, yet her pain is severe in several parts of her body. She has continuous pain in both her shoulders ranging in severity from 4 to 6 on the SUD scale, as well as pain in her right knee that never drops below a 7, and intermittent pain in her left ankle that frequently renders her unable to walk. She's desperate for a cure, yet her case has baffled doctors for years.

• A 55-year-old man who has experienced several losses in the past year. Two weeks ago, his best friend unexpectedly dropped dead of a heart attack while exercising on a treadmill at the gym. The two of them shared the same birthday. His mother died 3 months previously, and his father died 6 months before that after a protracted and agonizing illness. His wife divorced him just after his father's death, he is estranged from both his children, and he has just lost his job. He has been so buffeted by these losses that he has plunged into a deep depression. His SUD score for general depression is 7 and goes to 10 when he thinks about each particular loss.

• A female therapist who is also an EFT practitioner but who is completely unable to remember a single event in her childhood before the age of 12. She has tried hard to recover memories but has been unsuccessful, as have several other therapists who have worked with her. She is embarrassed about her "failure." She has an uneasy feeling when she tries to recall earlier events.

• A man is disabled by multiple sclerosis (MS). The disease runs in his family, and genetic testing shows that he has a high susceptibility to it, as well as to pancreatic cancer. The MS has become progressively worse, following a course similar to that of his father.

• A female painter in her 60s who lives in a tiny rented room and has never been able to make any money from her artwork or to save money from any other profession she's tried. Nearing retirement age, she has no savings. She recently had a bout of hepatitis that left her weak and demoralized, and saddled with medical bills that she can't pay. Her family was poor, she was raised in poverty, and her relatives are all, in her words, "financial basket cases." She feels overwhelmed by these problems and despairs of having a better future.

When clients have horrific experiences in their past, long-standing family patterns, or overwhelming losses, it's hard to believe that change is possible. Dealing with these issues is very painful, and fraught with the likelihood of failure. Yet in the hands of a skilled practitioner, EFT is able to address these problems and open up the possibility of emotional freedom, even in cases of people suffering deeply.

The Need for Gentle Techniques

One of the most satisfying experiences for any EFT practitioner is to work with people who have carried severe emotional trauma around with them for many years and witness how quickly it can lift after EFT. Sometimes a client has suffered from a problem for decades and, in a single round of tapping, it is gone. After such a session, a client may appear dazed, as though they'd just awakened from a trance. They may shed many layers of wounding in just a single session. They then move on with their lives, enjoying emotional freedom and no longer carrying around the heavy burden of suffering that had previously weighed them down.

Other times, just a small part of a problem dissolves during an EFT session. A single traumatic event may take multiple sessions to address. Persistent lifetime patterns might take a great deal of persistence as layer after layer of the problem is tapped away over a long period of time. Many of us have traumatic events that are so big and daunting that we hardly know where to begin, and we fear being swept away by the tide of negative emotion associated with them. The Gentle Techniques are useful for addressing psychological wounding that appears overwhelming to a client.

When you work with others in EFT, you will often run into traumatic childhood memories, and you may well have experienced trauma yourself. A U.S. government report found that 60% of older children had witnessed or experienced victimization in the past year. Close to half had experienced physical assault, and 25% had witnessed domestic or community violence (U.S. Department of Health and Human Services, 2012). Unresolved traumatic childhood memories are the foundation of adult maladaptive behaviors and limiting beliefs. More times than not, a person visits an EFT practitioner to address a current issue in their life and it leads them back to earlier pain, loss, and trauma. It becomes apparent that the current life stressor is being made worse by unresolved pain from the past. The previous examples are all drawn from actual cases reported in EFT workshops or recorded in the archives.

You'll find you often need techniques much less confrontive than EFT's basic instruction to "think about the problem." For this reason, EFT uses a suite of methods called the Gentle Techniques, and they're invaluable for these situations. The Gentle Techniques allow a client to tap without having to confront the trauma head on. They gradually reduce the amount of triggering over the course of several rounds of tapping, rendering the triggering event manageable.

There are three Gentle Techniques: Tearless Trauma, Sneaking up on the Problem, and Chasing the Pain. We'll describe each of these in turn. First we'll examine the characteristics that make an event traumatizing, and how these can be distinguished from a nontraumatizing event. We'll also examine how the psyche deals with overwhelming trauma in both functional and dysfunctional ways.

The Four Characteristics of a Traumatic Event

What distinguishes a traumatic from a nontraumatic event? There are several definitions, but there are four characteristics to watch for as you examine your life history and the life histories of your clients. If one of these four conditions is met, the psyche may encode the memory as a traumatic event. The event must:

- Be a perceived threat to physical survival.

- Overwhelm coping capacity, producing a sense of powerlessness.

- Produce a feeling of isolation, aloneness.

- Violate expectations.

Let's examine each in turn, starting with a perceived threat to survival. Some threats to survival are actual. If you're in a serious car accident, you experience an actual threat to your physical survival, and the possibility of death. If you're assaulted by a mugger brandishing a gun, you are faced with a clear threat to your physical survival. That's not a subjective opinion; it's an objective reality.

Such actual and *objective* threats to our physical survival are few and far between. We might experience one serious car accident in an entire lifetime, or one brush with an assailant wielding a weapon. Most of us will not have even a single such experience our entire lives. Yet we might have many *subjective* experiences that we perceive as threats to our survival.

Consider a 4-year-old girl whose father is a morose unemployed alcoholic and whose mother is a violent rage-aholic. The mother screams at the father regularly, and occasionally pummels him with her fists. Each fight drives him deeper into depression. One night the child is awakened by the sound of her parents fighting in the kitchen. She leaves her room and peeks around the edge of the kitchen door. Her mother is brandishing a knife at her father. Her mother catches sight of her. She turns toward the girl and transfers the target of her wrath to the child. "Get out of here or I'll kill you," she shrieks.

As you read this story (a variant of many similar stories told by participants at EFT workshops), you probably don't believe that the mother is really going to murder the child. Yet the child doesn't necessarily know that at the time. With adult judgment, you can interpret the mother's words figuratively. A child will often take them literally. The child does not know that the mother is not speaking literally, and is unlikely to carry out her threat. The child is likely to perceive the event as a threat to her physical survival, the first of the four characteristics of traumatizing events.

The second characteristic of a traumatizing event is that it overwhelms our coping capacity, producing a sense of powerlessness. A female therapist at an EFT workshop recounted that when she was 8 years old, her mother suddenly disappeared. Her father never provided an explanation. One day her mother was living with them, the next day she was not. Shortly after this her father remarried. At first she was delighted to have a stepmother, but her joy was short-lived. She soon discovered that her stepmother resented her. She behaved coldly toward the girl. One day when the daughter came home from school, her stepmother gave her a hard shove and said, "Leave this house! You don't belong here any more!" The distraught girl ran crying to her room, and when her father came home, told him what happened. His response? "You shouldn't have provoked your stepmother."

Consider how this type of experience fits the last three criteria for traumatic events. The girl took the most appropriate course of action possible by telling her father what had happened. That's the way she tried to cope with the assault and threat. Her father's response—to blame her—overwhelmed the coping capacity of an 8-year-old, who then felt powerless. She felt isolated and alone in her suffering, the third characteristic of traumatic events.

The experience also violated her expectations, the fourth characteristic. Children naturally have the expectation that they will be protected and nurtured by their parents. When a parent harms the child instead, or consents to or ignores harm being done to the child by someone else, this behavior violates the child's expectations.

Some people have the resilience to cope with extreme events, like rape or beating. Others are traumatized by what might appear to be a minor event. EFT Universe trainer Alina Frank provides this example: "Your mother is preparing a particularly stressful holiday meal, you are 4 years old and wanting her attention. You tug on her apron, but rather than her picking you up as usual, instead, for the first time ever, she unexpectedly turns and yells at you and sends you to bed without dinner. In that moment, all four of the criteria for trauma have been met. Had this happened to you as a 10-year-old, you may have successfully navigated sneaking back into the kitchen, getting some food, and talking it out with your sister. You may have then comforted yourself by playing a video game. With increasing age, resourcing for yourself typically includes a greater variety of options and strategies that reduce the odds of a life challenge becoming a trauma" (Frank, personal communication, 2013). But at the earlier age, without those resources, you're unable to cope. The crucial factor is not how traumatic an event appears to an observer, but the way it is interpreted by the person experiencing the event.

Even the withdrawal of parental attention can traumatize a child. In a series of experiments, mothers were asked to maintain a "still face" with their young babies for a brief period of time (Tronick, Als, Adamson, Wise, & Brazelton, 1979; Tronick, 1989). The babies responded immediately, even though they could not walk or talk yet. They waved their hands around, increased their level of vocalization, pointed, and performed other "cute" gestures that they knew from past experience would evoke an emotional response from the mother. When the mother was still unresponsive, they increased their efforts. When these still failed to evoke a response, the babies became distressed. They eventually collapsed into uncontrolled crying, extending to a loss of control of the autonomic nervous system. The experiments were repeated with fathers, and in different parts of the world, with the same effect. These studies were startling because they showed that it did not take active abuse to traumatize a young infant; the simple withdrawal of a caretaker's attention was sufficient. Infants have an inbred expectation that they will receive emotional connection from their caretakers, and when this is absent, their expectations are violated.

EFT Universe trainer and social worker Tracey Middleton, LCSW, says, "I have had countless clients say, 'I had a great childhood! Nobody ever beat me, nobody ever cussed at me, I was in a wealthy family, had good food, the finest schools money can by, and the best parents in the world, yet I don't love myself, I don't feel like enough, and I believe I am not lovable." As she patiently traces this back to early childhood memories, she often finds a withdrawal of attention on the part of the client's parents. She says that, "We need to train our ears to look for the subtle trauma that comes from an emotional environment that does not meet our most basic needs of being seen, heard, and understood, being loved consistently, with parents who are compassionately present and engaged. In therapy sessions, it's like an archeological dig to uncover a tomb. You get the brushes out and start sweeping little by little to arrive eventually at a pyramid that was dug out of a mountain. It includes all those games Dad missed (even though he bought me the best shoes and uniform), all the nights Mom was consumed by her work and didn't notice I came home with a black eye, and all the time with the maid who raised us because Mom and Dad were off making a million dollars. This leaves the child with limiting beliefs about self and the world, even though there may be few or no events that the client can point to as obviously traumatic. The client concludes that he or she isn't lovable, others can't be trusted, and the world isn't a safe place. Children develop a sense of self-esteem based on how others treat them.

"One client reported that it was very traumatizing when her parents would not talk with her when they were upset at each other. They withheld their love because they were preoccupied with anger. She interpreted their behavior to mean that, 'It is my fault Mom and Dad are not talking. I am a bad girl. There must be something wrong with me.' With countless events of her parents withholding their love when they were upset, she grew up with low self-esteem" (Middleton, personal communication, 2013).

The Trauma Capsule

Now retired, neurologist Robert Scaer, MD, was the medical director of a multidisciplinary pain clinic for 30 years. He estimated that 60% of his pain patients had been abused as children, and virtually all of them were depressed (Scaer, 2012). He identifies the ways in which children, with their limited resources, deal with early life trauma by encapsulating it.

When a traumatic event occurs, a child is not able to process it as an adult would. An adult has the cognitive ability to interpret and make meaning out of an event. If a man makes an unwanted sexual advance to a woman, she can say no, and if he persists, she has a variety of options to escalate the strength of her refusal, from calling for help to summoning the law. She can make meaning out of the advance, and choose her response.

A child lacks that ability. A child isn't able to formulate a cognitive frame for the event in the way an adult can, such as "Uncle Jim, who's exposing himself to me, is a sick pervert." The child is even less able to conceptualize a course of action such as "Next time he does that, I'm going to tell him to get lost, and if he doesn't, I'm going to call 911."

Instead, when confronted with a traumatic event, the best option a young mind can come up with might be to encapsulate the trauma. Putting a barrier around the event and dissociating from it is often the most useful and adaptive response the child can come up with. Scaer (2007) calls this the "dissociative capsule." In Clinical EFT training, we usually use the word "trauma capsule" to describe it. The unpleasant memory is wrapped in a protective sheath and buried in the subconscious mind or the body. The whole event is encapsulated in this way, from the beginning to the end. The child may remember events up to the neutral point of emotional calm before the traumatic event began, and also remember events subsequent to the neutral point at which the traumatic event ended, but nothing in between. In Figure 1, the vertical axis represents distress on the SUD scale from 0 to 10, while the horizontal axis represents time. Memory stops when the SUD level starts to rise and resumes after the last peak of negative emotion. Events before and after the traumatic experience are remembered, but the event itself is isolated in the trauma capsule.

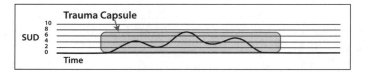

Figure 1. The trauma capsule.

Putting bad events into a trauma capsule allows the child to cope with the dysfunctionality of the family. The child can't escape the family the way an adult might. A 2-year-old can't say, "I'm going to pack my bags and rent an apartment to get away from Uncle Jim's abuse." The child has to live with the people traumatizing him or her. Isolating these events in trauma capsules allows the child to continue functioning in a hostile environment.

By the time a child reaches the teenage years, he or she might have formed dozens of these trauma capsules. The teenager might have a vague recollection that bad things happened earlier but can't recall the specifics. Yet the collection of traumatic events has shaped his or her worldview and attachment style.

Cognitive Processing: Shifts and How to Identify Them

Some events, even highly traumatic events, we cope with well. A useful guide to how well an event has been processed is the degree of emotion that is evoked in describing it. When you describe a troubling event from your past but you clearly view it in past tense and don't have a lot of emotional charge attached to it, you've probably reconciled yourself to it. You've digested all the unpleasant feelings you experienced at that time and the event is just a bad memory that no longer evokes strong emotion. You accept it, it's in the past, it no longer stimulates negative emotion, and it's part of your history.

If you still have strong emotion attached to the event, however, this may be an indication that you haven't processed it fully. Once I was doing EFT with a male psychiatric nurse in his mid 50s. He described an event in which he "lost the love of his life." He had been in a relationship and the woman had ended it. Crying uncontrollably, he described the last time he saw her. His high degree of distress made me assume the event was very recent, and I asked him when it happened. "Eight years ago," he replied. I did not say anything, but I was surprised that he still had such raw feelings so long after the breakup.

The event was so vivid in his mind that he shifted into present tense when describing it. "She's walking toward the jetway at the airport. I'm standing feeling nothing but stunned regret," he said, tears streaming down his face. His eyes were open but his gaze was focused far away, as he relived the event (Church, 2014d).

Within the trauma capsule, events are often frozen in time. Each sensory channel, sight, sound, touch, taste, and smell, may be part of the memory. The event may be recalled as though it were happening right now, full of emotional charge (Scaer, 2007). Rather than being recalled as part of the historical past, it's reexperienced as part of the living present.

After EFT sessions, clients often shift from describing the event in the present to describing it in the past. This indicates a cognitive shift. They've now come to terms with the memory, and as well as the SUD level going down, they perceive it through a different cognitive lens. The event is past, and they feel reconciled to it. It no longer evokes high emotion.

This phenomenon has been confirmed by research using EEG (electroencephalogram) technology (Diepold & Goldstein, 2008). The EEG showed that when a client was asked to remember a traumatic event, the memory evoked the brain-wave patterns associated with fear and distress. These normalized after a tapping session. Weeks later, when the client again recalled the event, brain patterns remained normal, indicating the permanent resolution of emotional distress.

Tapping on an unprocessed trauma can bring a cognitive shift toward feelings of being at peace, of having moved on, of being safe. The client may now imagine her or himself as a spectator witnessing the traumatizing event, rather than a participant. A memory that was vivid may become fuzzy, or the reverse; a fuzzy memory may come into sharp focus. A client may also shift from a victim perspective to feeling compassion for the perpetrator. All these are indications of cognitive shifts, and the observant EFT practitioner is alert to noticing them. The signal of a client shifting from present to past tense, or shifting from unfocused to vivid visual recall, is more subtle than the SUD rating but can be very revealing. When a client feels safe and describes an event in the past tense, without emotional charge, with a sense of perspective, perhaps even humor, it's likely that the trauma capsule has been successfully dissolved and its contents processed.

When working on a memory that takes the form of a trauma capsule, it's also important to tap on each aspect within the capsule. There might be several peaks of negative emotion within a single brief event. Imagine an event in which a client called David remembers being bullied in second grade. The bullies pushed the little David into the ground, breaking one of his teeth. Being a careful EFT practitioner, you search for emotional peaks as David tells you the story. You located the start of the story, when he was walking happily home from school, and his SUD level is 0 as he describes it during the session. The end of the story is after he gets home and is safe. You use EFT's Tell the Story Technique and David describes how the event unfolded.

The first emotional peak within the trauma capsule is when David saw the bullies walking in the opposite direction. As he recalls the event today in your office, he's a 7 for that segment of the trauma. They didn't see him at first, and he thought he had escaped. Then they noticed him and crossed the street to accost him. His SUD level shoots up to 10 as he remembers realizing that a confrontation was inevitable. That's the second emotional peak. The bullies taunted him, shoved him to the pavement, and broke his tooth. When David today recalls the taste of blood in his mouth, he's a 7 for that aspect of the experience, the third emotional peak. He went home after that and he remembers his mother comforting him. At the end of the story and the trauma capsule, his SUD score is again 0.

Figure 2 plots each segment of David's EFT coaching session. Time is on the horizontal axis and the SUD rating is the vertical axis. The bulge just after the start of the trauma capsule is the first emotional crescendo (seeing the bullies), the middle bulge is the second emotional peak (certainty of confrontation), and the final bulge is the aspect of tasting blood in his mouth.

You incorporate the first emotional peak into a Setup Statement, and tap on "Even though I saw the bullies, I deeply and completely accept myself." It may take several rounds of EFT, including the 9 Gamut Procedure, but eventually David's SUD on that segment of the trauma capsule goes to a 0.

You have him retell the story from the beginning till his SUD score peaks again. You incorporate the new aspect of the traumatic event in a Setup Statement: "Even though I knew confrontation was inevitable when they walked toward me, I deeply and completely accept myself." After you tap, you test your results and keep processing that aspect of the story till David's SUD level is 0 or at least a low number, 1 or 2.

David tells the story again, starting at the neutral phase at the beginning. This time you incorporate the third emotional crescendo into a Setup Statement: "Even thought I tasted blood in my mouth, I deeply and completely accept myself." The SUD level drops to a 0 after a single round of tapping.

To further test your results, you now have David tell the story again from the beginning. If he can get through it without going above a 2, you know you've cleared the trauma capsule.

You don't always have to go to a 0 for every emotional crescendo. I've noticed that I'll leave a client at a 2 for the highest peak, and then when I follow up an hour later or a day later, they're at a 0 for the whole event. Also, when the SUD score for one emotional peak goes down, the SUD scores for the others might drop too. In Figure 2, you can see that the SUD level for the second emotional peak drops after the first

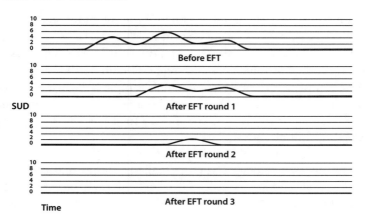

Figure 2. Clearing the trauma capsule with the Tell the Story
or Movie Technique.

emotional peak is zeroed out. This is due to the generalization effect
noted frequently in EFT; when you clear a trauma, associated traumas
tend to reduce in intensity, even though you haven't worked directly
on them.

EFT's Tell the Story Technique and Movie Technique (having
the client silently run the story in his or her head) are the basic and
most essential of the Clinical EFT techniques to learn, because they
force the practitioner to apply all of the core concepts to the session.
Identifying a movie makes certain you pick a specific event. Checking
the SUD level for each part of the traumatic memory ensures that
you identify and clear each aspect contained in the trauma capsule.
Getting the SUD rating at each junction forces you to test your work
frequently. Telling the story all the way through at the end ensures that
all the aspects have been dealt with and the trauma capsule has been
completely cleared. Though there are many useful techniques in the
body of methods included in Clinical EFT, the Movie Technique and
Tell the Story are ones you will return to again and again.

Dissociation

At one EFT workshop, we tested participant levels of emotional trauma before and after tapping. We used a questionnaire called the PCL, short for PTSD Checklist (Blanchard, Jones-Alexander, Buckley, & Forneris, 1996). Everyone's scores on the PCL went down after the workshop, except for two people, whose scores went up. One was a male therapist in his 50s, the other a female director of a psychiatric clinic in her 50s. They felt that they had made big emotional break-throughs in the workshop, and they were both very pleased with their results after EFT. Why did their traumatic stress scores go up?

The reason is that both of them had a history of dissociation. They had both experienced severe psychological trauma as children, and to cope with the abuse, they'd distanced themselves from their feelings.

Like forming a trauma capsule, the dissociative response makes perfect sense for a child. The child has to survive and live on in the abusive situation. He or she cannot escape, and the caregiver is often the abuser. The child resolves this paradox by pushing the bad experiences out of consciousness and into the subconscious mind. Carl Jung described the "shadow," that part of the self into which these "unacceptable" or unhealed traumas are stuffed. Poet Robert Bly calls it "the bag," and he says that we fill our bags with these unhealed experiences during childhood and drag the bag through our adult life like a huge burden that weighs us down and robs us of our joy.

Dissociation is described in the DSM-IV as "a disruption in the usually integrated functions of consciousness, memory, or perception of the environment." (American Psychiatric Association, 1994). Scaer (2012) describes dissociation more practically as a "confused, distracted state in your patient that prevents you from breaking through the fog into any semblance of meaningful contact. It's the patient 'leaving the room' [emotionally] losing contact with you when you've barely touched on the meaningful traumatic material, or when an obtuse reference to some supposedly benign topic causes a short circuit to a traumatic cue in their memory. It's the state of confusion and distraction that the patient describes, as if they've suffered a brain injury."

After a lifetime spent stuffing bad experiences into our shadow, or forming trauma capsules, and not truly feeling or processing our negative experiences, a person can develop a reflexive habit of responding to negative experiences this way. Such a person might feel very few of their feelings deeply, and perceive emotions as dangerous and disruptive. Their safety lies in dissociating.

When a person with a long history of using dissociation as a coping strategy and with a huge collection of disowned personality fragments stuffed into their shadow starts to learn EFT, these fragments may begin to emerge. Although the person might have managed to feel okay in the past by suppressing these fragments and associated feelings, and might have reported low emotional intensity, they're now feeling them fully, and reporting high emotional intensity. In this case, a rise in emotional intensity is actually a sign of healing, as long as the emotion is then fully processed, to the point at which the intensity subsides and the shadow fragment is reintegrated into the whole personality as an acceptable part.

Inducing Dissociation

Dissociation can be a useful therapeutic tool. When remembering an event is so terrifying to a client that thinking about it is impossible without fear, healing might be impossible unless some dissociation takes place. In these cases, dissociation can be deliberately induced as an interim measure to help a client approach the possibility of healing. EFT's Tearless Trauma Technique makes use of dissociation in this way. It gives the client permission to dissociate as far as is required by the traumatic memory in order to start the healing journey. Once some progress has been made, part of the dissociative barrier can be removed and, with the client's permission, another layer of healing can be attempted.

Scaer (2012) believes that several elements of EFT are effective for dealing with dissociation. These include the ritualistic nature of the affirmations used in the Setup Statement, which may anchor a client to reality even when the client tends to dissociate, and the integration of the functions of the left and right hemispheres of the brain through the 9 Gamut technique. My own experience with EFT is that the 9 Gamut is essential in cases of childhood trauma, which, as we have seen, is a factor for the majority of clients.

The Gentle Techniques give a client permission to dissociate temporarily as part of the healing process. With tapping, distress usually diminishes and, eventually, the feared event can be faced head on. The Tearless Trauma Technique erects mental barriers between the client and the fearful memory. Several layers of these dissociative barriers might be required before the client feels safe enough to start tapping on the event. The practitioner can induce this type of dissociation, suggest layer after layer until the client feels enough security to begin the work of healing. The following section explains how to perform the Tearless Trauma Technique.

Tearless Trauma Technique

1. Ask your client to choose a specific traumatic incident from the past to work on. For example, the client might say, "I almost drowned after my angry older brother threw me off the boat into the lake when I was 6." The phrase "My brother tormented me" is too general because the abuse may have occurred over the course of numerous incidents.

2. Ask your client to estimate (on the SUD scale of 0 to 10, with 10 being the most intense) what the emotional intensity would be if they were to imagine the incident. Tell them not to imagine it, but simply to guess what the intensity would be if they did. This estimate is useful, while allowing the client to avoid the emotional pain inherent in full memory. Write down the client's estimate. Make sure the client's eyes remain open, so they can see they're in a safe place. The way memory works is that we combine cues from the environment around us now with the old memory from the past. Keeping the eyes open during traumatic recall associates

the safety of the present moment with the trauma encoded in the memory.

3. Suggest an innocuous reminder phrase such as "the incident at the lake" that allows a layer of dissociation from the terror experienced in nearly drowning. Incorporate the phrase into EFT's Setup Statement and do a round of tapping. Avoid general statements like "brother torment" because it is so broad that it could refer to dozens of other events. Make sure the phrase is not too provocative, such as "the bloody knife."

4. After the round, ask the client to estimate again what the intensity would be if the client were to imagine the incident. Compare that rating to the original one. It is usually a significantly lower number.

5. Do more rounds of EFT, with new intensity estimates between each one. Three or four rounds bring most clients' estimates down to between 0 and 3.

6. When the client's guess has dropped to an acceptably low rating, do another round of tapping. Ask them to imagine the incident itself. Note that this is the first time you have requested them to do so (prior to this you only asked them to guess at the emotional intensity they would experience were they to imagine the incident). Now ask the client to rate the emotional intensity of the incident. Most people go to 0, but if your client does not, address the remaining aspects of the incident with the Movie Technique or Tell the Story Technique.

The Tearless Trauma Technique can be used in any case that involves trauma. It can be used with both groups and individuals. If your client has experienced abuse as a child, war, rape, torture, or other traumatic events, it's a good place to start an EFT session.

Here Australian therapist Steve Wells reports on his success the first time he tried using the Tearless Trauma Technique with a group. Participants were startled at how effective it was, even though they weren't receiving individual counseling.

Using the Tearless Trauma Technique in a Group
By Steve Wells

I just spent the weekend presenting a personal development seminar incorporating EFT and other energy therapy techniques. I tried out the Tearless Trauma Technique.

Sixteen people were asked to guess their SUD score when guessing the intensity of their trauma initially. All of them reported being between 8 and 10. Eleven went to 0 or near 0 after four rounds of tapping when asked to vividly reimagine the traumatic incident. The others were all at 4–5, and two more rounds took care of most of this. I offered to help during the break one woman whose SUD level remained at a 4, but she came up and told me she really saw how she could get beyond this herself and wanted to do so, as she felt empowered by the technique.

Most of the participants were absolutely astounded when they tried to reaccess the feelings and weren't able to. The most outstanding result, however, was by one gentleman who reported that an incredible feeling of sadness he'd been experiencing almost his whole life regarding his father was absolutely gone and he was now experiencing a feeling of complete peace. You should have seen the way his face shone. This guy had previously had a taste of EFT in another seminar I had run. He came to this one because after he used EFT to deal with his constant anger and anxiety, his wife said it was like getting a new husband. Needless to say, she was *very* happy for him to come and do more.

* * *

Further Layers of Therapeutic Dissociation

There are many traumatic events for which this single layer of dissociation—asking a client to guess at what the SUD score might be if the event were imagined—does not provide a safe enough distance from the event. A massage therapist at an EFT workshop wanted to dispel her fear of public speaking. She came up to work with me in front of the group, but I quickly noticed she was making little progress. Inquiry revealed that having her session watched by other people triggered her, so we turned her chair so her back was to the other workshop participants, which made her more comfortable.

When she tuned in to the body sensations that arose when she imagined making a public speech, she got in touch with a long-forgotten childhood memory. An uncle of hers had exposed himself to her when she was about 2 years old. She could not bear to think of the event. We used a further layer of dissociation by having her lock the event in a box. It was a yellow box with 10 padlocks holding it shut. Even then, thinking about the yellow box took her SUD level "through the roof." She decided to put the box inside a safe on an island in the middle of the ocean. Contemplating the island, her SUD level was a 9. Tapping quickly brought that to a 0, and she opened the safe. Her SUD looking at the box was back at a 9, but EFT quickly brought it down to a 1. We then used the Movie Technique, and she imagined the movie playing inside the box. Her SUD level went back to a 10 and we tapped till it was again a 1.

Not until she was ready and willing to open the box did we work on the movie. When she opened the box, the intensity of the movie was only a 6, and it quickly went down to a 1. The intensity of the images faded, indicating a cognitive shift.

I decided to test our results by having her turn to the group and give an impromptu public speech. She was happy to do this. She then stood up on a chair and continued speaking, laughing and waving her hands around as she expressed delight at her newfound emotional freedom.

Layers of dissociation, with the movie playing behind a curtain, or in a locked movie theater, or placing the movie theater inside a box, allow a client to diminish the intensity of a traumatic memory gradually. I've even had clients decide to place the box on a distant planet. That's as close as they can get to the personal tragedy locked inside. It usually surprises me how quickly they can retrieve the box, open it, and watch the movie. The safety that the Tearless Trauma Technique provides is key to allowing such rapid resolution of deeply disturbing events. Good EFT practitioners let clients proceed at their own pace, never pushing them to confront events that might overwhelm their coping capacity, and allowing them enough layers of dissociation and sufficient time to confront the event gradually. Practitioners sometimes have clients put the traumatic event back in the box for more tapping in the next session, or put the box back in the safe, or on the island, in order to provide the client with the assurance of safety between EFT sessions.

Exceptions to the Rule of Being Specific

The Tearless Trauma Technique presents an exception to the rule of being specific. The Basic Recipe instructs you to find a specific memory to work on. When the memory is too traumatic to contemplate, it's useful to dissociate, and it can also be useful to make general statements like "the lake incident." There are some other exceptions to the rule of being specific.

One is in cases of excessive emotional intensity. If a client is crying uncontrollably, it is wise to pull back from the specifics of the event and tap on general statements like "abandonment" or "misery." I sometimes use a very general statement such as "Even though bad things happened, I deeply and completely accept myself." The reason for the rule of being specific is to get clients in touch with their emotions. If they're crying, they're very much in touch with those emotions, and forcing them to remember traumatizing details of the event is counterproductive, risking the possibility of emotional flooding and retraumatization. My experience is that such clients remain very much in touch with their emotions even when the practitioner backs off from being specific.

Another exception to the rule of being specific is when a client has many similar events in his or her past, and you'd like to reduce the intensity of all of them simultaneously. For instance, a man who was beaten repeatedly by his father might find remembering a particular beating too upsetting. In this case, tapping on the general heading of "the beatings" might allow the intensity of the whole collection of beatings to diminish, especially if you use a method like the 9 Gamut technique, which experience shows can clear many similar emotional traumas simultaneously.

Sneaking Up on the Problem

Sneaking Up on the Problem is the second of EFT's Gentle Techniques. It's very simple yet effective. It's often used to address hopelessness, catastrophizing, resistance, and core beliefs that the problem cannot be solved. Examples of these core beliefs are:

I'm not lovable.
I'll never get over this problem.
Everyone in my family is like this.
Nothing I've tried has worked.
EFT isn't going to be able to fix this.
My pain will never go away.
Relationships aren't safe.
The doctor says my symptoms will get worse.
No one in my family has ever changed.
Working on this is hopeless.
I don't know where to start.
I've always been this way and always will be.

Such negative cognitions can also take the form of clichés, such as:

It's a dog-eat-dog world.
The apple never falls far from the tree.
No pain, no gain.
The higher you rise, the harder you fall.

Statements like these are not a promising start to a course of personal transformation! Yet while most of us have problems we've been able to solve, we also have problems that have defied our best efforts at solution. Perhaps everyone in your family is overweight. Perhaps no one in your family has ever gone to college. Perhaps your pain has never gone away before. Most people have a collection of issues that have not budged despite their best efforts over many years, and they may have no belief that change is possible. Nothing in their prior experience suggests it is, and they bring this mindset to an EFT session.

Sneaking Up on the Problem is a simple and elegant technique for dealing with these unhelpful beliefs and resistance. The practitioner simply agrees with the client! You incorporate the client's exact words into a Setup Statement, bracketing them with "Even though…" and "I deeply and completely accept myself." For instance, the client says, "I can never lose weight no matter how hard I try." The practitioner sneaks up on the problem by tapping with the client while affirming, "Even though I can never lose weight no matter how hard I try, I deeply and completely accept myself."

Clients are usually surprised or baffled that the practitioner is not attempting to talk them out of their negative belief. This technique is powerful because it acknowledges clients exactly where they are, not attempting to change them. The great client-centered therapist Carl Rogers said that the paradox of therapy is that the first step in transformation is accepting yourself just where you are (Rogers, 1957). EFT uses this observation to therapeutic advantage, by including even the most negative of cognitions in a Setup Statement. This both validates the client and opens the gateway of change. In my experience, these beliefs shift after just one or two rounds of tapping.

The Sneaking Up technique is also useful when a client states categorically that he or she is unable to remember specific events. You'll ask for one and the client may make a general statement like "I can never remember any specific events." You then build this into the Setup Statement, "Even though I can never remember any specific events, I deeply and completely accept myself." It's uncanny to observe how this use of Sneaking Up is usually followed by a client saying, "Something just popped into my head," after which he or she recounts a specific event. Another common response is "This probably has nothing to do with my problem, but I just remembered…" and the client goes on to describe an event that is key to solving the presenting problem. Sneaking Up seems to somehow change the client's sense of reality, broadening the scope of possibilities to include the element of healing.

It's also very easy to do, requiring no skill or insight on the part of the practitioner. The practitioner simply incorporates the client's exact words into a Setup Statement. There are occasional junctures in therapy when even the best therapist is stumped and can't decide where to go next. Sneaking Up is a good standby in these situations, and usually provides forward momentum to the session.

I took several classes from clinical psychologist Brad Blanton, who was one of the last students of Fritz Perls, the developer of Gestalt therapy. Brad is a brilliant therapist, and one of the ways he would address catastrophizing was to not merely agree with the client, but to take the argument one step further. If a client would say, "The pain will always be with me," Brad might extrapolate with a statement like, "It might even get worse. In fact, it could get worse and worse until you die of pain." This would usually evoke a reaction in the client such as, "Wait a minute, it's not that bad!" One of Brad's favorite sayings, after patiently listening to what he termed a client's "tragic story," was, "But wait! It gets worse!" Emphasizing the negative was a way to induce the client to argue for the possibility of positive change (Blanton, 2005).

This trick can enhance the effect of Sneaking Up. If a client says, "I'll always be sad," sometimes I'll agree, and affirm they'll get sadder. Taken to its logical conclusion, you can say, "Even after you're dead, people will look at the body in the casket and say, 'What a sad corpse.'" This usually produces a gale of laughter from the client, and the spell of the catastrophic trance is broken.

Alina Frank also views Sneaking Up as the outermost in a ring of concentric circles that surround the core of full healing. The outer ring often consists of fear or resistance that your client may have toward working on a traumatic event. By starting off with vague tapping statements such as "Even though I don't want to even think about that bad thing that happened" or "Even though that event was so devastating that EFT could never help me," we can ease the client's fears, establish a safe working relationship, and bring the intensity down sufficiently to allow the next deeper layer to be addressed.

As we move closer to the center, the statements can slowly become more specific, such as "Even though I feel this fear just talking about what happened to me when I was at the lake when I was 6…" Once a client's fears of addressing the event directly have been collapsed, the innermost circle consisting of the actual event may be addressed with the Tell the Story or Movie Technique (Frank, personal communication, 2013).

Chasing the Pain

The third and final of EFT's Gentle Techniques is Chasing the Pain. Often clients have more than one site of pain. There might be a pain in the shoulder rated at a 9, plus a pain in the lower back with a SUD level of 4, along with a sore knee rated at a 2. When Chasing the Pain, the EFT practitioner guides the client on tapping on each site of pain in turn. When the pain at one site goes down to a low SUD score, you tap on the next-highest pain, and on down the line. Clients might also become aware of new pains as old ones are tapped away. After you tap with a client on her sore ankle, which is a 5, she might tell you that the pain has shifted to her hip, which is an 8. You tap on the hip, after which the pain shifts to her stomach, which is a 4. The practitioner follows the client's lead, chasing the pain wherever it occurs.

The reason that Chasing the Pain is considered a Gentle Technique is that many clients use pain as a proxy for emotion. A grizzled veteran who is unable to share any emotions will readily describe his pain. Processing emotional trauma may be too difficult or triggering for a client to contemplate, or carry a stigma, while processing physical pain carries no such meaning. Physical symptoms like pain are thought of as objective medical realities, and few clients are unwilling to share them.

As the experience of Dr. Scaer and many EFT practitioners shows, much physical pain is tied to childhood abuse. Since the abuser was often the client's caregiver, feelings of anger toward the caregiver might be entwined with feelings of love and gratitude. A man might remember being beaten by his father, but also remember being loved and taught useful skills that helped him prosper later in life. Sometimes clients feel that talking about a parent's abuse is disloyal because the parent also loved them and provided for them. At a conscious level, a client may be unwilling to address abuse. Here tapping on pain can serve to dissipate that emotional material without needing to confront it.

Fritz Perls noted the link between physical symptoms and emotions after working with an artist on his repressed anger. The artist was extremely nearsighted. After Gestalt therapy sessions, his many symptoms resolved and his vision normalized. Perls observed: "Particularly if you get a combination of symptoms, like nearsightedness, lower back pain, anger indirectly expressed, instances of sexual impotency—you can have a noticeable positive impact on all the symptoms at once....[P]sychologically the overruling of the taboos against expressiveness allows for greater self expression, particularly of anger, then the eyesight improves, anger decreases, back pain goes away and sexual function is restored" (Blanton, 2011).

For some clients, pain offers a useful proxy for emotions. As pain after pain is tapped away using the Chasing the Pain technique, it is likely that a client unable to face his or her emotional trauma is making progress on resolving it in a way that is safe and non-triggering.

Sneaking Away from the Problem

Sneaking Away from the Problem is a technique for concluding an EFT session when it's apparent that the work is incomplete. One of the problematic issues in psychotherapy sessions is that a client is often feeling upset at the end of the appointment. A session might uncover major issues, but when the hour is at an end, they have not been resolved. One client said, "The end of some of my sessions with my therapist are like being on the operating table getting open heart surgery. Suddenly, the surgeon looks at his watch and says, 'Oops, time for the next patient. Sorry there wasn't time to finish the operation. We'll sew you up and get to you later.' I feel like I'm bleeding on the gurney. I leave my therapist's office crying, confused, upset, unable to function for hours afterwards."

Sneaking Away is a method of using EFT to name and describe this problem in such a manner that a client's process is honored, and affirming that there will be time later on to address the problem fully. Tapping and using Sneaking Away gives a client a sense of completion. Examples of Sneaking Away affirmations are:

> *Even though I still feel terrible, there will be time to work on this later.*
>
> *Even though I've just started to get in touch with this issue, I'll be fine.*
>
> *We'll put the problem back in the box, behind the movie curtain, till next session.*
>
> *Even though I didn't solve all of this problem today, there's time in the future.*
>
> *There's plenty of time for me to heal. I don't have to do it all today.*
>
> *This problem has been here for a long time, and what I've done today is enough.*
>
> *I don't have to demand from myself that I heal fully today.*
>
> *I can put this away and pick it up next time.*
>
> *There's always time and space for me to work on this.*
>
> *Even though I'm really triggered right now, I can manage till next time.*

In my experience, affirmations of Sneaking Away are enormously comforting to the client. Tapping and saying statements like this usually reduce SUD levels rapidly. Occasionally in practice sessions in EFT workshops, when I'm observing participants working with each other, time for the exercise will be up, but one person is still a 10. Sneaking

Away usually quickly reduces that to a 1 or 2, after which the participant can go on with the learning process of the workshop.

Sneaking Away can also be used to address the "doorknob effect," in which a client recalls a painful event when he or she is about to leave the session (Middleton, personal communication, 2013). This may reflect two contradictory urges present simultaneously in the client's awareness. One urge is to bring the issue to light by discussing it with the therapist. The second urge is to not discuss it because it is so traumatic. Unconsciously, the client resolves this dilemma by surfacing the issue at a time when it is impossible to process through to resolution. Sneaking Away can be used to sidestep the dilemma with which the client has presented the therapist. Tapping on a phrase such as, "Even though there's no time to address this now, I'm safe till our next session, and we can talk about it then," honors both of the mutually exclusive voices competing for the client's attention.

Touch and Breathe (TAB)

Touch and Breathe, abbreviated as TAB, is a development of TFT that is sometimes used in EFT as well. Developed by TFT practitioners in the 1990s (Diepold, 2000), it is the same as Clinical EFT, except that it does not use tapping. Instead, it uses a light fingertip touch on each acupoint accompanied by a breath. It is described in the book *The Energy of Belief* (Bender & Sise, 2007).

The indications for using TAB are when a client is uncomfortable with tapping. For instance, a rape victim in one workshop I offered was triggered by the tapping itself. The percussive nature of tapping on her body reminded her of the rape. So we used TABbing instead. Tabbing and tapping can be equally successful at reducing SUD scores.

Another EFT practitioner had a new female client, whom we'll call Jane, who was an Iraq veteran. After deployment, Jane had developed a slew of symptoms including multiple chemical sensitivities. This is a condition in which many substances common in the environment, such as soap and plastic, produce an allergic reaction. Jane's skin had become so sensitive that she could not tolerate wearing regular clothes, or constriction of any kind around her body. All she was able to wear were sack-like microfiber dresses of a certain brand. In her first session, Jane was unable to tolerate tapping on even a single acupressure point. The practitioner used tabbing instead of tapping.

By the end of the first session, Jane was able to comfortably tap on her collarbone point, using TAB for the other points instead. Midway through the second session, she was able to tolerate tapping on all the points. She also quickly lost her sensitivities and, after six EFT sessions, Jane's PTSD symptoms had normalized.

Posttraumatic Growth

While PTSD grabs the headlines, it's worth noting that terrible experiences can also produce posttraumatic growth. This is the phenomenon of people becoming stronger and more resilient in the wake of traumatic events (Tedeschi & Calhoun, 2004). PTSD is not inevitable. Roughly one third of veterans returning from Iraq and Afghanistan will develop PTSD, but two thirds will not (Tanielian & Jaycox, 2008). Research has shown a correlation between negative childhood events and the development of adult PTSD (Ozer, Best, Lipsey, & Weiss, 2008). Yet some people emerge from miserable childhoods stronger and more resilient than their peers.

Adversity can sometimes make us even stronger than we might have been had we not suffered it. New research is showing that people who experience a traumatic event but are then able to process and integrate the experience are more resilient than those who don't experience such an event (Stanley & Jha, 2009). A model developed by former General Loree Sutton, MD, former commanding officer of the Defense Center for Excellence and other authorities shows that such people are even better prepared for future adversity, and research that will be published in the coming years will confirm the value of posttraumatic resilience (Sutton, 2013). The way this works in your body's nervous system is that when you're exposed to a stress and successfully re-regulate yourself, you increase the neural connections associated with handling trauma. Neural plasticity, the phenomenon that we build new neural connections in nerve circuits we use frequently, works in your favor. You increase the size of the signaling pathways in your nervous system that handle recovery from stress. These larger and improved signaling pathways equip you to better handle future stress, making you more resilient in the face of life's upsets and problems.

Posttraumatic growth has only recently been named and identified, and has not yet received the research attention that PTSD has received. I believe that using EFT soon after traumatic events increases the likelihood that a person will be able to make positive meaning out of tragedy, and build the neural circuits required to handle future adversity. I also believe it's possible that further research will show that the events that trigger PTSD can later be reimagined with tapping in a way that promotes posttraumatic growth and generates growth in the neural networks that regulate stress.

One of the most provocative studies I was involved with looked at the experience of 218 veterans and their spouses (Church & Brooks, 2014). They attended a weeklong workshop that included 4 days of EFT and other energy psychology techniques. When they began, 83% of the veterans and 29% of the spouses tested positive for PTSD. After the retreat, these numbers had dropped dramatically, and they were retested 6 weeks later. At that follow-up point, only 28% of the veterans and only 4% of the spouses had PTSD. This represents a significant drop in their symptoms. It's also possible to see the results as a gateway to a new set of possibilities for these veterans and their spouses. Human potential that was circumscribed by suffering might be unleashed after liberation from that suffering. EFT can be used as a way to tip the balance after tragedy, away from PTSD and toward posttraumatic growth.

Resources

- The Still Face Experiments: StillFace.EFTUniverse.com
- Tearless Trauma: TearlessTrauma.EFTUniverse.com
- Touch and Breathe: EnergyOfBelief.com

Breaking the Habit
of Being Yourself

I'm about to jump into the ocean off the back of a dive boat. I'm 5 miles off the coast of Florida on a snorkeling excursion. The turquoise Caribbean water is calm and clear and I can see all the way down to the orange and purple coral reefs glowing on the seabed 20 feet below. The dive boat crew and captain are solid and professional, and the boat is state-of-the-art; their company has been offering expeditions to this area for 30 years.

Yet amidst all this perfection, I'm having a panic attack. The feeling in my body is like an old enemy; I know it well. I always feel this way when I'm about to snorkel. I think about how cold the water will be, and the fact that when I jump in my feet will not touch bottom. There will be a terrifying few moments when my head is below water, when I'm going down, down, down. I'll wait in agonizing suspense before the momentum of my jump reverses, buoyancy takes over, and I bob slowly to the surface.

I know there are sharks in these waters; I've seen them basking on the sand at the bottom of the reef on previous trips. My left brain knows that the chances of being attacked by one are statistically less than being hit by debris falling off an airplane, yet I'm still panicky. I know from past experience that I just have to tough it out. I remember that the panic phase subsides after about 15 minutes in the water. I always then become absorbed in the underwater scenery and forget my fright, or at least push it to the back of my mind.

This is just the way I am. When I was 2 years old, I was playing in the surf with my father and mother when a big wave came and knocked me down. My lungs filled with water as I tried to scream. At first, nobody saw my distress and, before I knew it, I was being carried out to sea. As I was moving away from the shore, my father saw me and grabbed me from the waves.

From that moment of half-drowning on, I had a fear of open water. Confusingly, it was intertwined with a love of water in general. I love hot tubs, pools, showers, baths, and lakes. I have a koi pond outside my dining room, I go to resorts with pools and hot tubs whenever I can. I go camping near the local lake frequently, and when my kids were young, I took them swimming in lakes, rivers, and pools as often as possible.

Let's now fast forward my autobiographical movie to the snorkeling expedition in Florida. I dangled my feet in the water behind the dive boat, trying to nerve myself to jump in. All the other snorkelers were overboard; as usual, I was the last to get in. Then a thought occurred to me. Use EFT!

"That's silly," my Inner Critic responded. "You've been afraid of open water your whole life and for good reason too. You had a bad childhood trauma. There's no way that silly tapping thing is going to overcome a lifetime habit. And anyway, you'll look like a fool tapping in front of the boat's crew. They'll think you're a nut case."

I got over myself and tapped anyway, right there in front of the dive boat crew. I jumped into the water and continued tapping. I still felt the familiar panic as I sank down under the surface, but it dissipated in about 10 seconds. I was soon swimming with the other snorkelers, absorbed in the beauty of the tropical fish and colorful reefs.

Ironically, I had learned EFT about 5 years previously, and begun teaching it 2 or 3 years later. Yet I never thought to apply it to my snorkeling dilemma. "That's just the way I am," I believed. "Open water is dangerous, that's just the way the world is."

Yet it isn't.

I was wrong.

That was not the way the world is. It was just the way my internal world was.

How often do we hold ourselves back with false messages like that?

How often do we tap for some of our issues, but exempt others, thinking that they are immune from change?

How often do we use EFT successfully for other people but not for ourselves?

When my friend Joe Dispenza, made famous by the movie *What the Bleep Do We Know!?* published a book called *Breaking the Habit of Being Yourself* (Dispenza, 2013), I was one of the first to congratulate him and to review the book. I was also struck by the brilliance of his title. We think that the way we are is the way the world is. We have a fixed habit of being ourselves, and we cannot imagine things being otherwise. In the early 1800s, philosopher Arthur Schopenhauer observed: "Every man mistakes the limits of his vision for the limits of the world." We can live with those limits for a lifetime unless we break the habit of being ourselves. We can suffer needlessly for decades simply because we're stuck in the erroneous belief that "thus it is" when it really isn't.

Imagine the vast collection of human potential that is lost to the world because of the limited thinking of seven billion people. If even 1% of them threw off the shackles of being themselves, dumped their suffering, and changed their assumptions, the creativity and joy unleashed could change the course of history.

EFT gives us enormous leverage over the old version of self. Tapping on our assumptions, we can change even parts of ourselves we believe are fixed and immutable. I passionately desire that this book leads you to challenge every assumption you have about the world and about yourself. My greatest wish is for you to throw off the shackles of your suffering and claim the life you were born to live. I want you to break the habit of being yourself, and embody a new self, the highest version of self you are capable of embodying.

Ask yourself these questions:

> *What stories do I habitually tell other people about my limitations?*
>
> *Are those limitations actually real?*
> *Are they just part of my boring old story?*
> *Who might I be if I dumped all those stories?*
> *Is the self-talk inside my head actually true?*
> *What parts of the world do I think are fixed in external reality, yet may just be projections of my inner reality?*

This chapter offers you techniques for changing all of these viewpoints and beliefs, and breaking the habit of being yourself. What you'll learn in this chapter is how to identify your core issues, the ones that are so central to your identity that you believe them unquestioningly. Our core issues form a frame of reference through which we see the world. For instance, if one of your core issues is "It's a dog-eat-dog world," then you will approach people and situations as though this were true. Rather than assessing people and situations objectively, you cram them into this subjective (and untrue) frame of reference. You are likely to have dozens of these core beliefs shaping your perceptions and your experience. Once you identify them, and tap on the events that created them, you change your experience. Clinical EFT contains powerful tools for helping us identify core beliefs and drop those that do us a disservice.

Finding Core Issues

While EFT can be useful for minor or peripheral problems, much deeper healing is possible if you assist your client or yourself in finding core issues. The events that bother us are only a problem because they resemble deeper emotional wounds usually dating from traumatic or painful events in our childhood. Rather than being content with using

EFT on surface problems, it's worth developing the skills to find and resolve the core issues that are at the root of the problem.

In the case example of Cindy, she encapsulates a theme in her life story with the phrase "I'm a doormat." A common thread to all Cindy's life events is that she cannot say no, she makes her needs subservient to those of others, she cannot articulate her wants, she's afraid of standing up for herself, and she has low self-esteem. Collectively, these events have led to the core belief that she's worthless, and one of her favorite sayings is "I'm a doormat."

Delving below the surface revealed several life events that contributed to forming Cindy's core belief. They are:

As a child during her first week in preschool, she needed to go to the bathroom and asked her teacher for permission to leave the class. The teacher told her that break was only 5 minutes away and to hold it till then. Little Cindy couldn't, and wet her pants. The other kids laughed at her, and the teacher punished her.

Cindy had two older brothers. They would make her play games with them, and she always wanted to please them. One of those games was Cops and Robbers. They always cast her in the role of the Robber and shot plastic arrows at her, aimed their toy pistols at her, and chased her. They would often tickle her, laughing while she writhed to try and get away. A couple of times they held her down and wouldn't let her move, and her panicked attempts to escape were of no avail. During at least one of these episodes, Cindy passed out.

In her current life, Cindy's husband and children criticize her mercilessly. In the evenings they watch TV or play video games while she takes care of all the chores. One day recently, she cleaned the whole house while they were away, clearing up layers of mess that they had created. When her husband came home from work, he commented on the one room of the house she hadn't gotten to yet.

Cindy's core belief of "I'm a doormat" was built up through dozens of incidents in her childhood, and she picked a husband who would perpetuate the pattern. Cindy thinks that's the way the world is, but in reality it's the way she is, projected onto the world. She trained her kids to carry on the family tradition, making them part of the problem. Cindy doesn't understand or believe that she trained them this way, yet she created a present that reinforces the world view built by her past.

When Cindy tapped on each of the traumatic events that led to the core belief, the SUD score of each of them went down. She tapped on about 50 events in the course of 10 sessions. After the fourth session, Cindy became extremely angry at the way she's been treated. By the seventh session, Cindy was furious at herself for letting herself be a doormat. She began to assert her needs at home, producing an uproar. Tapping made her strong enough emotionally to persist, even though her husband and kids weren't about to change.

With no family support for her transformation, Cindy decided to get support from outside the home. She joined a woman's group at her church, and a Master Mind group centered on finding your life purpose. She made many new friends and found plenty of people who respect and appreciate her. Cindy changed her inner story, no longer holding the core belief that "I'm a doormat." She now affirms, "I am a powerful and valuable woman." She's now busy creating outer circumstances that reflect the inner change. Over time, her new frame of reference will produce an outer reality that is diametrically opposite to her old one. Nothing spontaneously changed in the outer world first; it took inner subjective change for the outer objective world to begin changing. That's where change always begins: inside. When you change your story, you change your life.

Here are some questions you might ask in order to identify the events that have contributed to your core issues:

> *Does the problem that's bothering you remind you of any events in your childhood?*
>
> *Tune in to your emotions, and identify where in your physical body you feel the most sensation. Then travel back in time to the first time in your life you ever felt that same physical sensation in your body. Describe the event that was happening at that time.*

Think about the problem you have now. What's the worst similar experience you ever had in your life?

If you were writing your autobiography, what chapter would you prefer to delete, as though it had never happened to you?

Once you've made your list of the events that have collectively produced your core issues, tap on each of them in turn. They form a matrix that reinforces your core belief. As your SUD level for each event drops to 0, you weaken the matrix and, eventually, the whole psychological structure will collapse. Your core belief vanishes spontaneously, and a new set of beliefs emerges into your consciousness. Empowering and positive beliefs that were buried under the mass of traumatic experiences pop to the surface and become part of your picture of reality.

If the client tells you she can't remember the specific events that contribute to her core belief, ask her to simply make up a fictional event in her mind. This kind of guessing usually turns out to be right on target. She's assembling the imagined event out of components of real events. The imaginary event usually leads her back to actual events you can tap on. If it doesn't, tap on the imaginary event. It usually contains enough components of real events to be an effective target for EFT.

Identifying the Writings on Your Walls

The "writings on our walls" are the beliefs we picked up as children from those around us. When we asked for a new backpack for seventh grade, and Dad said, "Money doesn't grow on trees," we understood the principle of scarcity. Dad probably said that when Mom wanted a new dress or sister wanted to attend summer dance camp. We probably heard it from Grandma and Uncle Thomas as well. This phrase, written on the wall of your consciousness, became part of your world view.

Perhaps we heard a high school friend say, "All the good men are taken." We remembered when we overheard Mother and Aunt Peggy complaining about men, and about Peggy's contemplation of getting divorced. Eventually, she decided to stay with her abusive husband because the other models of husband were equally flawed. After all, all the good men are taken. In any case, the grass is always greener on the far side of the hill, there's no pot of gold at the end of the rainbow, every cloud has a silver lining, what doesn't kill you makes you stronger, and what goes around comes around. Perhaps you're laughing as you read that list of clichés, just the way I'm laughing as I write them, but they're instantly recognizable as pieces of folk wisdom that resonate for many people.

But are they true? Very often, we have writings on our walls that have long outlived their usefulness.

In the community where I live, there are a great many single women. Year after year, decade after decade, they can't seem to find the right man. They go to parties and meet new people. They subscribe to online dating services. They use match-making services to introduce them to potential mates. They're always hopeful, but their dreams never work out. After many years, despair sets in and, after decades of disappointment, they realize that Aunt Billie was right when she told them, "All the good men are taken."

I've also noticed that there is a small number of women in that same community who manifest the opposite result. They get divorced in their 50s or 60s after long marriages, meet many potential partners soon, and quickly find their ideal mate. They don't believe the proverb. Without that subjective frame of reference, they don't create that reality in their objective experience. The writings on our walls have a way of shaping the circumstances of our lives. We notice life events that validate our beliefs, and dismiss those that don't, a phenomenon that psychologists call "confirmation bias" (Nickerson, 1998). If you believe all the good men are taken, Mr. Right might be standing in front of you, but you can't see him past your belief.

The people who instilled your core beliefs in you when you were a child meant well. They were trying to protect you from harm. They were convinced that if they told you the dangers of the world, you'd become a prudent person and experience less pain than they had. They'd often had rough lives, had dysfunctional core beliefs, and shaped their reality accordingly. They're convinced the external world is that way, when in reality it's their internal world that is that way. They do their best to instill their sense of limitation in you, subconsciously hoping that you won't be damaged in the same way they were. Yet if they succeed in instilling these beliefs, they're likely to produce the very result they fear.

The problem is that the world can be either a place of pain or a place of joy, and a great deal of the difference is created by the writings on your walls. If your head is filled with convictions of limitation and suffering, you'll tend to reproduce those conditions in the outside world.

Notice whenever you use a cliché. Trace it back to where you learned it, and all the events that validated it as truth. Write these down in your personal journal, and tap on them. Rate how strongly you believe that truth. In the field of psychology, this rating of the degree of truth is called the "validity of cognition" or VOC and it uses an 11-point scale, similar to the SUD scale (Shapiro, 1989); in the case of the VOC scale, 0 represents no belief in the statement being rated and 10 represents unshakable conviction that it is true. What is your degree of belief in the following statements?

Money doesn't grow on trees.
No pain, no gain.
Life's a bitch, and then you die.
The world is a dangerous place.
It's a dog-eat-dog world.
All good things come to an end.
True love never lasts.

Let's try some positive statements. What's your VOC score for these?

The world is a safe and nurturing place.

The universe conspires for my good.
Everything turns out alright in the end.
I am a spiritual being on a material path.
I am abundant.
Money flows to me easily.
I am vibrantly healthy.

Once you've identified the writings on your walls, you can find the underlying events that installed them. We do this in live EFT workshops, and we find that even if participants have a very strong belief in a negative cliché such as "All good things come to an end," their high VOC score changes after tapping. We help them find the childhood events that installed the cliché, and tap on them. Once these events lose their emotional charge, the VOC around the cliché drops like a stone. They experience a makeover in the writings on their walls, walking out of the workshop with a revised internal belief system. Limiting beliefs are replaced by empowering beliefs. This can soon begin to produce a very different picture in their external objective world.

The Characteristics of Effective Affirmations

The practice of affirmations has a checkered history. Affirmations became popular in the 1970s. The idea was that you'd make an affirmation, and if you believed it strongly enough, it came true. Affirmations often didn't come true, however, and many people fell out of love with using them after their initial enthusiasm had died down.

In the process, we learned more about how and why affirmations do and don't work. We can now identify how to craft affirmations that are likely to succeed. When you combine affirmations with EFT, the effect is enhanced. There are several ways in which affirmations and tapping can be mixed. Here are some to experiment with:

• Tap while saying your affirmations. Start at the Karate Chop point and work your way down to the last point. Then start again at the Karate Chop point, tapping continuously while you affirm what you want.

- While saying your affirmations, notice any sensations that arise in your body. Tap on those sensations.

- Notice any objections your mind has to your affirmation. Tap on the objection.

- Make a list of your affirmations and say them daily while you also tap.

- Tap while formulating new affirmations. Notice how your body feels as you experiment with different wording for your affirmations. Choose the wording that produces the best physical sensation.

- Identify the objections that arise in your mind while thinking about your affirmations. In EFT we call these "tail-enders" because they pop up at the end of an affirmation, giving you all the reasons why the affirmation can't be successful. We'll focus on these in the coming section.

To have an impact, affirmations should be charged with high emotion. What's a way of stating your desire that engages your passion? Saying "I want a nice house" is a pretty limp statement. Saying "I want the house of my dreams" has more energy. Saying "I am now living in the white two-story house by the beach in Cape Cod with the wraparound deck" is far more concrete and is much more likely to get you emotionally fired up.

Affirmations should be stated in the present tense. Affirming that "I'm going to have plenty of money" pushes the event into the future. You might manifest your affirmation in 10 years. In 10 years, you'll still be in a state in which you're going to have plenty of money. Sometime, but always in the future. Saying that someday later you'll accomplish your dream means that you never reach the state in which it exists right here and now.

Affirmations should be vivid and detailed. If you're affirming health, what does health mean to you? Is it linked to outdoor activities like hiking, kayaking, and biking? Walking on the beach? Soaking in a hot tub? Being slender? Eating certain foods? Create a vivid and detailed picture of exactly what you want, and affirm that.

Affirmations should be crystal clear. Write them down and then refine them, becoming clearer with each revision. Affirmations should be positive, stating what you do want, rather than what you don't want.

I recommend creating affirmations after meditation or another spiritual practice that puts you into an elevated mental state. Otherwise, you're affirming and creating out of any limitations and fears that might occupy your conscious mind. First bring yourself into the highest possible state of consciousness. Napoleon Hill (1966) recommended this practice in his classic book *Think and Grow Rich*. He believed that when you do this, you are able to tap into awareness far beyond the scope of your limited local mind. That's the place from where to affirm the future you'd like to see.

Identifying Tail-Enders

When you state your affirmations clearly, in the present tense, with high emotion, in vivid detail, what happens? Say "I effortlessly maintain my goal weight" or "I manifest financial abundance" or any other affirmation you're working with, and notice what pops up in your mind right after the affirmation. This is the tail-ender. It is a negative and limiting statement that counteracts the affirmation. For instance, you say, "I effortlessly maintain my goal weight" and a little voice whispers in your ear, "…in your dreams." Examples of tail-enders are:

That's a laugh.
Who are you trying to fool?
Like you've never done before?
Not.
Are you kidding?
No way, Jose.
Don't be ridiculous.

Yeah, right.

Tail-enders are the true affirmation, not the statement you've just made. The tail-ender rings much more true in your consciousness. It has much more emotional power than the positive statement. Since the tail-ender represents your true belief, that's what you'll manifest. That's why after the first rush of enthusiasm for affirmations in the 1970s, people discovered that they didn't work as planned. They would say their affirmations daily and fervently, imagine them vividly, and then manifest the opposite. Paradoxically, this is a demonstration that affirmations can actually work, since the tail-ender, which is the real affirmation, comes true.

In EFT we turn this to our advantage. Say your affirmations, and locate your tail-enders. Write them down, and then tune in to your body as you say them out loud. That tail-ender is usually the result of limiting core beliefs and writings on your walls. You can find the childhood events that gave rise to the tail-ender, and tap on them till the SUD level goes down.

Once your VOC level for the affirmation is high and your VOC level for the tail-ender is low, then your affirmations have real power. Here Paul Zelizer tells about how he worked with a client who had self-sabotaging tail-enders around starting her own health practice.

Doubts about Her Holistic Health Practice
By Paul Zelizer

In the past few months, I've been contacted by an increasing number of people who have heard of EFT and tried it on themselves without success. These clients have read about the importance of finding the core issue and have tapped on many things that they think might be underneath their symptoms. However, for some of these folks, it just hasn't worked.

Jenny moved to a new city and was excited about starting a holistic health practice. However, she underestimated the cost of living in this new city, as well as the time it would take to build a successful practice in a new place.

When we first met, Jenny was very stressed out about money. She had gone through most of her savings, she had only a few clients, her health was declining, and she was starting to lose sleep.

While EFT made sense in theory to Jenny, she had no idea how she could use it to help with her money issues. In the course of several sessions, I taught Jenny the Using the Tail-Ender Technique.

First, I had Jenny decide on a statement that she would like to be true. In one session, she decided on "I easily earn $50,000 per year." Next, I had Jenny get in a comfortable position and prepared her to listen to messages that were about to come. In the counseling world, the messages that we tell ourselves are often called "self-talk."

Next, Jenny said aloud, "I easily earn $50,000 per year." Then, both Jenny and I remained quiet for about a minute while she listened to her own self-talk (tail-enders). What Jenny reported is that two messages were very clear. The first was "YEAH, RIGHT!!" and the second was "That's not a reality for me." We tapped on these using a variety of Setup Phrases.

Over the course of several months, Jenny has seen some big improvements. She found a part-time job in her field that pays well, has flexible hours, values her holistic skills, and allows her to continue to market her own practice. She is sleeping better and is less stressed overall. While Jenny says she has a long way to go, she now feels clear about how to use EFT for money issues and has a better idea of what to tap on.

* * *

Daisy Chaining, and Tapping and Talking

Frequently, EFT produces results so quickly and efficiently that the individual moves from issue to issue to issue, clearing each one. We call this pattern the "daisy chain." The resolution of a problem seems to call to mind another problem, offering the individual a rapid healing transit through a long chain of problems.

For example, a man might start with a spider phobia and, after tapping away the problem, he recalls his fear of heights. After tapping on that, he continues to daisy chain, moving quickly to fresh issues such as a car accident, criticism from a boss at work, and rejection by a lover.

This is a chance for dramatic healing to occur because multiple problems can be resolved in the space of one session. If you find yourself on a roll, keep tapping!

The daisy-chain effect is obviously in play when the client shares with you the new issues as they arise. The client may not know the value of telling you about subsequent memories that arise, however, so the healing opportunity is overlooked. This can be avoided by instructing your client in advance to tell you if other problems come to mind. Alternatively, asking a simple question can trigger the memory of additional issues in your client. When you have finished one issue, the simple question to ask is:

What does that remind you of?

With light probing in this way, you can set the daisy chain in motion. Ask the question again after the resolution of each issue. In some cases, you and your client might witness a long list of healing "miracles" in just one session.

A related technique is Tapping and Talking. That's all you do. In workshops, clients often start talking about a problem in their lives. I interrupt them immediately and say, "Keep talking, but tap while you talk!" What happens next is wonderful to watch. Rather than just recapping old problems, they experience breakthroughs. Talking about an old problem without tapping is likely to reinforce it. The neurons that process that information in your brain are firing as you speak, creating new synaptic connections and building up further neural capacity to carry that signal of emotional distress. If you tap, however, the emotional intensity of the event usually diminishes rapidly. Those neuronal pathways in the brain are then deactivated. You are literally reshaping your brain with every story you tell and every strong emotion you feel. EFT helps you release the pull of "your same old story" and opens up the possibility of creating a new story.

A handy rule of thumb is to tap whenever you are telling a story charged with negative emotion. The worst that can happen is nothing. The likely outcome is the discharge of the emotional energy associated with the event, and a new possibility of healing. Here's a story about how a client of mine daisy chained through many different issues in a long session.

Little Louise and Taxes

This client was a recently divorced woman. Her husband had completed the tax returns throughout their 35-year marriage, and this was the first year she'd had to face the task herself. She exhibited so many irrational fears that a structured conversation based on cognitions was virtually impossible. So I encouraged her to rant and tap, while holding in the other hand the tax information sheet her accountant had mailed her, and her checkbook. Here are some excerpts from the conversation. I've shortened it to make the daisy chain more clear, and inserted ellipses (…) where the transcript has been cut.

Client: Why are there taxes?

How can I be expected to do taxes?

I'm 60 years old and I've never figured it out.

Why do taxes exist? (crying)

Coach (I had an intuitive sense that the last sentence meant she'd already regressed to a childhood mental state): How old are you right now?

Client: I'm 5 years old. How can I know about taxes?…

I am overwhelmed.

I'm an abject failure.

I don't deserve to live.

I'm less than a dust mite in the carpet.…

Coach (noticing her looking at her checkbook): What do you feel in your body when you look at your checkbook?

Client: Panic. My brain freezes.

Coach: Where in your body do you feel it?

Client: My brain. My head....

Coach: If that feeling were a child, what would the child's name be?

Client: Little Louise.

Coach: Close your eyes and tap on her. Tell me about her.

Client: She wants to be taken care of. She doesn't think she can figure out business.

Coach: Show her the checkbook and ask her how she feels....

Little Louise never grew up. She feels stubborn. Not wanting to do that.

Coach: So she's choosing?

Client: She knows she's smart enough. She can do the math. She put her foot down, she said, "I am not going to do that." (Note the cognitive shift as she realizes that not doing her taxes is a choice, not an inevitability.) She knew enough to write down checks in her check register.

Coach (noticing a detail from the checkbook and being impressed): You wrote down a balance after every check. Wow!

Client: It's fun. I guess if writing down checks is fun, it could be fun to learn how to do taxes. We can make it a game (another cognitive shift)....

Coach: What number are you on not being an organized person now, after tapping?

Client: 2.

Client: Because I love myself anyway, and I can get organized when I need to, like when I used to study for tests.

Coach (wrapping up session): What number are you about "I didn't keep good records?"

Client: 2. Little Louise did the best she could. I still didn't keep good records, but I'm still okay. I forgive myself. I was going through a divorce. I was grieving.

The client left me a voice mail 2 weeks later to say she'd finished her taxes, 3 weeks before the government deadline. She said it was easy!

* * *

The Generalization Effect:
Identifying It, and Adjusting the Setup Statement

The generalization effect is the tendency after tapping on an event for your SUD level to go down for all similar events. Perhaps a client has had dozens of negative experiences with his bosses at work. He has a pattern of getting into conflict with them, and eventually quitting or being fired. He's decided to find an EFT practitioner to work on his problem and he's found you.

In the first session, you help him identify the worst three events with a boss and tap on them. You then shift the focus, and have him pick the first bad event with a boss, which occurred when he was flipping burgers at a fast-food restaurant as a teenager. His boss, Terry, screamed at him when he burned a batch of fries. His SUD level is now 0 for all four events. It's likely that his SUD score on all the others will then go down even though he has not tapped on every single one.

It's also possible that his SUD level around being yelled at for burning the fries goes down slowly. It's a 10 to start, and after a round of tapping, it's a 4. His first Setup Statement was "Even though Terry screamed at me for burning the fries, I deeply and completely accept myself." After his SUD level goes down to 4, you can adjust the Setup Statement to be "Even though I still have some emotional intensity around Terry screaming at me for burning the fries…" When his number is down to 1, you can say, "Even though I still have a little bit of emotional intensity…" and so on. You adjust the Setup Statement to reflect the client's progress. EFT Universe trainer and social worker Tracey Middleton recalls one Vietnam veteran who remembered hundreds of firefights. After tapping on the four that were the most traumatic, the rest no longer bothered him.

Notice the generalization effect when you're working with clients or working on yourself. If, for instance, you worked on the bosses during the first session, ask your client about those four events when he arrives for the second session. He might still be a 0 on all four. You ask about other similar events with bosses, and find that few or none of them now have any emotional intensity. So you might need to shift the focus of subsequent sessions to a different issue.

The Apex Effect

The Apex Effect is a term coined by Roger Callahan (1985) to refer to a phenomenon frequently observed in energy psychology practice. Clients tend to dismiss the effectiveness of tapping because once the problem is solved, they have difficulty believing or remembering that it was once severe. When offering EFT to veterans at the Veterans Stress Project, therapists sometimes remark on the Apex Effect. After a veteran has had four or five sessions of EFT, he may be feeling much better. He might say something to the therapist like, "I don't think I ever had PTSD to begin with." Therapists in the research program keep records of their sessions, including PTSD scores, and they then show the veteran their intake forms. Veterans are often shocked at how severe their PTSD was when they started treatment, and they realize how far they've come. When a problem is solved, it can be difficult to remember how bad it was to start with.

A related phenomenon is the tendency by clients to ascribe their success to something other than tapping. I was working with an executive team at a large family-owned company. Before we began, I assessed their levels of anxiety and depression using a standardized test. I worked with the treasurer on several deeply disturbing emotional events. We were using an office with a beautiful view overlooking a flower garden. The man was a good candidate for EFT and his SUD scores dropped quickly. He felt much better after the session, and the improvement was reflected in his second batch of test scores on the anxiety and depression scale. "I feel great," he said at the end of our time together. "This office is so cheerful, and the view is so pleasing, that it's really improved my mood." I didn't disagree with him, but I chuckled inside. He ascribed his improvement to the view, an implausible explanation given that he'd seen it many times before.

Here are two case histories from the EFT archives that document the Apex Effect. First, EFT Master Carol Look shares a story from "Sara" who burned herself badly while boiling vegetables. Sara used EFT not only to lessen the pain, but also to deal with the redness and possible blister. To her surprise, the next day there was not a blister—not even a red spot. It was as if the burn had never happened at all. In the second case, psychologist John Digby describes his client forgetting the fibromyalgia symptoms she'd tapped on.

A Skeptic's Use of EFT for a Burn
By Carol Look, LCSW

"Sara" burned her finger very badly by touching a metal pot in which she had been boiling vegetables. She said she heard her finger "sizzle" and she physically shuddered from the pain. She immediately applied ice to her finger but was shocked by the severity of the burning feeling that persisted in spite of the ice. I had taught her EFT for anxiety issues, so she knew the routine. She was still a little skeptical, however, and reluctant to try it on herself, by herself.

Feeling desperate, she decided to tap anyway on the burn pain. Sara reported feeling greatly relieved from the throbbing and pain immediately after using EFT on herself. She continued to apply the ice for the next half hour but, based on previous experiences of burning her fingers in the kitchen and applying ice as the only remedy, she didn't expect much relief. She anticipated that her finger would still hurt or throb later in the evening, feel tender and sore at night, and eventually blister the following morning.

Sara was amazed to find herself free of pain that evening. She wasn't even mildly distracted from leftover sensations from the burn. The following morning she reported she was able to grab onto the holding bar of the treadmill during her workout, because she basically "forgot" she had injured herself in the kitchen. Her finger did not feel sore or tender and never blistered or even looked as if the skin had been hurt.

Sara is no longer reluctant to try EFT on herself. Illustrating the Apex Effect, however, she said, "Maybe it was just the ice..." While Sara admitted that ice alone had never given her this kind of relief from a burn before, she still didn't feel entirely comfortable attributing her speedy recovery to EFT.

* * *

Client Forgets Symptoms of Fibromyalgia
By John Digby, PhD

In my practice I have become known as a specialist in fibromyalgia and chronic fatigue syndrome and regularly address support groups for these conditions. In these events I have the assistance of one of my first "cures" in the way of a lady called Tina, who, since her recovery, has also become a practitioner.

After explaining how EFT works and demonstrating with a member or two from the group, I open the floor to a Q & A session. This week a gentleman in the audience asked Tina exactly what symptoms she tapped on to get rid of her fibromyalgia. She quickly replied that although the consultations we had were just over a year ago, she had no recollection of specific symptoms and went on to explain that this was the Apex Effect in action.

Her fibromyalgia had been severe, and she had been diagnosed with depression, receiving pharmaceutical treatment for depression for 14 years. But she had so completely dissolved the issues causing the symptoms that she could not connect with that "other Tina" who had had the condition.

The Apex Effect never fails to enthrall me and, after a few early jitters as a therapist, I now smile when a patient experiences it, as I know then that the healing is total!

* * *

There are several possible explanations for the Apex Effect. One is that the conscious mind does not believe that healing is possible, or that it could happen so quickly. I remember doing my first telephone session with a client as part of a radio program. The client's SUD level dropped quickly. I did not believe it, even though I had been doing EFT for years and I was the practitioner in this case. After the show, I phoned the client and asked if her SUD level really had dropped that fast, or if she was just trying to please me on the air. She assured me that she'd reported her distress honestly and accurately. In that case, it was me who suffered from the Apex Effect!

I am frequently startled at how quickly clients heal. My conscious mind is sometimes reeling, unable to accept what clients are telling me about their levels of distress. My logical mind tells me that such rapid healing of physical pain, for instance, isn't possible. Yet I've witnessed hundreds of people going from high to low SUD levels for pain in just a few minutes, despite my skepticism.

In the documentary film *The Tapping Solution,* producer Nick Ortner wanted to include a woman named Patricia who'd had severe and long-term physical pain. Patricia had been in a car crash that severely injured her back. Subsequent operations inserted rods and screws in her back, and she called the pain a "constant heavy presence." Nick's sister, Jessica Ortner, who was collaborating with him, did not want her included, arguing that her physical injuries were so severe, and of such long duration, that EFT was unlikely to have much effect. If I had been part of the debate, I would probably have sided with Jessica. To their credit, Jessica and Nick took the risk and included her in the group. Her pain completely vanished, the Ortners captured the transformation on video, and when they followed up a year later, Patricia had maintained all the progress she'd made in the earlier session. The movie is inspiring and a great way to introduce newcomers to EFT (TappingSolution.EFTUniverse.com). Clinical psychologist David Feinstein believes that one reason that mental health professionals have been so slow to adopt EFT is that nothing in their prior experience suggests that such rapid healing is possible (Feinstein, 2010). Given my own difficulty in accepting these seemingly miraculous results, I can sympathize with these professionals.

Sometimes clients recognize that they've had a life-changing event, and they're awed and grateful. Other times they ascribe their changes to the view, the weather, the chair, the flowers, or something else. That's one reason why EFT places such emphasis on collecting SUD scores. They're a way of demonstrating progress to both client and practitioner, despite the Apex Effect.

Shifting the Setup Statement as the Client Rapidly Shifts Aspects

Given the speed with which client distress can vanish with EFT, the alert practitioner is attuned to the client, noticing changes in the client and shifting her approach to match. EFT practitioners, especially experienced therapists, can have a clear idea of the direction a treatment session should take at the outset. Clients often make mincemeat of our plans as soon as we start tapping. Clinical EFT is a "client-centered" approach and we place great emphasis on following the client's lead, not pulling the session in the direction we believe it ought to go.

A client may rapidly shift aspects. A client working on a car crash might identify the smell of blood as 10 on the SUD scale, with the sound of tearing metal as the next-most-triggering aspect with a SUD of 8. You'll then formulate the Setup Statement, "Even though I smelled the blood…" and start tapping. In less than 10 seconds, the client may drop to a 0 on the smell of blood, and shift aspects to the sound of tearing metal, the scream of a passenger, or some other aspect entirely. If you're the practitioner, trust the process, and shift your language to match the client. Do this even if you're thrown off balance by how rapidly the client shifts aspects. It's also very common for clients to remember additional aspects of an event that they did not mention at the start of the session. The client with the car crash might recover a memory fragment about being yelled at by the passenger in the other car, or being afraid of being arrested by the Highway Patrol officers because they had drugs in the car, or one of a thousand other possibilities. Once the remembered aspects are tapped to a SUD score of 0, many unremembered aspects may present themselves for healing and release.

Our brains and bodies contain much innate wisdom on how to reprocess traumatic events, and when we tap and start the healing process, they may rush to heal, upsetting the neat conceptual frameworks a practitioner may have on how the session should unfold. If you as a practitioner follow the client's lead, listening intently and adjusting the Setup Statement as the aspects shift, you'll match the client's pace of healing.

Customized Setup Phrasing

When you're learning EFT, you begin with the Setup Statement, "Even though [problem], I deeply and completely accept myself." Embodying the effective techniques of exposure and cognitive framing, this Setup Statement works well. As you gain experience, however, you'll begin to experiment with a variety of Setup Statements. Ideally, they should all contain both exposure (the problem) and the cognitive frame of acceptance (I accept myself). But otherwise they may look nothing like the classic Setup Statement you first learned.

Here are some other setups that focus the client on exposure using different words:

"If only…"
"What if…"
"Suppose that…"
"I choose…"
"Even if…"

Though they don't use the classic "Even though I have this problem…" format, they activate that part of the client's neural network that is processing the traumatic memory. Activating those neural signaling pathways is the purpose of this part of the Setup Statement, not the use of a particular set of words. Here's how these alternate setups might be used in practice:

> "*Suppose that my wife leaves me for another man, I deeply...*"
> "*Even if I lose my job, I deeply...*"
> "*I choose to accept myself even if the value of my retirement plan decreases.*"
> "*If only I'd kept my cat Molly in the house, she'd be alive today, but I still deeply...*"

It's clear that all of these might evoke a strong emotional reaction in the client, which can then be addressed with EFT. As you apply EFT, you'll begin to find creative ways to modify the Setup Statement to work for you, as psychotherapist Timothy Hayes explains in this story.

Using "It's In Here" in the EFT Setup Phrase
By Timothy J. Hayes, PsyD

Each time I say to someone, "You make me so angry," I am choosing to focus on them and their behavior as the cause of my anger and discomfort. In doing this I prevent myself from seeing the true cause of my anger, which is always inside of me. It is my thoughts that cause my emotions, not the actions or reactions of anyone else. Each time I tell someone that they have offended me, I block myself from seeing the actual process of how I have chosen to take offense and then feel offended by what they have said or done.

I have discovered an added benefit of the EFT process. When you are tapping or rubbing on the acupressure points on your body, and repeating an affirmation that pairs the problem with acceptance, love, and forgiveness of self, you are physically pointing to the source of your discomfort! You are continually tapping on your body. You are not tapping on the body of the person who did something you chose to get angry about. You are tapping on your body, as if to say, "It's In Here! The source, and therefore the solution to my pain, Is In Here!"

I have found that adding "It's In Here!" to my affirmations has helped reinforce the knowledge that I am creating, and therefore can eliminate, most of my pain and discomfort, whether it is physical, mental, or emotional. I alternate using this affirmation in addition to, and instead of, the standard affirmation format recommended in *The EFT Manual*. When I focus on the anger I am feeling, about something someone said or did, I begin tapping and say the Setup Phrase:

Even though I am angry about what they said, I deeply and completely love, accept, and forgive myself, and I know "It's In Here!" Then my Reminder Phrase is something like "This anger, that's In Here." Remember that whenever you are using EFT, you are physically pointing to the source of your pain and discomfort. It may help to verbally remind yourself that "It's In Here!"

* * *

EFT Master Carol Look, LCSW, suggests that sometimes adding "what if" to the Setup Statement opens up new possibilities. Examples of this type of setup are:

Even though I get nervous when I'm about to kick and so I always miss the goal, what if I didn't get nervous this time?

Even though job interviews make me so anxious that I stutter and avoid eye contact with the interviewer, what if this next interview I felt confident?

EFT Master Patricia Carrington, PhD, developed a related variant of the setup, called the Choices Method (Carrington, 2000). She introduces the concept of choice into the language used. She recommends you formulate a choice that is the exact opposite of the problem. For instance, if your issue is "I'm afraid of public speaking," then your Choices Method Setup Statement might be "Even though I'm afraid of public speaking, I choose to feel wonderfully at ease when presenting to large groups of people." You can follow this with the Choice Trio: one round of EFT on the negative only, one round on the choice only, and a final round alternating negative and positive.

Dr. Carrington makes the following four recommendations for using the Choices Method. The first is to identify specific events, just like in normal EFT. The second is to create "pulling choices" that entice and compel you toward them. Make your choices as attractive as possible. The third is to strive for the best possible outcome. Taking the time to develop pulling choices makes them effective against tail-enders. Don't compromise or dilute what you want. Finally, like affirmations, choices need to state what you do want rather than what you don't want. Rather than saying, "I want my boss to stop yelling at me" you say, "I choose an employer who always speaks to me with care and respect." You can find out more about the Choices Method at Choices. EFTUniverse.com.

Flowing Setup Statements

Eventually, Setup Statements become second nature. You conduct a session not even thinking about them or analyzing what you're doing. This leads to flowing Setup Statements that interact smoothly with the words the client is offering you. You tap and talk with the client in an uninterrupted flow, not using the structured Setup Statement but nonetheless keeping the client focused on the problem (exposure) and the acceptance (cognitive shift).

When you watch a session offered by a very experienced practitioner, it may look more like a conversation than a therapy session, with a dynamic ebb and flow in which practitioner and client are both participants.

In the following example, an EFT practitioner goes from one issue to another, allowing her mind to "free associate." She finds some surprising associations, one of which leads to the quick remission of her bladder infection.

Experiments with the Setup and a Urinary Tract Infection
By Christine Cloutier

Recently, I received a phone call from my brother telling me that he was going to commit suicide. It is never a great phone conversation, but it is not the first time. He has his own problems.

What was different about this phone call is that recently one of my cousins did commit suicide and my mother was very distraught about this. I started thinking about my brother calling our mom every month or so with his suicidal ideas and I got very angry about it. How dare he do this to our mom…she is getting older and cannot take these phone calls anymore.

In order to calm myself down, I decided to take a long warm bath. In the bathtub, I started to feel the pressure to urinate and I knew the feeling. I was getting another infection. You don't forget the symptoms.

It was late at night and I did not want to go to the emergency room to get pills. I decided to tap on it. Every time I would go to the bathroom for my two drops of relief, I did some tapping. It amounted to about every 5 minutes.

> *Even though I have this urinary tract infection…*
> *Even though I still have some of this urinary tract infection…*

It was reducing the intensity level a bit but not by much. On a scale of 0 to 10, it went from a 10 to an 8 and would go back up quickly. I went back to what happened before it started to see if I could find an emotional counterpart to this. Of course, the phone call came up.

> *Even though I am angry at my brother for disturbing our mother's peace of mind…*

It was still there. This was very annoying and I told myself that I would find the proper words to say because I knew it could work. What else could I do? I tried:

> *Even though I am pissed off at my brother…*

Right away, I felt this warmth around my urethra and the symptoms of the infection disappeared like magic. That is what I call a miracle. Instant healing. I had a hard time believing it was for real, so for good measure I tapped on:

> *Even though I am afraid this might come back…*

It did not come back. I hope this story can help some other person not to give up on themselves.

* * *

Techniques for Working on Your Own Issues

One of the questions people frequently ask is, "Do I ever get to the end of my emotional processing?" It's like the question asked of a notorious French courtesan, "Does your sexual appetite wane as you age?" She replied, "How would I know? I'm only 85 years old!"

I learned EFT in 2002, though I'd learned energy medicine techniques much earlier. I was 15 years old when I took my first class in an energy healing technique called Attunement. Though I use EFT, I also still use Attunement occasionally, as well as techniques learned from many schools of psychotherapy, spirituality, and personal transformation.

I went to a gathering recently at which I met many members of my ex-wife's extended family, most of whom I had not seen for 20 years. I was surprised at how triggered I got, and I did a lot of tapping on the way home. I couldn't even remember many events, but the feelings were still there. Though you might make progress by leaps and bounds after you learn EFT, issues will keep on arising in your life for many years into the future. With some, you might not be successful at resolving them with EFT, and require other methods. A few years back I hired an Imago therapist to work on a particular issue that regular EFT could not budge. Imago therapy, developed by Harville Hendricks, is often very effective for childhood issues (Hendricks, 1993). The therapist did Imago therapy while I tapped, and she was amazed how fast I progressed. Tapping seemed to accelerate the Imago work. Many psychotherapists trained in other schools add tapping to their toolkit and report that, suddenly, everything else they do has more impact.

So the answer to the question is yes, you're going to need to keep working on yourself for as long as you're alive, with EFT and with other methods, since life seems to continually present us with fresh challenges.

Besides using the Clinical EFT techniques in this book, and getting help from an experienced practitioner when you feel stuck, how do you work on yourself? One challenge you'll have is that certain clients will trigger you. You might be overweight, and have a client who's struggling with weight issues. Tapping with her on her issues brings up all of your issues. Perhaps a client reminds you of your mother or another family member, and you have a flood of triggering memories as the client tells her story. A client may bring up an event such as assault or molestation that echoes a similar incident in your childhood. You might get an uncomfortable feeling in your body when working with a certain client and not be able to identify its origins. A skilled practitioner is aware of these body sensations while simultaneously remaining tuned to the client. It is imperative that you not allow the feelings you are experiencing as the practitioner to interfere with the session. If your feelings become the main focus of your attention, then you are no longer present for your client. While it's not appropriate to work on your issues during the client's sessions, it's essential to pay attention to your own triggers. Make a note in your journal whenever you're triggered, and work on the problem later.

This is a case in which it's useful to solicit the perspective of another person, such as an expert therapist or a trusted colleague. Getting advice from such a source, called supervision, is an essential part of keeping yourself on track. When difficult client issues, or ethical problems are involved, supervision can provide you with the perspective to avoid making mistakes.

The Personal Peace Procedure is an essential practice for working on your issues. The more you clear, the less emotional debris stands in the way of you being truly present for your clients, your loved ones, and your friends.

I recommend tapping on yourself every morning. I do this while clearing specific worries as well as general ones. Many meditators report better results if they tap before beginning their meditation. Tapping to clear your emotional body before the day begins helps remove impediments to expressing your full potential.

I also recommend tapping if you feel emotionally triggered during the day. I meditate every morning, as well as tapping and doing energy exercises like qigong. This practices establishes a mindset of joy and power at the outset of the day. Things happen during the workday, however, to upset the applecart. If I feel myself off balance, rather than pushing myself to continue working, I stop. I know from hard experience that the work I do while in an impaired emotional state will not be my best. I take a walk, or make some tea, tap, meditate briefly, or do something else to center myself before returning to work. Tapping is an essential part of self-care in this way.

Keeping a personal journal is invaluable in charting your emotional and spiritual growth. You will notice recurring patterns that are hard to change, as well as record your breakthroughs. Your journal is where you reflect on the events of your life, large and small, and it helps give you perspective. Record in your journal your before-and-after SUD scores for troubling events. This will encourage you to tap for new challenges that arise. Reading in your journal about your success with old challenges will inspire you when you're faced with new ones.

If you're a practitioner, it's vital to work on your own issues with another practitioner as backup. You might be successful with many problems applying Clinical EFT on your own. Yet you'll find that another pair of eyes on the problem often illuminates new solutions. I was working with my practitioner on a problem with my business during a phone session recently. I'd mapped all the ins and outs of the problem for her, and I frankly didn't see how she could help me. She responded, "Well, obviously what you need to do is…" and she told me a solution.

The effect of her words was approximately the same as if someone had stuck me with a pin. "What?" I exclaimed, "Can you say that again?" She was puzzled, and said, "Well obviously…" and presented the same solution.

"That might be obvious to you," I told her, "but it never occurred to me!" The solution that was immediately apparent to her had never crossed my mind, even though I'd spent weeks looking at the problem from every angle. Even if you've had great success with EFT with clients, it's essential to keep working on your own issues, and do so in the context of the support that a community of practitioners offers.

Practitioners who enroll in the Skinny Genes weight loss program often say, "I've used EFT successfully with clients and for most of my own issues. But I can't seem to get it to work for weight loss." Others enroll in the Tapping Deep Intimacy relationship course with variations on the theme: "It works great with clients and for most of my issues, but my love life sucks." We all seem to have quick and easy personal growth in some domains of our lives, while other domains present lifelong challenges.

This is where persistence pays off. If you keep on working at your challenges, exploring every possible angle, you set yourself up for a breakthrough. It might not occur in the time frame you want, or be as dramatic as you'd hoped, but peeling off layer after layer of a problem eventually exposes the core. The breakthrough might take years or even decades, but if you don't take the first step, you will make no progress toward your goal. When using EFT with your own issues, make what progress you can, use the resources you have, and persist. My father, a priest and Bible scholar, has a favorite saying inspired by the example of Shamgar, the third judge of the ancient Israelites: "Start where you are, use what you have, and do what you can." That's the beginning of breaking the habit of being yourself.

Interrupting Your Tragic Story

The feature that the techniques covered in this chapter have in common is that they interrupt our stories. By the time we're adults, we have fixed stories and beliefs about our successes and failures, our personalities and our circumstances. We've learned roles, and we play them faithfully. In each of the five major areas of life—work, relationships, money, health, and spirituality—we act out the script we've written for ourselves. By the time we're 20 or 30 years of age, we have a habit of being ourselves, and it can be very hard to change.

EFT breaks our habit of being ourselves. It interrupts the continual reenactment of our old stories. Tapping disrupts our old realities, challenges our limiting beliefs, and opens us up to change. When we lose the habit of being ourselves, the possibility of a new self emerges. This new self can embody all the potential that was previously imprisoned within the old self. When we tap on our patterns, they start to change and, like a butterfly emerging from a chrysalis, a new being emerges. This often produces major shifts in our outer experience. I'll leave you with a final inspiring story of how inner change can lead to outer change.

From Abandonment to Engagement
By Alina Frank

A client named Susan contacted me from Switzerland after learning of EFT through one of my online articles. Susan said that she wanted desperately to get rid of her absolute terror that her boyfriend was going to leave her. The first half of her first EFT session was spent tapping on her fear, and the intensity level dropped from a 9 to a 2 on the SUD scale. Upon reflecting on the session midway through, I discovered that Susan had shifted aspects and was focusing instead on the divorce she had gone through a few years earlier, so we then tapped on the scenes related to her past relationship and how he had abandoned her. By the end of our first session, Susan was at a 0 when imagining her boyfriend leaving her. She was also completely neutral when I had her recount several events from the time her ex left her, which we'd also worked on.

During the subsequent session, I asked Susan if this pattern of men leaving her went back even further than her failed marriage. There were a few clues that this was indeed the case, including a statement she had said during one of her tapping rounds: "They always leave me." When statements from clients (or from yourself when working alone) include words such as "always" or "never," suspect that you are uncovering a core issue. Susan said that she had felt a sense of dread that people would always leave her, and it showed up often and strongly for seemingly insignificant reasons—a coworker transferred to another department, her regular public bus driver being reassigned, amongst others. Because she didn't consciously know where this belief had originated, I had her tap on the global statement "Even though people always leave me..." (Sneaking Up Technique). Midway through that round, Susan burst out excitedly, "I know where this started!"

Susan recalled being born to a teenage mother. Her mother left her to be raised by her grandparents but drifted in and out of Susan's life throughout her childhood. Her mother would be out of work for a while, then she'd move in to connect with Susan and then leave a few months later. Susan's mother wanted to go back to school to get a degree and so she moved back home to save money, attempted to reconnect with Susan for a few months, and then left 6 months later. Live-in boyfriends would prompt her mom to move home and, well, you get the picture. This pattern of being attached to someone only to have them leave was set up in the first 7 years of Susan's life, a time we know is when you are most susceptible to forming the most important attachments and the foundation of your world view.

We spent the next two sessions working through some of the most painful scenes from Susan's childhood. By the end of the fourth session, she felt a tremendous sense of freedom from the fears and anxiety that had plagued her entire life. Two weeks after the end of her final session, I received a blank e-mail from Susan with picture of a bouquet of flowers attached. I wrote her back saying thank you for the photograph. She wrote back, asking me to zoom in on the bouquet. When I did, I was delighted to see that in the center of the bouquet was an engagement ring, proof positive that we had indeed collapsed the pattern!

* * *

Resources

- Core Issues and How to Find Them: CoreIssues.EFTUniverse.com
- Daisy Chaining: DaisyChaining.EFTUniverse.com
- Choices Method by Patricia Carrington: Choices.EFTUniverse. com
- Skinny Genes: SkinnyGenesFit.com
- Tail-Enders: TailEnders.EFTUniverse.com
- Tapping Deep Intimacy: TappingDeepIntimacy.com
- Tapping Solution Movie: TappingSolution.EFTUniverse.com

Special Populations

As you gain experience with EFT, you'll run into situations where you need to adapt the Basic Recipe or other techniques to the needs of the people with whom you're working. Experience using EFT with children, for instance, has shown the usefulness of modifying language that might be perfectly appropriate for adults. Working with a golf pro on lowering his handicap requires an approach that is completely different from that required for using EFT with a very sick patient in the hospital. This chapter examines some of the specialized groups with whom you might find yourself using EFT, and shows how to adapt the basic tools of Clinical EFT to meet their needs effectively.

Age-Appropriate Techniques for Using EFT with Children

How you use EFT depends on the age of the child. For infants, no language is necessary. You don't need to formulate a Setup Statement to use EFT with a crying baby. Tapping without words is most appropriate for very young children. While you tap, you can certainly make soothing statements like "Everything's okay," even if the child doesn't understand your words. They'll understand your tone of voice and your peaceful intent. Famed biologist Rupert Sheldrake, author of *Science Set Free* (2013) and nine other books, has suggested that one reason for

EFT's calming effect is that tapping around the eyes mimics the way a mother wipes away the tears from around a baby's eyes.

I also recommend tapping very gently with infants, barely brushing the skin with your fingertips. When tapping on babies, I am often rewarded by a puzzled frown at first, followed by relaxation of the facial muscles. Babies recognize a soothing experience and respond. You can also use Touch and Breathe (TAB), in which you rest your fingertips lightly on each point and take a breath. I recommend knowing where the acupoints are, and using one fingertip rather than two, since the area you're tapping is much smaller than on an adult.

Many parents and other adults use surrogate tapping with babies. Surrogate tapping involves tapping on yourself as a substitute for tapping on the baby. The mechanisms of action of surrogate tapping are unknown, though clinical psychologist David Feinstein assembled 100 case reports of success with surrogate tapping, and speculates on how it might have an effect (Feinstein, 2012b). There are many stories in the EFT archives of people who tapped surrogately for babies and found it calmed them down.

For elementary school children, use a Setup Statement that is simpler than the formula prescribed in the normal Basic Recipe. Stick to concrete events rather than concepts. Examples of concrete events might be: "Even though…

Johnny hit me…
The teacher sent me to the principal's office…
I have a tummy ache…
The other kids laughed at me…
I wasn't picked for the team…
I failed the exam…
Sister bit me…
I can't tie my shoelaces…

With children in this age bracket, you can also use a self-acceptance statement that is simpler than "I deeply and completely accept myself." Any reassuring phrase can be effective. Examples are:

...I'm okay.
...but I'm still a good kid.
...I love myself.
...I'm fine now.
...I'm still an awesome kid.

With children of high school age and older, you can use the regular Setup and tapping routine. Some in this age bracket perceive tapping as cool; others perceive it as decidedly uncool. There are many YouTube videos of teens tapping, and you can encourage a teenager to tap along with those rather than being guided by an authority figure such as a parent or teacher. This minimizes the possibility that a teen might rebel against tapping, refuse to do it, and suffer needlessly as a result. There are also stories in the EFT archives of parents whose teens refused to tap, and the parents tapped surrogately on themselves with success. Reading those stories will give you creative ideas for using EFT with your own children.

In his article on surrogate tapping, Feinstein (2012b) discusses some of the ethical issues raised by this practice. Generally speaking, it is not ethically permissible to tap on another person, even surrogately, without their consent. It is ethically permissible, however, for parents to tap on or with their minor children. There is a gray area in between, such as being in a crowded airplane and tapping surrogately for a crying baby who is not your own child. Feinstein's paper encourages you to explore the ethical considerations inherent in these situations.

Daily Releasing with Children

Most of us as adults have a huge collection of traumatic events stored in our awareness. We weren't taught to deal with negative events as they occurred, and we stuffed them and stored them in our minds, our memories, our subconscious minds, and our bodies. Personally, I think of the years of my life from 0 to 15 as the time of acquisition of negative experiences. During the next 30 years, from the age of 15 to 45, I struggled to heal the old dysfunctional patterns I'd learned early on—while often repeating and reinforcing them. Those 30 years were a determined personal growth journey on which, through meditation, psychotherapy, group work, and reading transformational books, I began to break free of some of the patterns of thought and behavior that sabotaged my intentions and gifts.

During this agonizing process of catharsis, I fantasized about what my life would have looked like if I had not had to spend 30 years digging out from under the "mountain of dung" that had been shoveled onto my head in the early years. I could have blossomed early and accomplished great things in my 20s and 30s, I imagined. I certainly became determined that my own children would not have to spend decades shoveling their way out of a mountain, and raised them accordingly. It's been a joy to see them blossom early.

I strongly believe that it's very worthwhile to work with your children daily to release any negative experiences right after they occur, rather than letting them settle into the psyche. Carine, a soccer mom, told me recently that her daughter Tiffany, who plays goalie for her elementary school team, had missed a ball during an important match. The coach lost his temper and screamed at Tiffany, "How could you miss that ball? It was coming right at you!" After the game, Carine tapped with her daughter, both of them very angry at the coach. That night, Tiffany still remembered the coach yelling at her but told her father that she'd in fact caught almost every other ball coming toward her, saving her team many times. The next day, Tiffany had another soccer match and excelled at her job as goalie.

This story stands in stark contrast to the many stories of kids who've stopped playing a sport they love because they were so emotionally traumatized by criticism and failure. Without tapping, Tiffany's path could have gone in that direction. She could have been so nervous the next day that she missed several saves, and quit soccer shortly thereafter. Releasing the emotional intensity of a negative experience helped her develop her gifts rather than giving up. Tapping with your children each day frees them of the emotional hold that negative experiences might have over their consciousness. Daily releasing ensures that, though life might throw the occasional negative experience a child's way, tapping brushes it aside, and the bad stuff does not accumulate into a mountain that stifles the promise of a young life.

The Daily Peace Procedure for Children

The Daily Peace Procedure is simple. Each night, while tucking their children into bed, parents ask: "What good and bad thoughts did you have today? And what good and bad things happened to you today?" As the child is describing the thoughts and events, both good and bad, the parents tap the EFT points lightly and lovingly or rub them gently. As children describe bad events, they are tuned in to the emotions of the problem. Tapping ensures that these emotions are dispelled rather than reinforced.

Children are constantly absorbing information from the environment, which includes from their parents, teachers, peers, television, the Internet, and other media. Much of this information is negative. By the time a typical television-watching American child reaches the age of 18, he or she will have witnessed about 200,000 dramatized acts of violence including 40,000 murders (Grossman & DeGaetano, 2009). Even comedy shows often get their laughs through vicious attacks on others. This daily barrage of negative images and words fills a child's consciousness and subconscious mind. A parent who performs the Daily Peace Procedure with a child can empty the garbage can by tapping. Here are examples of bad experiences children might report:

"Daddy scared me when he yelled at me."
"I saw a monster killing people on television."
"My teacher thinks I'm dumb."
"I can't run fast like Billy."
"I'm not as pretty as Susan."
"The preacher said I won't go to heaven if I'm not good."

These are just a few of myriad statements that reflect the feelings and events that can become entrenched in children's psyches. It doesn't matter whether the child's interpretation is reasonable by adult standards. What matters to children's psyches and the effect of the events on them is how they felt when they had the experience.

As you are tapping or rubbing the points, you can continue to probe, asking, "What else happened today?" You can also reframe the event for the child, providing another way to look at the event, such as, "Monsters on TV aren't real." Doing this while tapping makes it far more likely that your child will absorb the message than if you simply talked about it.

This EFT procedure for children can also be used with infants. Even though babies are unable to tell you what is upsetting them, their crying or other indicators of distress when all their physical needs have been met let you know that tapping could be beneficial. There may be fear, trauma, or physical discomfort, the source of which is not apparent. When infants are in the midst of distress, they are tuned in to the problem and therefore ready for tapping. The addition of EFT tapping to the usual murmured soothing language can interrupt the accumulation of negative events and feelings by infants.

Tap the EFT points while children share the good as well as the bad thoughts and events of their day. The reason for this is that when describing a positive event, there is often an unspoken negative worry or counterpoint to the event. For instance, when the child says, "My teacher complimented me today in front of the whole class," the underlying worry might be "But sometimes she scolds children or ignores them and I am afraid that will happen to me."

Although the tapping is happening while the child speaks about being praised by the teacher, EFT is simultaneously reducing any fear associated with the underlying negative possibility. For this reason, the procedure calls for tapping on both "good" and the "bad" thoughts and events.

Though children are the focus of the discussion of this procedure, the technique is useful for all ages. It's never too late to start! You can do this procedure nightly on yourself, tapping on all the good things and bad things that happened to you that day, or alternate the parent and child roles with someone else, tapping on each other's days.

Borrowing Benefits

Borrowing Benefits refers to the phenomenon that when you tap while watching another person's EFT session, your SUD levels usually go down too. It might seem farfetched that, while watching a man tap on the emotions associated with his divorce, for instance, the pain in your foot goes away. Yet that's precisely how Borrowing Benefits works.

Borrowing Benefits was first noted in the late 1990s when psychotherapists using EFT reported that they felt fine at the end of the day. Previously, they had felt burnt out at the end of a workday listening to other people's tragic stories. Some of the emotional energy sticks, and after a day of offering therapy, they would typically feel exhausted and depleted. This did not happen if they were doing EFT. They were tapping on themselves as they showed clients how to tap, and just as the clients discharged the negative energy they carried, the therapists discovered that they discharged any they were taking on as they tapped along too.

There have been several studies that quantified the usefulness of Borrowing Benefits. The earliest was performed by Jack Rowe, PhD, a professor at Texas A&M University (Rowe, 2005). He studied 102 participants at a weekend EFT workshop. He found that symptoms of psychological conditions such as anxiety and depression dropped significantly, and remained lower than before in the months following the workshop. Several other studies involving hundreds of people have measured the value of Borrowing Benefits. A study of 216 health care workers found that the intensity of their psychological symptoms such as anxiety and depression dropped by an average of 45% after a one-day EFT workshop, and remained lower thereafter (Church & Brooks, 2010). Those who tapped more in the ensuing months experienced the greatest benefit. Veterans with PTSD and their spouses also got much better after a weeklong EFT retreat where they borrowed benefits (Church & Brooks, 2013).

There are several ways to borrow benefits. One is to take an EFT workshop and tap along with the other participants. Here's an account of what happened with three people who did this.

Simultaneously Resolving Childhood Issues in Three People

Tracy told about how when she first learned to drive, she decided to buy her mom tickets to a classical music concert and drive her there, as a surprise gift. Her mom suffered from depression, and there was usually plenty of drama in her household. The concert was one of Tracy's many attempts since early childhood to make her mom happy.

When she told her mom, her mom exploded in anger and ridiculed Tracy. The trip to the concert didn't happen. I asked Tracy to name her event, and she named it "The Concert." Her intensity was a 9.

Markus talked about a time when his mom left him alone when he was 5 years old. She went to the store, telling him she'd be back in a few minutes, but didn't return for several hours. He became afraid. When she returned, he told her how scared she was and her response was to laugh at him. He named his event "Left alone." He reported his emotional intensity as a 9 when he thought about the event.

Kathy had memories of many events during which her parents fought. I asked her to recall a particularly traumatic one and she said, "The Day the Police Came." Her intensity was a 10.

I tapped only with Tracy. We tapped on each of the aspects of "The Concert," till her intensity rating was 0. I had the whole group, including Markus and Kathy, tapping at the same time. Both reported a 0 intensity on their issues when we were finished, even though I hadn't worked with them individually.

* * *

Another way to borrow benefits is to watch videos of people tapping and tap along with them. A third way is to tap along with members of a "tapping circle." These are groups of people who agree to get together periodically and tap together on their issues. There are tapping groups all over the world, and there are even some online. Some are free, while others, usually under the guidance of a life coach or psychotherapist, charge a modest fee. You'll find them listed at TappingCircles.EFTUniverse.com.

While you're likely to experience the value of Borrowing Benefits yourself by tapping along with videos or online presentations, I recommend you take an EFT workshop first. That way, you'll know where the points are, how to formulate a Setup Statement, how to focus on specific events, and the other essentials of successful use of EFT. With that solid groundwork in place, you'll be well equipped to tap along with others and experience just how far you can get with the Borrowing Benefits technique.

Working with Groups

After learning EFT and experiencing the power of Borrowing Benefits, you might decide to tap with a group yourself, or start your own group. Groups can be formal and structured, such as a psychotherapy group, or informal drop-in leaderless groups. There are many venues in which emotional clearing as a group can be helpful. These include:

- Workplace groups, usually meeting during a break, or after work.

- Church groups, often meeting after a service or one evening a week.

- Therapy groups, in which EFT is used along with a structured therapeutic approach.

- Mastermind groups.

- Life coaching and performance groups.

- 12-step groups.

- Play and art groups, in which EFT is used to tap away the barriers to creativity.

- Prison and jail groups.

- Hospital and outpatient groups.

- Sports teams.

- Social service groups such as Rotary, Lions, and similar groups.

- Youth groups such as Scouts and 4H Clubs.

- Women's groups and men's groups.

- School and university groups.

When forming a group, here are some questions to bear in mind as you decide on the structure of the group. How often does the group meet? Is the group closed or open to new members? Is there a standard for how many sessions a member must attend or might miss, or is this a drop-in group? How will you qualify new members of the group, and how will you handle the eventuality of a member being unsuited to group work? Is there a leader, a rotating leadership, or some other method of guiding the group? Is there a donation or fee required to attend? What will you do if a group member has a severe psychological breakdown? What happens if a group member fails to keep agreements? Is there a book, value system, or philosophy that guides your group? Are there written guidelines to how the group is structured, and do all members know these?

This is not a comprehensive list and there are many other facets to running a successful group. There are many good books and online resources describing how to run a group effectively. It is my dream to see EFT groups in all the places listed, with members using tapping to support the other personal work they're doing and smooth their path to success. Some therapists and group leaders believe that emotional problems clear faster in a group than they do using individual psychotherapy. In fact, EFT Master Carol Look terminated her private practice after making this assessment and now does only group work. There seems to be some kind of collective effect in which participants reinforce the power of change in each other. I encourage you to seize any opportunity to start or join a group to accelerate your process of emotional healing.

Cravings and Addictions

One of the most frequent uses of EFT is for cravings and addictions. What's the difference between them? A craving is a momentary desire, such as an urge to eat ice cream. An addiction is a long-term pattern of giving in to cravings, such as eating a tub of ice cream every day. Cravings usually pass, given time. You might crave ice cream now, but if you pick up an engrossing novel, you might forget all about it. Addictions are long-term behavioral patterns and they require determined effort to change. Clinical psychologist Roger Callahan, who popularized acupoint tapping, believed that cravings and addictive patterns mask anxiety. You're anxious in a social situation, so you pick up a cocktail. You're nervous before a job interview, so you eat a piece of chocolate. You feel a sense of lack in your life, so you visit the ice cream store. He believed that the way to treat cravings and addictive patterns was to address the underlying anxiety.

Clinical experience suggests that some addictive patterns disappear quickly with EFT, while others resist change no matter how much tapping you do. For example, therapists who specialize in helping clients quit smoking tell me that they're usually successful in just a few EFT sessions. Those working with alcohol addiction, such as Dr. David Lake, say that EFT alone is rarely effective for these problems (Lake, 2013).

My personal experience is that EFT is very effective for releasing momentary cravings. The data are clear on this point. In the Health Care Workers Study, we incorporated a craving segment into the EFT workshop (Church & Brooks, 2010). The workshops were held in hotels, and we arranged with the management to supply frequently craved substances at that point in the workshop. Wait staff brought in trays of chocolate, cake, sweets, and alcohol. Proximity allowed participants to get powerfully in touch with their cravings, and many were at or near a 10 on the SUD scale. After tapping, however, cravings simply collapsed. The average reduction in SUD was 83% in the course of about 20 minutes. Participants whose hands had been trembling as they picked up a piece of chocolate before EFT made comments like "This is repulsive." After the workshop, we cleared the room, and all the chocolate and cake went into the trash. One therapist with whom I've stayed in touch has never forgiven me for completely removing her lifetime love of Reese's Peanut Butter Cups!

Because EFT is so effective with cravings does not mean it can magically cure long-term addictions. Addiction is a generality, and tapping on general patterns doesn't give you any target to focus on. Tapping may make a craving go away, but the craving will arise again and again. To be successful, you have to tap each time. You might reach the point where you never crave the substance again, but many people report still having the craving even years after their first tapping experience. Modifying addictive behavior can take years or even decades even with consistent application of EFT. That's the way to address addiction: Tap whenever you have a craving. In this way, you might successfully cut your consumption of your craved substance. For instance, you can simply hold a cigarette up to your nose and tap, or smell the chocolate and tap. Measure your craving on the SUD scale before and after to determine if you're making progress.

The second and deeper way to use EFT is to dig for emotional events associated with the craved substance. Emotional associations can take many forms. Here are some questions you can use to uncover them.

What age was I when I first began to consume this substance? What events were occurring in my life at that time? For example, one woman loved hot fudge sundaes. When she asked herself this question, she remembered that after her parents got divorced when she was 4 years old, each time her father picked her up from her mother's house, he would take her out for a hot fudge sundae. Love and fudge sundaes became entwined in her little mind. After tapping, she still had fond memories of her dad, but lost her taste for sweet ice cream.

Do I have associations between the craved substance and celebration, connection, acceptance, or happiness? For instance, did eating cake with the family mean we were having a good time? Was drinking a beer with Dad a rite of passage that signaled acceptance? Did smoking cigarettes behind the bushes in junior high school indicate the approval of my peer group? Did my Jewish mother cook to show her love? Was getting pickled with my friends a way to rebel against the restrictions of my family?

What losses did I experience in my life that might relate to the craving? Was there a friend or loved one early in my life who was tied in to the pattern of eating or drinking? What did I used to have in my life that I don't have now? Is it associated with the craving? (Think Great-aunt Carla's cinnamon rolls.)

What triggers the craving? You aren't craving the substance 24/7. There are periods of peak craving. When are they, and what information does that timing hold for you? Are there times of day when you crave that jelly donut? Do you crave a martini when you're in the company of "the girls?" Do you need to down a shot of tequila after a stressful business meeting? Do you splurge when your favorite sports team wins, or when they lose? All these triggers are laden with information about the origins of your craving, and you can follow the trail of clues till you get to the earliest events and tap on those.

There's a great deal more to consider on the topic of EFT for cravings and addictions. To avoid making this manual 1,000 pages long, however, I must stop here. I encourage you to take a workshop, and work with a practitioner. The practical experience you obtain in those ways will provide you with great insight into and leverage over your cravings and addictions.

Multiple Phobias

You might well encounter clients with multiple phobias. They might not just have a fear of heights (acrophobia), but also a fear of enclosed spaces (claustrophobia). It's not uncommon for someone with a fear of snakes to also fear other reptiles, and small mammals like rats and mice. If you're working with a person with many phobias, how do you know where to begin?

This is an occasion when "the worst and/or the first" can be a useful guide, especially when linked to body sensations. Ask such clients to imagine vividly the feared item, and then find out where they feel the strongest sensations in their bodies. Find out the first time in their lives they ever felt that physical sensation. You've then successfully made the transition from a general phobia to a specific event. Tap on that event till it's a low number. Test your work by having clients again imagine the feared item. If their SUD score is 0 or near 0, that phobia may be gone. If not, find another event, and tap on that. Keep tapping on events till the phobia is gone. Testing using imaginary exposure to the feared stimulus is useful, but it's even better to test in a real-life situation if possible. If your client has claustrophobia, ask her to step into an elevator or closet and rate her SUD score. If he has acrophobia, have him take an elevator to the top floor of a building and look out the window. They can keep tapping while they do this. When they can expose themselves to the feared situation in real life without a rise in SUD, you know your work is done.

Once one phobia is cleared, others may clear faster because of EFT's generalization effect. If the other phobias are still present, use the same procedure to find specific life events, and take them down to 0. Work through the list, phobia by phobia, and you'll usually find that they disappear. Three randomized controlled trials of EFT for phobias have been performed, and they all showed that phobias disappeared after a very brief period of treatment (Wells, Polglase, Andrews, Carrington, & Baker, 2003; Baker & Siegel, 2010; Salas, Brooks, & Rowe, 2011). Treatment time frames ranged from 15 to 45 minutes, and when participants were followed up, they'd maintained most of their gains.

Because EFT usually eliminates phobias in a single session, the experience can be very gratifying for the practitioner. It's also a good demonstration for a client of EFT's potential. Though most psychological conditions require more work and extended sessions, phobias are an area in which you'll consistently experience "one-minute wonders."

EFT for Physical Symptoms: How the Approach Differs from EFT for Psychological Symptoms

EFT is widely used for physical as well as psychological symptoms, and many people write in the EFT Universe archives of success tapping on problems like migraines, rashes, and burns. Though superficial tapping on the symptom may result in it diminishing or disappearing, it's usually necessary to dig below the surface for emotional issues. The physical symptom is often being held in place by an emotional problem. While it might be the physical symptom that has led the client to EFT, it's usually more productive to focus on traumatic events if the client is willing to go there.

Wrist Fracture Pain Tied to Resentment

While presenting to about 100 medical professionals at a conference at Massey University in New Zealand, I worked with a group of five people with pain.

One of them was a 52-year-old German physician with a fractured wrist. The broken wrist had occurred during a camping trip 2 weeks prior. I asked her how severe her pain was on the 0-to-10 scale, and she said 7.

When I asked her to identify an emotionally triggering incident associated with the fracture, she was puzzled, and couldn't find one. She said she'd slipped while walking across a log that served as a bridge over a brook. She grabbed a branch, but fell anyway, twisted her arm, and broke her wrist.

I asked to mine the circumstances around the fracture for any possible emotional factors. After thinking long and hard, she said, "I was camping with my daughter. I didn't want to go hiking that day, but she made me go with her. I was resentful about that," though on the actual hike she reported that she had been "having a good time." I asked her to recall her resentment of her daughter, and identify where that feeling was located in her body. She pointed to her solar plexus, and rated it a 7 out of 10 in emotional intensity.

I then asked her to recall the first time she had felt that same feeling in her solar plexus. She responded that it was when she thought about her father, and that he had often acted toward her in angry and demeaning ways. I kept on asking her questions, till we uncovered a particular incident that had occurred in elementary school.

She was so intelligent that she had scored second in her entire class during their initial test. She took her examination results home and proudly presented them to her father. His comment was, "Why weren't you first?" The doctor rated this incident as a 10 out of 10 in emotional intensity in her solar plexus.

Since I am usually short of time during these demonstrations, I try and hit as many angles as possible in a brief session, having the subject make as many statements as possible that might trigger emotional aspects of the problem. So as well as tapping on the test incident, we tapped on the look on her father's face, his body language, the sound of his voice, all the other times he put her down, and also on some positive reframing statements such as "My father was doing the best he could figure out how to deal with me."

I then asked the doctor to reassess the feeling in her solar plexus. It was 0 intensity. "And by the way," I enquired, "what's the level of pain in your wrist now?" She moved her wrist back and forth, then the other wrist. She looked puzzled, as she struggled to locate the pain. Then she said, "Well maybe it's a 2 now, I don't know, I can hardly feel it."

* * *

There's a good deal of emotion and psychology in the ways people describe their physical ailments. You can use these descriptions as a way to test the progress of EFT. Ask a client in pain, for instance, to describe the pain exactly. They might say something like: "I have this sharp blue humming pain the size of a coin just below the center of my right shoulder." Build that description into a Setup Statement, for example, "Even though I have this sharp blue humming pain the size of a coin just below the center of my right shoulder, I deeply and completely accept myself."

After tapping, these descriptions often change. A pain the size of a beach ball becomes a basketball becomes a tennis ball becomes a Ping-Pong ball becomes a spot, then vanishes. A heavy black mass of pain becomes a gray pool becomes a white mist and blows away. A solid block of pain becomes a wavy box becomes a vibrating line and finally disappears. These images are another way of testing. If EFT is having no effect, the beach ball remains a beach ball. When it changes size, color, or consistency, you're usually making progress.

A useful question to ask in cases of persistent physical symptoms is: *"If there were an emotional issue behind this, what would it be?"*

Sometimes clients tell you readily. At a conference I attended, a doctor described his time as a resident in a cardiac unit at a hospital. Almost all the patients were men, and they had been admitted after suffering heart attacks. He asked them a simple question: "Why are you here?" He expected to hear "Because I had a heart attack." Yet none of the men said that. They gave him responses like, "There's no way I could stand another day in that horrible job" or "I would do anything to escape my marriage" or "My kids are driving me crazy." All their reasons were emotional. He speculated that their heart attacks were, in part, a desperate attempt to escape from emotionally intolerable situations. Ask your clients the same question: "Why do you have this symptom?" or "What emotional causes might lie behind it?" You might get surprising answers.

If your client is unable to find an emotional issue, have him or her guess. These guesses are often right on target. The content in the guess can come only from the client's actual life, and forms an adequate starting point for an EFT session.

Techniques to Use When Regular EFT Does Not Reduce SUD Level

Sometimes you'll use all the classic approaches of Clinical EFT and yet the client's SUD level doesn't decrease. Here are some recommendations for where to go next.

Check for aspects you might have missed. Our brains encode trauma in surprising ways. One therapist worked with an Afghanistan veteran whose armored Humvee had been blown up in combat while protecting a convoy of supply trucks. He had been thrown clear of the vehicle and survived, injured, in the middle of a firefight for several hours before he was rescued. He was having recurrent nightmares that featured the symbol of a triangle. Neither he nor the therapist could find any association between the nightmares and a waking problem. The therapist tapped on all the aspects of the Humvee disaster, but the veteran's SUD level did not go down. Suddenly, the veteran remembered an aspect of the attack that he had previously forgotten. After he was blown clear of his vehicle, he lay crushed against the burned-out hulk of a supply truck. The symbol of the supply convoy's unit was a black triangle. The triangle was the element of the event with which has brain had associated all the fear encoded in the entire event. Once they tapped on the triangle, the SUD rating for the whole event dropped immediately to 0. If you haven't been successful with EFT for an event, search for aspects like the triangle that you might have missed.

Describe additional details of the event. Perhaps your client is working on a car crash without the SUD level lowering. Ask questions like "What else do you remember about the event?" or "Describe this part of the event in more detail." You can also ask the client to slow down and give you a detailed blow-by-blow replay of the event. Watch your client's face and body language carefully, and you might notice some detail that evokes high emotion. Tap on those details, since the trauma might be encoded there.

Drink water. Our bodies are 70% water, and water is a primary conductor of electricity in the body. When we're stressed, we can become dehydrated. You'll notice this symptom when you're nervous and your mouth dries up. That's part of the stress response, and dehydration by itself is stressful. Sometimes the SUD level drops after the client drinks water. Personally, I drink around a gallon of water each day of an EFT workshop, and find it helps process the emotional shifts that are occurring all around me.

Dig for other events that resemble the presenting event. A client might tap on an event without the SUD rating dropping because the presenting event is a pale shadow of a much more troubling event, or many similar events. The SUD level of the presenting event is propped up by all the other events behind the scenes. To uncover events that resemble the presenting event, ask questions like: "Was there a time it was worse?" or "Did it happen often?" Once you've found an event with bigger emotional impact, tap on that first.

Make the problem worse. This often makes it better! If the SUD rating of a pain isn't going down, for instance, you could tap on, "This pain will get worse. Much worse. Worse and worse until it fills my entire body." This and similar statements often make clients laugh, disagree, insist they'll improve, or get worried, or produce some other shift in emotion that allows the session to move forward.

Intensifying the problem can help clients get in touch with the emotion. Their SUD levels may not be dropping because they haven't really made visceral contact with the depths of raw emotion in the scene. They may have a degree of protective dissociation from the event. Making the problem worse can put them in touch with the emotion.

The problem can be made worse in a variety of ways. You can take an argument and extend it to the point of absurdity. You can raise your voice, scream, swear, exaggerate, and catastrophize. You can rant and rave. Here are some ways of adding emphasis to the problem in order to activate the emotion to be tapped away.

Dramatize and catastrophize. Turn a problem into a major life drama or even a catastrophe. For instance, "I'm always losing my keys…[add] and I want the whole world to stop what it's doing and help me find them!" Another example: "I'm nervous about this math class…[add] so I'll probably fail, drop out of school, never find a job, and become a homeless person."

Generalize and exaggerate. Expand the size of the problem to include a whole group of people, not just the offending individual. For example:

"He should have loved me more" becomes "All men should love me more."

"She must not leave dishes in the sink" becomes "No one should ever leave dishes in the sink."

"He ought to have been more considerate of my feelings" becomes "Everyone should always be more considerate of my feelings."

Emphasize to the point of absurdity. For example:

"All women are angry bitches…[add] including Mother Teresa and the Tooth Fairy."

"The outdoors is always dangerous…[add] even in Disneyland and the Garden of Eden."

Speak emphatically, raise your voice, swear, scream or yell. Shouting the setup, or simply raising your voice, sometimes produces profound emotional shifts. I was recently working with a woman in a group who was abused while growing up, and also by her husband. Once we'd made a breakthrough in the session, she spontaneously said, "I am a powerful woman." She was speaking softly, so I asked her to repeat the statement loudly. "Make me believe it!" I urged, and she said it again loudly, confidently, and emphatically. "Tell everyone in the group!" I urged, and she turned to the group and said it emphatically again, this time adding several swear words for emphasis. She burst into laughter and the whole group applauded, giving her public validation for her strong statement of self-worth.

Rant and tap. Ranting is a lot like daisy chaining, except that clients have permission to raise their voices, swear, generalize, run on at the mouth, and generally say everything they've been suppressing. It's a liberating experience for many clients, and tapping provides them with a felt sense of safety. Tapping also discharges the emotion, rather than simply reinforcing the anger, as might happen with ranting alone. They feel the cathartic nature of the rant, giving them permission to process these feelings.

We don't often have permission to be angry, but we still are. Men especially mask their anger for fear of the consequences. Ranting and tapping is a great opportunity to let all that old anger out in a controlled environment, with a safety valve that prevents it from damaging those around you. We may also have unspoken fears. Clients may reveal their small fears and their rational fears, but not their big or irrational ones. Ranting and tapping allows them to say the things they dare not think. Here's one of many examples from the EFT archives of an actor who used emphatic EFT and got more than he bargained for.

Emphatic EFT Clears More Blocks Than I Imagined
By Rex Jantze

I had my first, real, amazing breakthrough last night with EFT when I used a not-so-subtle technique. I could honestly call it an OMW (one-minute wonder). I have had chronic low back and hip pain for the last year, unsure of where and when it began. It manifested during a summer tour of a theatre mask troupe I was performing in, which forced me to resign the following fall.

Last night, while perusing the recent EFT newsletter, I went back into the EFT website to look up more articles on pain issues. I remember having seen articles where people had success by putting more emphasis on the Setup Statement, speaking it loudly or shouting it, putting more emotion into it than they could honestly feel during the session.

I have learned that memory and learning is more successful if the person puts emotional energy into what he or she is learning or reading. This is why traumatic memory is the most persistent and untenable of memories, creating powerful filters by which we receive and transmit all other events and situations in our lives.

My friends and family regard me as a generally calm, relaxed, humorous person. Almost non-emotional. (Not that things or events don't move me; I just don't get as worked up about them.) As an actor, though, I know how to get my blood boiling convincingly without being actually angry; I can weep without being actually sad. I can get the chemicals and molecules of emotion flowing in my brain and body and actually feel it—the tension, the passion, the tragedy or humor—though I know I am just faking it.

I say this now more in retrospect (I didn't really pre-plan this session) because that is what I did with EFT last night—I completely exaggerated my frustration and anger and sadness associated with the pain in my back (especially the frustration), not really knowing if it would work. Without waking the house, I shouted my frustration in my head, I tensed my body and made it feel almost psychopathically angry and upset about my pain issue, violently stabbing my Karate Chop point as hard and fast as I could for my Setup Statements, then continuing the exaggerated feelings and hard tapping (if you tense enough and throw enough emotion into it, you won't really hurt yourself) as I blustered and pissed and pleaded my way through the Reminder Phrases, struggling with my faux deep frustration at how it just won't go away and I really want it to and my life is ruined if it won't cease, etc.

Now, a round would consist of one set of Setups and two to three sets of tapping, including the fingers and eye movements. I swear that in four rounds of this I had a pain of 8 out of 10 reduced to a level of intensity of 2 out of 10. And before this, I could barely budge the pain with my usual EFT program, thinking and believing I had some deeper core issue I couldn't find therefore wasn't addressing.

Follow-Up #1, Day 2: I have been noticing even more subtle effects from that short session than I could have dreamed. Several things I've wanted to change and have worked on previously all seem to be manifesting. My writing block has gone away. My bad food and eating habits changed dramatically, for the better—another set of issues I have desired to change.

Follow-Up #2, Day 4: I have done nothing else other than that short session 4 days ago. My back remains about a 1 to 2, though I am now able to exercise and not hurt myself further and strengthen those areas that are weak. As a residual effect, my relationship with food has entirely changed; it seems I am connected with and collaborating with my body on a new level. My poor eating habits (food choices, eating too much at one time, eating too fast, eating when I'm not hungry) have all shifted or collapsed. I kid not! I am trying to lose about 10 pounds; this has been a remarkable start to see that happen. And I wasn't even working on that issue at that time, though it has been an emotional issue I've been trying to deal with.

My sleeping pattern has changed, and I sleep more deeply and comfortably without tossing and turning so much—another issue I wasn't even focused on during the session. It just got better, more naturally on its own. There have been several other subtle or profound positive residual effects on other problems I have been trying to change. I am also calmer overall. I will experiment with this again in a few days, when my skin desensitizes and heals a little more from that first crazy session.

* * *

Mental Tapping

There are some situations in which you can't tap. In a courtroom. In the middle of a tennis match. In a business meeting. While delivering a public speech. Yet you can tap mentally in all these situations.

Mental tapping is simply tapping on all the EFT points using your imagination. Making the image of tapping vivid can increase its effect. If you're an experienced tapper, the mere memory of tapping can set your body up for change. Here's an example from the EFT archives of success with mental tapping.

Mental EFT Stops Migraine in 10 Minutes
By Eswar

I was introduced to EFT less than a year back. I came across your website when I was on the lookout for a solution to my son's severe "fear of falling." I ordered the books and since then have been avidly studying EFT in earnest. Recently, I had a new experience with EFT.

Whenever I travel in the sun, especially with all the pollution in our land and clime, I get a mild form of migraine headache. This goes away with a cup of coffee. But the other day it started mildly but steadily increased in intensity.

I thought of tapping, but I could not bring myself to tap, as I felt totally helpless and immobile. I just could not move my hands. I reclined on the seat when suddenly the thought came to me to tap mentally. So I focused on the Karate Chop point and silently said:

> *Even though I have this terrible headache.*
> *Even though I feel so helpless and not wanting to take action, I forgive myself completely for whatever contribution I have made to this awful pain. I deeply and completely forgive anyone else for whatever contribution they might have made to this problem.*
> *Then I closed my eyes and imagined tapping on the EFT points silently, telling myself: This terrible headache; this feeling of nausea; this feeling of helplessness; this splitting pain in my temples, and so on.*

I must have done it for around 10 minutes when I noticed that the intensity dropped all of a sudden. Then I felt a vomiting sensation rising from the middle of my navel. I continued to imagine tapping as the feeling became powerful, but, very strangely, I could watch the sensations with nonattachment, as though it were happening to somebody else. As I prepared myself with a plastic bag for the eventuality, nothing came out except some gas. I felt a great relief, though exhausted.

The headache completely disappeared. I went home and lay down on the bed and imagined a white light surrounding me inside as well as outside and did progressive relaxation. I did not know when I slept, but after 15 minutes when I woke up, it felt as if nothing had ever happened!

Oh boy, EFT worked! And it worked like a miracle! Thank you so much, for you are basically giving it away to everyone, even the intricate points, without holding back anything. Cheers!

* * *

Secret Tapping

Secret Tapping is tapping surreptitiously in triggering situations. For instance, you're at Christmas dinner with your relatives. You're stuffed to the gills. The hostess brings out her special homemade apple pie. You know you'll feel uncomfortably bloated if you attempt to cram one more bite into your mouth. You're also afraid of offending her by refusing a portion. As the pie is being sliced, you use secret tapping. You tap on your hand points under the table.

After EFT, your mind clears. You say to your hostess, "What an outstanding meal! I really want some of your famous pie, but I can't eat another bite. Can you save me a slice to take home?" After tapping, the emotional charge around the situation disappears, and you come up with a solution that honors your needs and hers.

Imagine being in a business meeting around a conference table. The discussion has become heated and everyone in the room is becoming upset. You're triggered too. You secretly tap your hand points under the table and calm yourself down. You're then able to suggest a reasonable compromise that breaks the gridlock.

Secret tapping is usually done under the table, but sometimes I'll rub my collarbone points or eye points in public. It's a natural gesture and doesn't call attention to itself.

EFT for Sports and Business Performance

EFT has become increasingly popular in amateur and professional sports, as well as in business. Businesspeople and sportspeople are by nature competitive, always seeking techniques that will provide them with an edge. EFT has made its way into rugby, soccer (football), golf, wrestling, tennis, American football, baseball, and a variety of Olympic sports. Several sports entertainment channels such as ESPN have captured tapping athletes on video. Many businesspeople use EFT personally in their workplaces, and sometimes with their teams.

In a study of championship basketball players that I performed with EFT sports expert Greg Warburton at Oregon State University, Greg tapped with the EFT group on a variety of worries. These included conflicts with parents, breakups with girlfriends and boyfriends, concerns about academic performance, and awareness of physical limitations such as height and strength. The control group received a placebo intervention consisting of an article on tips and advice from a top basketball coach. After just 15 minutes of EFT, there was a 38% difference in free-throw performance between the EFT group and the control group.

A randomized controlled trial by EFT Master Tam Llewellyn and his wife, Mary Llewellyn, replicated these results with soccer (football) players practicing free kicks. They found significant improvement in goal-scoring ability following a short EFT session. In a follow-up 6 months later, they reported: "Both teams we worked with are currently top of their divisions, and the Under-16's have won every single one of their matches since they learned EFT. They are now so far ahead that none of the other teams can catch up, so they will win the league cup. They have scored 147 goals (a record for one season) and their striker (main goal scorer) has scored 57 herself—another record."

Another study I collaborated on, with Darlene Downs who collected data at Ursuline College, compared the confidence levels and psychological trauma levels of female volleyball players. We found that after a 20-minute EFT session, their levels of confidence increased significantly, their degree of physical and emotional distress about traumatic sports experiences dropped significantly, and they looked forward to future games.

The book *EFT for Sports Performance* (Howard, 2014) goes into great detail about how to apply EFT to sports. It's used to remove performance blocks such as anxiety about the sport itself as well as other areas of the athlete's life. Besides the primary text, there are also supplements such as *EFT for Golf* (Church, 2014c) that apply these principles to specific sports.

Performance is as important in business as it is in sports. Businesspeople are under pressure to perform in many ways. EFT is widely used in business for problems such as interpersonal conflicts, meeting sales goals, presentation anxiety, and workplace stress.

Applying EFT to business and sports performance requires a focus quite different from that used for mental health problems such as anxiety and depression or physical health problems such as pain. When tapping for health, clients typically have a deficit they want to remedy, such as wanting to escape from pain. In contrast, when it comes to performance, clients may already be highly functional and bring to their EFT sessions a strong degree of motivation to excel above their current baseline.

A wise EFT coach usually starts the process, however, by looking for the blocks and limitations that impede performance, rather than tapping on positive affirmations of better achievement. Clients will naturally achieve more once their blocks to attainment have been tapped away. Clients often have subconscious barriers that prevent them from performing to their full potential, and an expert practitioner can identify these and work with the client on releasing them.

Once these blocks are gone, a client's potential for peak performance may be released.

Just as EFT is transformative when applied to health settings, it can radically improve both sports and work experience. When the barriers to excellence are tapped away, and people live their potential minus the stress that previously impeded them, they are capable of great achievements. For this reason, EFT will increase its presence in sports and business in the coming years.

* * *

Resources

- Tapping Circles: TappingCircles.EFTUniverse.com
- Borrowing Benefits: BorrowingBenefits.EFTUniverse.com
- Addictions: Addictions.EFTUniverse.com
- Working with Children: Children.EFTUniverse.com

Professional
Practice Techniques

There are a number of techniques that are highly useful for those with professional EFT practices. Nonprofessionals can also use them, and none of these techniques is beyond the reach of the novice practitioner, though they all presuppose a base of experience with EFT's foundational techniques. They can be used independently of each other; there is no requirement that you master one of them before experimenting with another.

Maintaining Client-Centered Focus

EFT is a client-centered practice. This means that the center of gravity in EFT sessions rests with the client, rather than the practitioner. Sessions begin with clients describing a problem they're facing, and continues with the practitioner offering Setup Statements and tapping with the client. The flow of the session, however, is best controlled by the client. One way of assessing the skill of a practitioner is if clients believe they made all the breakthroughs themselves. The purpose of teaching EFT is to empower the client to solve his or her own problems, rather than cultivating dependence on the practitioner to solve them.

When considering intervention by the practitioner, less is more. The simpler and less intrusive the direction offered by the practitioner, the better. An expert practitioner may guide and occasionally suggest but provide the client with plenty of space and time to come up with the solutions from within. Self-generated solutions are usually far better matches for the client's circumstance than solutions conceived on the outside. They are congruent with the client's existing neural network and behavioral patterns.

For this reason, teaching the client to tap is better than having the practitioner tap on the client. Learning to tap on 12 acupressure points is simple and very easy for a new client to learn. Only rare cases require the practitioner to tap on a client. In many jurisdictions, such touch by mental health professionals is not permitted even with permission from the client. Shifting the locus of power to the client empowers clients to take healing into their own hands (literally!). It provides clients with a tool that they can use in real-life stressful situations, rather than fostering dependence on a professional to solve these problems.

If a practitioner is faced with a choice between following a path that he or she has plotted for a session, or following the client's lead in a different direction, it's preferable to validate the client's chosen path. This plus tapping can give clients the confidence to pursue their journey of transformation.

A client-centered focus also avoids the power differentials inherent in the therapist-client relationship. In such a relationship, the therapist is the expert. EFT emphasizes that the client is the expert when it comes to his or her own internal states, and the role of the practitioner is to teach a self-help tool. A good practitioner cultivates a peer-to-peer relationship with the goal of fostering self-sufficiency in the client. This approach avoids the power differentials inherent in conventional therapist-client relationships.

Self-rating versus Observer-rating

The word "rating" is used to describe the assessment of the severity of a problem. The SUD scale, which EFT borrows from the work of psychiatrist Joseph Wolpe (1958), is the most common way to rate that severity. EFT relies on the client, not the coach or psychotherapist, to rate the problem. This places the task of evaluating the results of a session firmly in the hands of the client.

If you're a coach, you might occasionally sense that a client is rating the severity of a problem lower than nonverbal signals indicate. Perhaps a client says a problem is a 2, but you observe shallow breathing, tense shoulders, and perspiration. In such cases, it may be appropriate to ask the client to rate again, saying something like "You look upset. Are you sure you're only a 2?" This provides the client with an opportunity for reflection. The client may then scrutinize his or her feelings, and agree with you that the number is higher. Then again, the client may not. In either case, accept the client's rating of the problem, rather than declaring, "I can clearly see you're a 10."

The whole focus of EFT is to put the power back in the hands of clients, even if they are just learning the skill of rating the intensity of their emotions. If the coach or other practitioner grabs the reins and tells clients what their SUD number is, they remove the power from clients' hands. Some clients may have difficulty providing accurate SUD scores when first learning EFT, but it soon becomes second nature. If you think the client isn't accurately reporting SUD, make a mental note but don't invalidate the client's rating. Learning to rate their emotions might take clients some time, and a coach's support and validation plays a large role in the development of clients' confidence.

When Self-acceptance Is the Problem

I remember a striking EFT session with a famous actress. I was teaching a workshop in Los Angeles and the organizer asked me to do EFT with an actress friend of hers. She drove me to a beautiful Beverley Hills mansion, and introduced me to her friend. I was star-struck to be in the presence of someone I'd seen in movies. The actress was tall, willowy, and beautiful, with a powerful personal presence.

I was moved and saddened to hear details of her chaotic childhood with an absent father, mentally ill mother, and physically abusive siblings, all lived in the Hollywood limelight. I formulated a Setup Statement, and asked her to tap on, "Even though [problem], I deeply and completely accept myself." To my surprise, the actress burst into tears. It turned out that self-acceptance was one of her core issues. This woman, with millions of adoring fans all over the world, admired for her stunning beauty, was filled with so much self-loathing that she could not even choke out the words, "I deeply and completely accept myself."

This phrase is part of EFT's Basic Recipe. What do you do with a client who can't say the words? There are several less confrontive versions you can experiment with. While a client might not be able to say those words, they may be able to make a more tentative statement. Examples of these are:

I'm doing the best I can.
I'm a good person.
Many parts of me are okay.
I'm improving all the time.
My Higher Power loves me.
I'll like myself someday.
I am working on accepting myself.
I feel compassion for myself.

These less forceful versions of the Setup Statement are acceptable substitutes. Suggest one that matches the client's current level of self-acceptance. In my experience, clients are able to say, "I deeply and completely accept myself" within a few rounds of tapping.

The self-acceptance problem is why we say "accept myself" and not "love myself." Many clients are triggered by "accept myself," but many more are triggered by the words "love myself." We begin with self-acceptance, and introduce self-love when the client is ready. Usually within a session or two, clients can say "love myself" even if they couldn't even say "accept myself" at the start.

The Role of Insight

Insight is a cornerstone of the psychotherapy of the past century. Insight is the ability to link events and beliefs in a tapestry of meaning. Perhaps a male client has an aversion to balancing his checkbook. An expert therapist assembles details of his early childhood experiences, including the client's poor performance in high school math classes. The therapist asks the client if he was ever punished for poor math performance, discovers that he was, and has an "aha" moment. His insight is that, as a child, the client was punished for calculating sums. Declining to balance his checkbook is an extension of his childhood experience that attempting to add numbers was likely to result in punishment. These insights can be very valuable to a client's understanding of the source of his behaviors.

Unfortunately, they may go no further. Sigmund Freud believed that insight produces change. Insight may produce change, but simply knowing why you have a problem does not always bring a solution. At a recent conference, I was fortunate to share a number of meals in the faculty lounge with Stanislav Grof, MD, a psychiatrist who was one of the earliest experimenters with LSD. After LSD was made illegal, Grof sought nonpharmaceutical methods of altering consciousness, and developed a technique called Holotrophic Breathwork. He described how, as a young man, he went to Freudian psychoanalysis three times a week for 7 years, but it failed to produce change. It certainly produced insight, but he described the overall result as mistaking the map for the territory. He had an excellent map of his psyche but no idea how to alter his course. He joked that taken to its logical conclusion, psychoanalysts might eat the menu, mistaking it for food.

Insight may produce change, but knowing exactly how you got so messed up psychologically does not necessarily provide you with any clues about how to repair the damage. The process of discovery also takes a very long time.

EFT places s little emphasis on insights generated by the therapist or life coach. The focus is not on how you got messed up, but on how you can heal. That's why EFT tests relentlessly, asking clients if their SUD scores have gone down. The earliest proponent of SUD, Joseph Wolpe, was equally disenchanted with psychoanalysis after observing that it failed to provide relief to veterans of WWII suffering from PTSD. Like later proponents of EFT, Wolpe was intensely practical: he wanted methods that made people feel better, and fast. In at least one study of anxiety, the Diaphragmatic Breathing method favored by Wolpe was as effective as EFT (Jain & Rubino, 2012).

EFT does not require insight to make progress, though insight can be useful. Particularly useful are insights that emerge spontaneously from within the client's experience. When tapping clients have an "aha" moment and link their current problem to a childhood pattern or belief, they're usually excited by the insight. They now understand a new facet of their inner world, and may experience a feeling of satisfaction and integration.

As a coach, you're likely to have many insights while working with clients, but I urge you to share them sparingly. Let the insight emerge from the client if at all possible. You might see the links, but they're much more powerful if the client discovers them without your help. It might take the client much longer than it takes you, but emerging organically from within the client's consciousness, the links and insights have much more power than if you offer them from the outside. When the client exclaims, "I just realized the reason I feel so reluctant to balance my checkbook is that I was punished for doing my sums wrong by Sister Lorenzo in third grade!" he is in control of his own restorative process.

You might have powerful insights that will impress a client, but dazzling the client with your brilliance is not your job in an EFT session. Less is more. Letting clients dazzle themselves with their brilliance is far more valuable. Letting them have the insight, and own the insight, even if it takes longer, places the power firmly in their hands. That's where it belongs.

Collarbone Breathing Exercise

One of the many techniques borrowed by EFT from TFT is the Collarbone Breathing Exercise. It's used in cases in which the Full Basic Recipe is not producing a reduction in the SUD level. It takes about 2 minutes to perform, though the instructions are complicated and should be followed exactly. Here are the instructions.

During the Collarbone Breathing Exercise, keep your elbows and arms away from your body. The exercise uses your knuckles and fingertips; these should be the only parts of your arm that touch your body.

Place two fingers of your dominant hand on the Collarbone point on that same side of your body. With the first two fingers of your nondominant hand, tap the Gamut point (in the groove in the bones that anchor the last two fingers) continuously while you perform the following five breathing exercises:

1. Breathe all the way in and hold your breath for 7 taps.
2. Breathe half way out and hold your breath for 7 taps.
3. Breathe all the way out and hold your breath for 7 taps.
4. Breathe half way in and hold your breath for 7 taps.
5. Breathe normally for 7 taps.

Then place the first two fingertips of your dominant hand on your nondominant side's Collarbone point and, while tapping the Gamut point continuously, perform the same five breathing exercises.

Bend the fingers of your dominant hand so that the knuckles of the second joint stick out. Place them on your dominant side Collarbone point and tap the Gamut point continuously while doing the five breathing exercises. Repeat this after placing the knuckles of your dominant hand on the Collarbone point of your nondominant side.

You are now halfway through the Collarbone Breathing Exercise. Repeat the same procedure starting with your nondominant side. When you're finished, proceed with the Full Basic Recipe. Many practitioners have reported significant shifts in SUD levels after using this exercise, even with clients who had been going nowhere before.

The Floor to Ceiling Eye Roll

This technique is for use when a client is at a low SUD number, perhaps 1 or 2, but is not getting to 0. It takes only around 6 seconds to perform, so it's faster than doing the Basic Recipe. Here's how to do it.

Tap the Gamut point on the back of the hand. Tap it continually, hold your head steady, and repeat the Reminder Phrase while performing the following eye movement. Start with your eyes looking all the way down at the floor, with your head held straight. Keeping your head still, raise your eyes slowly to the ceiling, taking around 6 seconds to do so. Clinical practice has found that this is often enough to bring the SUD level to 0.

Reframing

Reframing refers to changing the frame through which a client sees an event. You can't change past events, but you can see them through different lenses. Imagine looking at an old photograph of a family on vacation. You place it in a dark and somber frame. It seems depressing. You take it out and place it in a happy-looking frame ringed with smiley faces on every side. You might perceive the same photograph as joyful. That's the power of reframing: same event, different emotional tone.

Reframing is a useful technique in EFT sessions. Clients often spontaneously reframe an old event after tapping. An event that previously seemed traumatic to a client may be placed in a neutral emotional frame. I worked with Jacques, a man whose father had spanked him with a belt on several occasions. He was angry and resentful toward his father. After EFT, Jacques said, "I know my father loved me, he was doing the best he knew how. Compared to the way his father, my granddad, beat the crap out of him, what he did to me was just his best effort to keep me in line. I was a handful." Jacques had flipped to perceive the spankings as an example of his father's restraint, rather than abuse.

Either the context or the content of an event can be reframed. The context represents the meaning of the event. Here's an example. Before EFT, Roberta exclaimed, "I am so angry at my mother for not protecting me from my father's abuse. I can never forgive her." After EFT, Roberta saw the same events in a different context. She said, "Mother was trying not to get assaulted herself, knowing that her survival was all that stood between us kids and Dad's craziness. She also knew Dad was a good provider, and the family couldn't survive without Dad's paycheck."

The second kind of reframing involves the content. Janie first said, "My sister tried to pull my hair out when she got angry and jealous." After EFT, Janie saw the content differently, and put it this way: "My hair is strong and thick to this day, despite my sister's efforts to destroy it."

The client or the coach can do the reframing. A simple reframe by a coach might be to add the words "and you're safe now" to a Setup Statement. This places the traumatic event in a context of safety and of the present moment. Coach: "Even though your mother threw things at you, she had terrible aim, and she always missed, and here you are safe and sound."

Cognitive shifts by the client often result in spontaneous reframing while doing EFT. As a client taps, she may shift her perceptions of the people and events that troubled her in the past. She may go from describing the two bad things that happened on vacation to the six good things that occurred. The bad things fade in intensity after tapping, allowing the good things to predominate in memory.

Preframing

Preframing refers to the practice by the coach of providing a context to the next phase of the session. The coach might say, "We've made great progress on your anger toward your sister for the way she acted at Thanksgiving. Now we're going to nail all the remaining aspects of that event." This type of statement by the coach sets up the expectancy in the client that she will, in fact, completely release all the unpleasant emotions lingering since the event.

One of the most elegant preframes was developed by hypnotherapist Milton Erickson. It's called the "Yes Set." He would ask a client three questions in a row, the first two having an inevitable answer of yes. He would then ask the client the third question, to which he wanted a yes. The previous two questions would preframe the outcome of the third. For instance:

Erickson: It's a nice day, isn't it? Client: Yes.

Erickson: Are you comfortable in that chair? Client: Yes.

Erickson: Are you ready for change?

The client was now in the rhythm of answering yes. Erickson would also use the word no in a similar way, a technique known as Erickson's No Set.

Preframing can be used to reinforce either a positive or a negative expectation. In the Thanksgiving example, the coach set the client up for positive change. An EFT practitioner can also reinforce the negative. An example of this might be: "We've tapped successfully on the superficial aspects of the problem. We can probably make great progress on the deeper aspects, so let's go there."

Identifying Tables and Legs

One way of conceptualizing the difference between general problems and specific events is the analogy of tables and legs. General problems are the tabletops, while events are the table legs. Examples of general problems are procrastination, low self-esteem, anxiety, depression, disappointment, and lack of self-confidence. There are many others.

Though clients may come to us driven by a desire to solve a tabletop-type problem, as EFT practitioners we look for the table legs.

The legs are the events that gave rise to the tabletop. For instance, a client might have a tabletop of a lack of self-worth. You dig for specific events, and discover that her father put her down for being good at school, believing that a woman's place is in the home and academic performance is irrelevant. When she showed him her second-grade report card, he said, "When you're barefoot and pregnant, that won't matter." She remembers many similar incidents. Her mother became competitive with her when she reached puberty, and when she put on a skirt and makeup for her first date, her mother said, "Wipe that stuff off. You look like a slut." The client remembers nothing other than being put down for being precocious and beautiful. All these incidents combined to create the tabletop of low self-esteem. But the tabletop did not spring to life fully formed. It was built gradually, the culmination of dozens or even hundreds of specific events. The client is aware

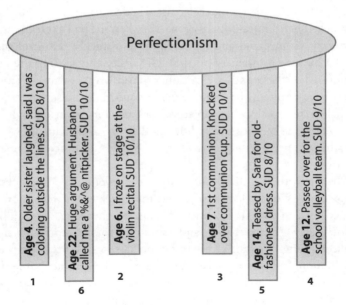

Figure 1. Tabletop and table legs.

that she has low self-esteem and is seeking counseling for the problem but has not traced it back to the individual events that gave rise to the problem. If you tap on the tabletop, your success will be limited. Just as the tabletop was created by individual events, it must be collapsed by removing the emotional charge from those events.

A client might see this as a daunting challenge at first. If there are hundreds of events, do you have to tap on each and every one? This is where EFT's generalization effect comes into play. Once you've removed the emotional charge from a few of the major legs through tapping, you destabilize the whole table and the top comes crashing down. You don't need to tap on every event, just enough events to collapse the tabletop.

Take a look the table and legs diagram in Figure 1. Perfectionism is the tabletop. The table legs consist of several events. The first one is at age 4, when the client's older sister saw her coloring outside the lines and mocked her. The last one is at age 22, when she had a terrible argument with her husband and he called her a nitpicker. Three of them are a 10 out of 10 intensity on the SUD scale, and reading the brief descriptions of the events, we can understand why they might cumulatively have resulted in a habit of perfectionism. She also has various core beliefs reinforcing her tabletop, such as "I'm never enough," "I always get punished no matter how hard I try," and "Murphy's Law: If anything can go wrong, it will." She believes all three statements very strongly.

We tap with the client on the first two events, and she goes to a 0 for both. We check in again, and the other events have now all dropped by 2 points in intensity. We tap on the First Communion memory, her SUD goes to a 0, and goes to a 1 for the remaining three without tapping. We didn't have to tap on all seven events. After we've tapped on only three, we ask the client how big her problem of perfectionism is, and she exclaims, "I'm perfect just the way I am, warts and all. I enjoy my life even if I never change." This indicates a cognitive shift, a reframe of how she perceives the world. Once we've tapped on some events, her intensity goes down for all the remaining events, and some go to 0 without tapping at all.

You test your work further by assuring her that she'll "always get punished no matter how hard I try." She disagrees with you vigorously, even though she held firmly to this core belief at the start of the session. She tells you that other people appreciate her and what she does and usually praise her rather than punish her. This shows that her core beliefs shifted when enough legs were knocked from under the tabletop.

Here's an example of distinguishing tabletops from legs written by expert EFT trainer Jan Watkins. Jan is a former attorney and psychotherapist who earns rave reviews from students for her Level 1, 2 and 3 workshops, and you can see evidence of her fine mind in the following story. When the client resolves old childhood events, she gains a fresh perspective on the challenges she faces in her life right now.

Tabletop: "I'm Unlovable"
By Jan L. Watkins, JD, MSW

Laura came to an EFT practitioner because she was overwhelmed with life generally. She expressed disappointment in her lack of accomplishments in her movie production career, her failure to keep pace with her friends, who had successful careers and children, and her disconnection with her father and stepfamily. Laura's family was quick to blame her for just about everything. Additionally, Laura was uncomfortable in her community, and she reported, "It doesn't feel like home" and "I feel all alone here." She was sensitive to social feedback and constantly worried that she had done something to alienate her friends. Her story revealed several tabletops or core beliefs, including: "Something's wrong with me," "I'm unlovable," and "I'm alone."

Initially, the practitioner had Laura use continuous tapping while explaining her dissatisfaction with her relationship with her father, the issue that troubled her the most. Laura felt unloved by her father and his new family. She was excluded from certain family photos, and was criticized for not having advanced degrees. One family member even told her that everything was "her fault." Laura had a tabletop belief that she was unlovable, and many table legs, or specific events, supported that belief. We addressed many specific family experiences separately with EFT. Setup Statements included, "Even though he said, 'You have to work hard like your siblings to get ahead,' I deeply and completely love and accept myself" and "Even though I'm not in that family portrait, I deeply and completely love and accept myself."

Other core beliefs were revealed during Laura's sessions. Laura had undergone many unsuccessful infertility treatments. She had heard many discouraging statements from professionals, such as, "You're too old" and "Your body isn't properly equipped." She reported during an EFT session, "There's just something wrong with me! I've always felt that way" and "I'm so alone." These core beliefs represented additional tabletops that had formed as a result of Laura's early experiences.

As Laura felt the experience in her body of "something's wrong with me" while tapping, she was flooded with unpleasant memories of early childhood experiences that had led her to conclude that she was flawed. She was embarrassed when she moved to a new area and kids made fun of her southern accent, and humiliated when kids made fun of her for needing special help with schoolwork. She was tested repeatedly and labeled as learning disabled at a very young age. She felt responsible when her father moved away after her parents divorced when she was in elementary school. As an only child, she was often alone, as her young divorced parents had active social lives. These early table-leg experiences supported the tabletop, or core beliefs, "Something's wrong with me" and "I'm alone." Laura used EFT on these and other early childhood memories. Setups included: "Even though I was called in by the teacher during recess to be tested, I deeply and completely love and accept myself" and "Even though I played alone with my new Christmas toys, I deeply and completely love and accept myself."

The emotional charge was initially very strong on many of the early table-leg experiences. During each session, we addressed specific childhood events with EFT until there was no remaining charge. Laura's circumstances began to change. The tension eased between Laura and her family. Laura was surprised when her father invited her to a special occasion and her siblings unexpectedly began to communicate in respectful and loving ways. Eventually, Laura reported feeling more comfortable in her community. She developed more compassion for herself and began painting and exploring new interests. She decided to put her plans to start a family on hold, as she rediscovered herself and reexamined her goals and vision for her future.

* * *

The type of shift described by Jan, with a client gaining a new perspective on her current life after old events are tapped through, is typical with EFT. It's important to tap on each leg separately as Jan

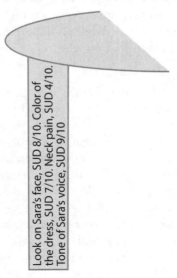

Figure 2. Aspects within a table leg event.

describes. Within each leg, you might find several aspects (see Figure 2). For instance, as an EFT practitioner working with the client who has the tabletop of perfectionism, you would look for different aspects of the client's experience at 14 when Sara teased her for her old-fashioned dress. The client may be at an 8 for the look on Sara's face, a 7 for the color of the dress, and a 9 for the tone of Sara's voice. You tap on the first two, but then she says she has a sudden pain in her neck, a kinesthetic aspect that emerges in the middle of the session. You tap on the pain as a separate aspect, and perhaps you use the Movie Technique or Tell the Story on the Sara memory as a whole. You might find that when you tap on one aspect, such as the pain, EFT's effect generalizes to all the other aspects. You might find some go to 0 even without tapping. Eventually, testing reveals that all aspects of the event are now a 0, and you move on to the next event.

It's well worth getting clear on the differences between tabletops and table legs, and between legs (events) and aspects. Knowing and exploring these distinctions and tapping on each piece of the event until all the emotional intensity clears is important to being thorough and to getting good results for your clients.

Becoming Extremely Specific

When you're not sure if a client is fully in touch with the emotion that underlies a traumatic event, you can find out by becoming extremely specific. If the client has told you there were bodies lying on the ground after an auto accident, and says he's now at 0 for the accident, ask him how many bodies there were, and in what positions they were lying. If he's truly discharged the emotional intensity, his SUD scores won't go up. If they do, you may have missed an aspect, and you have more tapping to do.

You can ask very detailed questions about what the client saw, heard, and experienced. For example, if the client says, "Dad yelled at me" you can ask for the exact words that he used. If she says, "He hit me," you can ask "How many times?" This kind of specificity tests how thoroughly you've cleared out the trauma capsule. If it's clear, a client is able to recall even horrific details of a traumatic scene without becoming emotionally triggered.

Targeting the Problem from All Angles

Especially if I'm short of time, after identifying specific events, I may use many versions of the Setup Statement in quick succession, as I seek to clear as many possible aspects of the problem quickly. Some of these might resonate with the client; others might not. I watch their faces carefully and notice when one seems particularly potent. I then follow it up with more along those lines. I might use 10 to 20 different statements a minute, after which time we'll have exhausted most of the possible ways of targeting the problem. In the case of the German doctor with the wrist injury described in an earlier chapter, whose father criticized her for not coming first in her school in her exams, I used phrases like:

My father's angry face.
His angry eyes.
His angry words.
Full of anger.
Life is full of anger.
I am full of anger.
He never approved of me.
He never approves of me (switch to present tense)
I never approve of me.
I'm never good enough for him.
I'm never good enough for anyone.
I'm never good enough for myself.
He doesn't love me.
I don't love me.
Nobody loves me.
Nobody will ever love me.

… and so on. These phrases, repeated while tapping and especially while performing the 9 Gamut routine, can clear the emotional impact of many similar memories in a very short period. The goal is to formulate every possible variant of the statement, eliminating emotional charge from each of them. This technique starts with specifics, like Father's angry eyes, and then spirals outward in a progressive swirl of generalities, each of which may be linked to the event we're targeting.

In Vivo Testing and Confrontive Questions

The most common form of testing in EFT is Joseph Wolpe's (1958) SUD scale. This is by no means the only way we test our results in EFT. There are many other ways of testing the results of a session besides the 0–10 scale. Two of these are in vivo testing and confrontive questions. *In vivo* simply means "in life," as in "in real life." If you have a client who's afraid of heights, ask her to look out of a high-rise window after an EFT session. That will tell you quickly how successful your work has been. If your client is claustrophobic, ask him to step into an enclosed space such as a closet. If his SUD level stays low, you've used a real-life situation to test the results of EFT. If you're teaching a workshop and a demonstration subject has a fear of public speaking, ask her to make a speech to the class after her EFT session. You'll immediately establish whether or not your approach has borne fruit.

Confrontive questions are another method of testing. If a client was assaulted by Uncle Bob, a family member, you can ask confrontive questions like:

> *What was Uncle Bob wearing at the time?*
> *What exactly were his words?*
> *When will you see Uncle Bob next?*
> *Imagine the future scene vividly. What will you say to him?*

If you've truly cleared the emotional impact of the old assault, the client may be able to answer these without a rise in SUD scores. If not, you might have more work to do on the past event. Confrontive questions might even reveal a cognitive shift from powerlessness to powerfulness. It's not uncommon for abuse victims to now perceive themselves as large and the perpetrator as small. They may feel empowered enough to plan to tell Uncle Bob what they think of him. Successfully passing this test means that the client has cleared the emotional impact of the traumatic event.

When Your Client Feels Worse

Usually after an EFT session, clients report great improvement. This is not always the case, however, and sometimes a client might report feeling worse. Does this mean EFT isn't working?

It's important that EFT practitioners validate client experiences. If a client reports feeling worse, treat it as an opportunity to go deeper. Just as you might be delighted when a client's problem gets better, be curious when a client reports getting worse. Encourage the client to report his or her progress honestly, without overt or subtle insistence on reporting only positive experiences.

An alert practitioner will use the situation as a way of facilitating deeper healing, rather than treating a report of "feeling worse" as a problem. The following are some of the common reasons that clients report feeling worse after an EFT session, and what action you can take.

They're dissociating, and EFT has put them in touch with their feelings. Clients with a history of traumatic events often dissociate. Dissociation serves a protective and adaptive function in young children, allowing them to function in the midst of their chaotic families. Dissociation may become the standard way a client deals with emotional difficulties and the pattern of dissociation may persist into adulthood.

Dissociative clients may start to get in touch with their long-suppressed feelings after they start using EFT. A dissociative client might initially provide you with a low SUD score for a horrific event. They may, for instance, describe a childhood rape, and then say, "But I don't feel anything, I'm a 2." When they start to tap, their SUD level may start to rise as they get in touch with the trauma encoded in the event.

It might seem that EFT isn't working because that 2 might become a 10. In reality, EFT is providing them with a safe space in which they can reopen old wounds, reexperience bad events, and tap them through to a place of emotional resolution. If you suspect dissociation, follow the Clinical EFT procedures for working with a dissociative client. In these cases, the SUD level typically rises, then falls again as all the aspects of the memory are addressed.

They have permission to feel negative emotions for the first time. Throughout our lives, we are taught to think positively. This is exemplified in sayings like "When the going gets tough, the tough get going," "If life gives you lemons, make lemonade," and similar admonitions. A relentless drumbeat of positive thinking permeates popular culture. If you're sad, you're reminded things will get better: "This too shall pass." Growing up, phrases like "Big boys and girls don't cry" communicate to us that our negative emotions are unacceptable. There's no room for them, and rather than being taught how to process them, we're taught to stuff them. When a negative emotion comes to the surface, it triggers adult caregivers, who often try to suppress it as quickly as possible. The media presents us with images of heroes and heroines as people who stay positive, keep the faith, and overcome adversity.

We have a habit of pushing away uncomfortable and difficult experiences. These then wind up in what Carl Jung called the "Shadow," the part of the self that has been suppressed or disowned. These elements of our shadow are often festering just below the surface, begging for attention and healing.

When we start to use EFT, these shadow elements may come to the surface. After the first few positive experiences with EFT, our psyche might realize that it has a safe way of processing old emotional trauma. Aspects of the shadow start to emerge, in order to be healed. Parts of ourselves that were too dangerous or overwhelming might crowd into our awareness, so that they can be safely reprocessed and integrated into our larger personality. This might show up in an EFT session as "feeling worse."

Think of an EFT session as a safe space in which a client can process this backlog of negative emotional experiences. It may take many sessions, but allowing these experiences to come out of the shadow, be reexperienced, and emotionally digested is an ultimately healthy experience, even if the client feels worse when he or she starts to feel long-suppressed feelings.

You're tapping on the tabletop, not the table legs. Clients often state problems in broad terms such as "anxiety" or "self-esteem." EFT is rarely effective when used on these generalities. Instead, you have to find the specific events that gave rise to the general problem. As discussed previously, the general problem is like a tabletop, supported by many legs. The legs are the specific events. A tabletop such as procrastination, for instance, might have been created out of hundreds of individual events in which, as a child, the client was invalidated. You do EFT on each of those events. As noted, you don't typically have to work on every single one, because when you collapse enough legs, the whole table crashes down. Sometimes it takes tapping on only one or two legs to collapse many others. Some practitioners work on "the worst" or "the first" leg; the worst of the many experiences, or the first time that type of experience ever occurred.

When you tap on a tabletop, you might sensitize the client to the problem, without resolving the emotional intensity held in the legs. In such a case, the client might report feeling worse. The solution is to make sure you're targeting the legs, and all the aspects contained in each leg.

You're tapping on an adult issue, when the real problem lies in the client's childhood. On the first day of one EFT workshop, a practitioner worked with a woman who was greatly triggered by a male colleague who treated her dismissively. The woman's intensity went way down. The next day, however, she reported that it was right back up again. An expert practitioner then worked with her, and ignored the situation with the woman's colleague. This second practitioner delved deeper, and found a similar event that had occurred during kindergarten, when a male teacher had disparaged her work.

After EFT, the childhood issue was resolved. When the woman was then asked to think about her adult colleague, she said his behavior was "just silly," and she had no emotional intensity around it. The real problem was the childhood issue, and tapping on the adult problem the first day produced no lasting change. When the childhood event was addressed, the intensity of the adult issue vanished, even though it hadn't been tapped on that second day. If a client feels worse, you might be overlooking a childhood issue in which the trauma is rooted.

The client is rating a different problem rather than the original one. Often a practitioner will have an experience with a client that goes something like this:

Practitioner: *Where is your pain, and how intense is it?*

Client: *It's in my shoulder, and it's a 7 out of 10.*

They do EFT.

Practitioner: *Are you feeling better now?*

Client: *No. I feel worse. My pain has gone up to a 9. EFT clearly isn't working.*

Practitioner: *Really? The pain in your shoulder is now a 9?*

Client: *The pain in my shoulder? Oh, that's gone. The pain in my hip is a 9.*

This might sound funny, but it often happens. The client perceives that the problem has become worse, and reports a higher number, because they've shifted their attention to another problem, after the first problem has been quickly resolved with EFT. Make sure, if the client reports feeling worse, that they're focusing on the same area in their body or the same experience in their psyche that they were reporting on initially. Chasing the Pain, one of the Gentle Techniques, is appropriate to use in these cases.

The client has shifted aspects. The client might have been picturing the face of a perpetrator who assaulted her. When first providing a

SUD score, she tells you it's a 7. After tapping, it's a 9. She concludes that EFT isn't working. You inquire what her number is for the perpetrator's face, and she tells you it's a 1, but the smell of his breath is a 9. She's shifted aspects. The first round of EFT was, in fact, successful, but the client shifted aspects rapidly. She's not trained to look for them, but you, as the practitioner, are. You find the new aspect, tap on that, and the number goes down again. A client may switch between many different aspects in the course of processing an event.

Cautions. When clients report a higher SUD score after a round or rounds of EFT, it's vital to validate them. Virtually all clients wish to please their practitioners, whether the practitioner is a medical doctor or an EFT expert. A client wants to get better, you want the client to get better, and this produces psychological pressure to report lower SUD scores. When clients report a higher SUD score, validating them supports their confidence in tuning in to their bodies. This establishes trust, reliability, and a good working relationship. You can go on from there to find out why the SUD score might be rising, but it's vital to validate the client's experience first.

Energy Toxins and Allergens

Energy toxins and allergens are substances that interfere with the effectiveness of energy psychology treatments. They aren't necessarily toxins or allergens in the conventional sense of the words. They may be innocuous yet still prevent EFT from having an effect. In a series of cases presented by Roger Callahan and colleagues (Pasahow, Callahan, Callahan, and Rapp, 2014), one was a 38-year-old male client who was successfully treated for insomnia using Thought Field Therapy. In a subsequent session, he told his therapist that for the previous two nights, his insomnia had mysteriously reappeared. On investigation, they discovered that the client's wife had begun using a new detergent that was harsh and heavily scented. After a subsequent application of TFT, and his wife switching to an unscented detergent, his insomnia disappeared for good.

Soaps and detergents can be energy toxins. So can certain fabrics. Perfumes can be energy allergens. During one visit to Washington, DC, to testify before a congressional committee, I left the hearing room feeling elated that we'd effectively presented EFT in a conventional forum. With two colleagues, I got into a cab and I made some cell phone calls on the way back to our hotel. An air deodorizer strip hung from the cab's rearview mirror, and the fragrance felt sharp to my sense of smell, despite the many odors of a busy city. After a few minutes, my nose began to close, then my sinuses, then my throat. I tapped while I was talking, but I felt as though I could not breathe. I became nervous despite tapping. I felt as though I was drowning, and I was surprised the tapping had so little effect. That fragrance was clearly not toxic or a conventional allergen, but it was an allergen for me. If you find you aren't making progress with a client, or if progress is suddenly reversed, scan the client's environment for possible energy toxins and allergens. The client can eliminate fragrances, soaps, oils, detergents, and fabrics, one by one, till the culprit is identified.

Massive Reversal

Some clients are so massively reversed they're hard to work with. In cases of massive reversal, psychological reversal isn't an occasional impediment to success; it's a way of life. There are clients for whom psychological reversal is their normal state, and any other energy configuration feels foreign to them. With experience, you'll be able to spot these clients easily. They are often very intelligent, and have a difficult time accepting progress with EFT on a mental level. They may feel a change physically, but their minds will argue that such changes are not possible, or at least be very puzzled.

Clients may have massive reversal generally, or in one specific part of their lives such as food. Some obese people go into reversal whenever they're around food, and find it very difficult to respond to normal cues involving taste, smell, or satiety. Reversal blocks out the usual signals. Others go into reversal when it comes to other parts of their lives, such as work, money, or relationships.

Working with a client who is massively or chronically reversed is a challenge because they can't readily perceive the usual signposts indicating successful progress. I recall working with one brilliant researcher during a workshop. I sensed shortly after I met him at the start of the workshop that he had massive reversal. I observed that his face did not reflect emotional shifts the way the faces of other participants did, as though he perhaps had Asperger's syndrome. His body moved woodenly, without free articulation of the joints. His questions reflected mental puzzlement about the course curriculum. He had difficulty connecting emotionally with the other participants. He had trouble performing the Cross Crawl, an exercise drawn from the field of energy medicine (Eden, 2012). Reversed clients typically have difficulty with this exercise, or are unable to perform it at all. I decided to work on him during demonstration, partly to show others in the room that EFT is not a panacea and doesn't always produce a dramatic result. Though I applied all the best EFT techniques, his SUD score dropped only slightly.

My subjective experience during the demonstration echoes that of other cases with clients who are massively reversed. I found myself becoming drowsy, and the air seemed thick, as though made of syrup. I found myself becoming drawn into his internal arguments that EFT couldn't work, and becoming unsure myself whether EFT would work. My mind became foggy, and I had trouble remembering the techniques I planned to demonstrate. I felt as though I were fighting an invisible force throughout the session. The force seemed determined to block any progress, fluidity, thought, or movement.

With experience, you'll learn to recognize massive reversal quickly. In these cases, it's important to tap long and often on the Karate Chop point to correct psychological reversal. I might spend two thirds of the session on that one point, returning to it again and again. Rubbing the "Sore Spot" on the chest just below the point where the collarbones join the breastbone is also effective for psychological reversal. Energy medicine has further techniques for correcting massive reversal when EFT fails (Eden, 2012). Though there are few clients in whom reversal is so massive that EFT makes little or no progress, most practitioners will eventually cross paths with one, and knowing that this condition exists prepares to you deal with it when it arises.

Physical Symptoms That Resist Healing

Many people have used EFT successfully on physical issues such as rashes, headaches, sore throats, and similar problems. Sometimes we can tap directly on the physical problem, creating a Setup Statement with the words, for instance, "This migraine." There are often emotional factors underlying our physical symptoms, however, and it's usually much more fruitful to dig for those.

You might try tapping on the physical problem first, or you could search for the emotional problem first. If you're an experienced EFT practitioner, you'll probably work with your clients' emotions, even if you believe the physical problem might be resolved by tapping on it, because it's an excellent way to dramatize to the client the contribution emotional factors make to our physical symptoms.

A key question to ask if a physical ailment doesn't yield to tapping is: "What emotional experience might underlie this physical issue?"

Sometimes a client will immediately describe one. A client might say something like "These migraines began just after my husband asked me for a divorce." Other times, a client is unable to come up with any emotional experience associated with the symptom.

In these cases, ask the client to guess. These guesses are usually close to the target. One young man in an EFT workshop could not identify any emotional event linked to his migraine headaches but had a word that triggered him: "injustice." We asked him to make up an event, and asked who might have said words of injustice to him, or been a headache in his early life. "My mother," he replied. "What might she have said?" we asked. "You can't have what you want," he told us. We asked him to visualize her face, and asked how old he was. He replied that he was 8, and his mother was telling him he could not use his yellow bicycle. He'd saved up and bought the bicycle with his own money, and when he transgressed, his mother wouldn't let him use it. These questions helped him evolve from a guess, to an actual event, to an emotional contributor to his migraines. Once he tapped on the event, the migraine headache that had developed during the EFT workshop went away.

Though it's possible to get some success tapping on physical symptoms alone, don't stop there. Find the underlying emotional issues, and you'll usually have long-lasting success with EFT.

Guidelines for Serious Diseases

You aren't likely to see "one-minute wonders" with serious diseases. Though these have been known to happen, and it's essential for the practitioner to be mentally open to a client healing, serious diseases usually require time, persistence, and collaboration with the client's healing team. Serious diseases often take many years to incubate, and may take quite some time to reverse. The average cancer grows for 12 years before it is detected (Jemal et al., 2011).

Yet up to 30% of cancers resolve spontaneously by themselves, without any medical treatment or intervention (Challis & Stam, 1990). This shows that your body has a remarkable ability to heal itself and reverse even serious diseases like cancer. The amount of time between the first cancerous cells arising and when cancer is detected can be substantial. That serious cancer growth was not created overnight, and expecting it to disappear in a flash of tapping is unrealistic. Serious diseases usually require support from the client's entire health team. This includes doctors and mental health practitioners, as well as health coaching and tapping.

Conventional medicine excels at treating emergency conditions such as infections, wounds, and mechanical injuries. It often fails with chronic and autoimmune conditions. Many diseases such as type 2 diabetes are called "lifestyle diseases" because they're propagated by the patient's lifestyle rather than medical causes. Stress plays a big role in lifestyle, chronic, and autoimmune diseases, and this is where EFT can help. But EFT cannot be used as a substitute for lifestyle change. EFT may reduce a client's stress, but if the client continues to make lifestyle choices like an unhealthy diet and no exercise, EFT cannot counteract the long-term effect of these choices.

Here are some recommendations for using EFT with serious diseases.

Tap daily. Tap in the morning on waking with the intention of releasing anything other than positive thoughts and beliefs about the day ahead, and about life in general. Personally, I tap this way for 5 to 10 minutes every morning. I'm not awake enough to formulate Setup Statements, so I tap generally, intending to release anything other than my highest good. Tap in the evening just before going to sleep, releasing all the stress of the day, intending to have good dreams and sleep well.

Tap whenever you think about the disease. A simple Setup like "Even though I have chronic arthritis, I deeply and completely accept myself" doesn't require much imagination. If you tap every time you notice your pain from arthritis, you get into the habit of associating the disease with the stress-reducing effects of tapping. This can reduce your stress level around having the condition. Mentally, you go straight from the problem to stress reduction, which promotes your overall sense of well-being.

Tap for negative thinking. Whenever you find yourself catastrophizing, or extrapolating into the future based on the suffering you now feel, tap. When you allow your mind to harbor negative thoughts and beliefs, your body is immediately affected. An extensive body of research shows that your autonomic nervous system, which regulates every major organ system in your body, shifts from repair mode to stress mode when you think negative thoughts. When you find yourself in negative mental mode, start tapping even before you formulate a Setup Statement. While tapping, decide what direction you want your thoughts to take.

Get rid of negative influences in your life. When you're faced with a serious disease, you need all the positive support you can get. You also need to cut the cords linking you to any negative influences that drag you down mentally and physically. This can mean jettisoning friends, social events, movies, books, television programs, video games, and other media that exert a negative pull on your emotional state. You might be in the habit of listening to the news, and reluctant to let go of your need to "stay informed." Tap on that. A friend of mine recently, and aptly, referred to radio and television news shows as "fear porn." They propagate mental distress, yet they are fascinating. You can do nothing about the problems they describe, while they distract you from the positive influences in your life.

Make a list of what lifts your spirits, and what depresses them. If you're dealing with a health crisis, it's time to jettison the concrete boots that pull you down. Your healing is far more important than the junk you're letting go of. Tap on any worry about the habits you're throwing away in order to support your healing journey.

Tap directly on symptoms. You can tap very simply on the symptoms themselves, before going deeper. This often provides partial relief. An example is "Even though I have this migraine headache..." or "Even though my blood sugar level is over 300..." or "Even though my blood pressure is 185..." The EFT archives contain many cases in which this simple form of tapping on symptoms changed them quickly.

Describe symptoms in detail. Describe your symptoms precisely, and get as vivid and detailed as possible. Describe their shape, size, temperature, consistency, and color. I worked recently with a client with fibromyalgia who had pain in many places, and her feet hurt the worst. She tapped on "Even though I have this square brown block of pain with bright yellow lightning bolts stabbing through my feet..." A detailed description while tapping on the pain plus several highly emotional events brought her pain from 7 to 0.

Tap on the emotions behind the symptoms. Ask yourself what emotion is linked to the body part that feels pain or is symptomatic. An example is "I have this swollen right knee. I am so angry at my knee and about how it restricts my movement. Even though I'm so angry..."

Tap on the events behind the emotions. If you're angry, tap while describing various events that made you angry. If you're feeling helpless, take your mind back to an early event in which you were helpless. Clear as many events as possible. Use the symptoms as a useful stimulus. They can serve the purpose of unearthing painful early memories, so you can tap away their emotional intensity.

Sneak up on the problem. Identify your most hopeless beliefs and thoughts, and incorporate them into a Setup Statement. You might believe your condition is hopeless, that it's genetic, that it runs in your family, that it's bigger than you, or that it will get worse. You can simply take your exact words and add "Even though" at the beginning and "I deeply and completely accept myself" at the end. Examples are:

> Even though [this disease is 100% genetic and there's nothing I can do about it]...
>
> Even though [the doctor said my case is hopeless]...
>
> Even though [my mother, grandmother, and great-grandmother all had it]...
>
> Even though [this problem is overwhelming]...

This practice of using your negative thoughts in a Setup Statement while tapping transforms them from hopeless impediments to your healing to stress-reduction tools. Clients usually report a marked shift in the intensity of their negative beliefs, and some make a 180-degree turn after tapping, arguing that their decline is not inevitable.

The Personal Peace Procedure. This is useful as homework for clients. They make a list of every emotionally troublesome event they can think of in their lives and tap on them. Even if there are over 1,000 events, if you tap on three per day, in a year you'll have tapped on them all.

Use emphatic language or shout the Setup Statement. This can engage an increased level of emotional energy, and shift the problem.

Search for secondary gain. There's often some benefit to a person from staying sick, whether it's increased attention from important people like doctors, the financial reward of disability benefits, or the escape from unwanted social obligations. Here are some questions you can ask to identify secondary gain:

- What would it be like to have none of your symptoms?
- What benefits are you getting from this illness?
- What would you have to give up if your illness went away?
- Why might you believe you deserve this illness?
- Who would you be without this story?

Use questions to identify core issues to tap on. Here are some questions you can ask to identify them:

- If there was an emotional contributor to that symptom, what could it be?
- If you had life to live over again, what person or event would you prefer to skip?
- Who or what are you most angry at?
- What are the three worst things that happened to you?
- How has this disease shaped your life?
- What comes up when you say, "I am in perfect health"?

Chasing the pain. Sometimes after tapping, physical discomfort changes location and/or intensity or quality. For example, a headache, initially described as stabbing pain in the temples at an intensity of 9 can shift to a dull ache in the jaw at an intensity of 7. In this case, the tapping strategy is to chase the pain. Tap for the new location and quality. Each time the number goes down, find the next site of pain.

Use humor. Sessions working on serious diseases can feel very heavy and grave. Laughter can break up the intensity of the session.

It's almost as if both client and practitioner go into a trance, which can be broken by laughter. Laughter often characterizes the transition from tapping on the severity of the problem to considering the possibility of healing. Great sensitivity on the part of the practitioner is required when using humor or laughter, so that the client does not feel the practitioner is making light of a serious situation. What sometimes works well is when the practitioner outdoes the client's catastrophic conditions. In the previous case of the fibromyalgia patient with painful feet, the healing transition came when I agreed with her that her foot pain would never get better. We tapped while saying, "It will get worse." Then I said to her, "Yes, even at your funeral, people will look down at the corpse and say, 'Her feet are in such terrible pain.'" The client laughed at this absurd scenario, and the pain began to lift.

Professional Standards in a Coaching Practice

As EFT coaching and practice has evolved, a body of knowledge has emerged about how to care for clients and for practitioners. Two excellent textbooks describe the professional standards to which EFT coaches aspire. They are *Creating Healing Relationships* (Hover-Kramer, 2011) and *Ethics Handbook for Energy Healing Practitioners* (Feinstein, 2011). Clinical EFT training also includes an ethics module and practitioners must pass an ethics examination in order to become certified. The following sections review briefly some of the procedures that facilitate a happy and healthy professional practice. They are covered fully in the two textbooks and live trainings.

Self-care. Caring professionals such as social workers, psychotherapists, and life coaches are usually excellent at giving to others. They give time, attention, and their best insights to their clients. They're often less adept at caring for themselves. It's important to include yourself among the people you care for. This might include establishing healthy professional boundaries such as hours when you're unavailable to clients, adequate vacation time, and clear payment and refund policies.

Case study write-ups. When becoming certified, it's required that you record your client sessions in writing. You're encouraged to continue this practice after you're certified too. Provided you respect client privacy and the laws of your jurisdiction and mask the identity of your clients, you can write up case histories to post in the EFT archives and on your own website. These give you a record of your progress, as well as provide potential clients with a sampling of the types of problem in which you specialize.

Record keeping. Professional records such as session times and billing, and referrals to other practitioners, are an integral part of a coaching or psychotherapy practice. There are many software packages that guide you through the process of capturing the details required to maintain professional records.

Scope of practice. The scope of practice of a coach is quite different from that of a psychotherapist. For instance, life coaches are not qualified to diagnose or treat mental health conditions. There are many other differences between the two. Similarly, psychological trauma might be beyond the scope of practice of a psychotherapist, who might refer traumatized clients to specialists who have such training. Regard for your clients makes it essential to be aware of the limitations of your scope of practice and observe these boundaries.

Supervision. You are likely at some point in your practice to face puzzling professional dilemmas. You might be uncertain whether to coach a family member, or how to prioritize clients, or whether to communicate troubling news you've heard about a colleague. You don't need to figure out these problems alone. Having a wise mentor with whom you can discuss issues puts a new and more experienced pair of eyes on the problem. Having a source of such supervision is required of psychotherapists in most jurisdictions, and life coaches also benefit from having the resources of an experienced supervisor to draw on.

Ethics codes. Professional organizations publish ethics codes. Be familiar with the ethics codes of organizations you belong to, since these principles will steer you clear of many ethical pitfalls of which you might otherwise be unaware. Organizations also publish procedures for filing complaints against practitioners who might have committed ethical violations. Familiarity with the ethical guidelines of your organization makes it much less likely that you will have a complaint lodged against you.

Interactions with other professionals. If you're a life coach practicing EFT, you'll come into contact with other members of the healing professions in your area, such as physicians, nurses, psychotherapists, and alternative medicine practitioners. Conducting yourself professionally shows that you're a responsible member of the healing community. You'll also find yourself referring clients who need help that lies outside your scope of practice. An example of such a referral is a client who comes to you for business coaching, and you identify symptoms of PTSD in his behavior. You recommend he work with a local psychologist trained in treating psychological trauma; for his own safety, you might even make appropriate mental health treatment a condition of him continuing with you as a coaching client. If you conduct yourself professionally in these circumstances, you'll become a respected member of your local healing community, and you're likely to find mental health professionals referring clients needing coaching to you, as well as the other way around. We want the profession of EFT practitioner to be highly regarded by all the other members of the healing community, and responsible interaction with other professionals is key to establishing a good reputation.

* * *

Resources

- Collarbone Breathing: CollarboneBreathing.EFTUniverse.com
- Floor to Ceiling Eye Roll: FTC.EFTUniverse.com
- Serious Diseases: SeriousDiseases.EFTUniverse.com
- Tables and Legs: TablesLegs.EFTUniverse.com
- When Your Client Feels Worse: ClientFeelsWorse.EFTUniverse.com

Confronting Massive Human Suffering:
Humanitarian Work and Research

The amount of suffering in the world is hard for those who live in developed countries to comprehend. One way of making the statistics comprehensible comes from an organization called 100 People (100people.org/statistics_100stats.php). They imagine the world as a village of 100 people. In that village, here's how people fare:

- 83 would be able to read and write; 17 would not.

- 77 people would have a place to shelter them from the wind and the rain, but 23 would not.

- 1 would be dying of starvation.

- 15 would be undernourished.

- 13 people would have no clean, safe water to drink; 87 would.

If you have a roof over your head, a few hundred dollars in your bank account, food in the refrigerator, and warm clothing, you're among a fortunate minority of the people in the world.

Compassion for the suffering of others, coupled with the recognition that EFT can help ease this suffering, has let to many humanitarian efforts by EFT practitioners. These have ranged from teams that work with local and international non-governmental organizations

(NGOs) in helping trauma victims to individual efforts toward helping the survivors of disasters. Individual EFT practitioners offered help to survivors of Hurricane Katrina, the 2008 Pakistan earthquake, the 2004 tsunami that hit Thailand, and other disasters, traveling to those areas and working with aid agencies to offer EFT sessions to survivors. Organized teams have been to Rwanda several times to work with children whose parents and other relatives were killed in the 1994 genocide. In the wake of the Sandy Hook school shootings in 2013, Nick Ortner, an EFT practitioner and online marketer who is the largest single donor to EFT research and humanitarian efforts, set up an organization that offered EFT to the whole community. The use of energy psychology for disaster relief has been surveyed in a key paper (Feinstein, 2008). In this chapter, we'll hear from some of those who have organized these humanitarian efforts, and get a glimpse of how much human suffering might be reduced as EFT comes into widespread use to help survivors.

Highly Traumatized Populations

When a tragedy strikes an individual, it often affects the entire future course of that person's life. When a tragedy involves a whole community, however, the "field effect" can reinforce the suffering to produce psychological dislocation that persists for generations. Haiti is one of the world's poorest countries. Researchers estimate that a large percentage of the Haitian population had PTSD even before the devastating earthquake of 2010 (Gurret, Caufour, Palmer-Hoffman, & Church, 2012). PTSD can result from natural disasters such as earthquakes and tsunamis. It can result from social conditions such as poverty and political repression. It is also rife in the human-caused disasters of invasion, war, and occupation.

There are many examples of the mental health toll exacted by human-caused disasters. The Rwanda genocide in 1994 resulted in close to a million deaths. It left the whole country traumatized (Stone, Leyden, & Fellows, 2009). Following the Serbian army's actions in Kosovo in the late 1990s, a high proportion of the Kosovar population reported traumatic events, and showed a high level of PTSD and a decrease in mental health (Cardozo, Vergara, Agani, & Gotway, 2000). In a study of Palestinians living under Israeli occupation, 89% of children exposed to military violence had symptoms of moderate to severe PTSD (Qouta, Punamäki, & El Sarraj, 2003).

Whether due to natural causes or human action, large-scale disasters can result in a whole population or even an entire country being highly traumatized. It is a measure of EFT's effectiveness that it is able to make dramatic improvements even in these extreme circumstances. Here are some examples of EFT humanitarian initiatives that offered relief to large groups of people.

The Veterans Stress Project

The Veterans Stress Project (www.StressProject.org) was set up soon after the first group of U.S. veterans began returning from deployment in Iraq. Reports began to filter in from psychotherapists that they were treating veterans with PTSD using EFT and other energy psychology techniques with great success. A group of practitioners volunteered to offer free or low-cost treatment to veterans and their family members, many of whom were also affected by PTSD. The practitioners' names were listed on the Stress Project website, so that veterans and family members could find help. Since then, the Stress Project has grown to encompass hundreds of practitioners in many parts of the world. It helps not just veterans of recent wars such as Iraq and Afghanistan, but also those from earlier conflicts such as in Korea and Vietnam. Several WWII veterans have discovered EFT through the project. They've used it successfully, even though they are in their 80s and have had PTSD for over 60 years.

Veterans find the project through online searches, through community groups, or through media broadcasts. They contact practitioners and work with them, either in person or long distance via phone or videoconferencing services. Two pilot studies and two full-scale randomized controlled trials have shown that over 80% of veterans who go through six EFT sessions recover from PTSD, and that the results

results hold over time (Church, Geronilla, & Dinter, 2009; Church, 2010b; Church et al., 2013; Geronilla, McWilliams, Clond & Palmer-Hoffman, 2014). The Veterans Stress Project is a program of the National Institute for Integrative Healthcare (NIIH.org), which I chair.

Twice, I've testified before committees of the U.S. Congress on the effectiveness of EFT for PTSD and the work of the Stress Project. Several U.S. congresspeople have written formal letters to the head of the Department of Veterans Affairs advocating EFT. Here is one story by a veteran who worked with Marilyn McWilliams, one of the most active coaches in the Stress Project. Without Marilyn, and my colleague Deb Tribbey who works in the NIIH office, the Stress Project would never have been so successful. By taking the lead in research, Marilyn has helped pave the way to healing for thousands of veterans. The author of the following account, David S., served in both Iraq and Afghanistan, and had many psychological and physical challenges.

Vulcan Voodoo with Marilyn
By David S.

My life was in shambles. I was in the middle of a disastrous divorce. My youngest son was born and I was not allowed to be present. I had angry outbursts, migraines, nightmares, flashbacks, and bouts of depression regularly. My mind and my body began suffering from the affects of the VA medicines (i.e., lack of libido, weak and dizzy in the morning hours, and vertigo every time I blinked my eyes). I had no emotions or compassion anymore. I was falling apart with no hope of gaining control again. Thoughts of suicide entered my mind daily. All I had were my combat memories. I felt alone.

I began to explore the thought of attempting this EFT psychobabble therapy. Skeptical is an understatement…What did I have to lose? Besides, it was free, and I was rock-bottom broke at the time anyway. It was this or the end of a rope…I chose life (a big step for me).

I was in Texas; Marilyn was in Oregon. We scheduled our first face-to-face appointment via Skype. I broke my neck in Iraq and had suffered from excruciating migraines, sometimes as many as three a day, ever since. On a scale from 1 to 10, and 10 being the most horrible pain imaginable, I had a 10-size migraine for our first session. Marilyn's first priority was to prove to a skeptic that the EFT works on everything...even migraines. "Whatever, let us get this over with so I can swallow a bottle of Excedrin Migraine and go to sleep!"

Within 10 minutes, I was a believer! For the first time in 5 and a half years, I was migraine free! Amazing! Her Vulcan mind meld and voodoo witchcraft worked on me, and I wanted more. We began to work on one of my top five worst experiences. I fell asleep that night easily and stayed asleep for more than 2 hours, which was unheard of for me at the time. I felt a difference the next morning in my memory of the story I told. Funny thing, it was just a memory now, not a living nightmare. I felt free for the first time in years. I was already excited for the next week's session.

The day arrived where I was going to tap on my worst memory yet. This was the memory that put me over the top. This event changed my life forever; it caused me to retreat into myself; it cost me my personality, my marriage, my job, and worse, my children. We removed my emotional response to the memory that had haunted me for over 6 years. That was the first time I ever spoke about what happened that horrible day in Iraq. Marilyn, again, allowed me to take charge. We tore the story apart and tapped every chance we could. We missed nothing that night...not even the smallest detail. We did it!

Because of the Veterans Stress Project and EFT, I can sleep at night without the aid of sleeping pills. I have only had two migraines of low intensity in the past 11 months. I am no longer on antidepressants. My ex-wife allows my boys extended stays with me. I lost 40 pounds. I have friends, and the best of all, I have my life back! For the first time since my combat days ended, I can share my stories with my loved ones without the fear of my own emotional responses. I now have the ability to face my past and my memories with confidence and security that I will be safe and comfortable.

I continue to use EFT as a means to defuse stressful memories and other activities that may cause me discomfort or an emotional response. I have spoken of the Veterans Stress Project in my VA PTSD group sessions and to the VA counselors as a means to end the pain and suffering of veterans everywhere. I wish to "pay it forward" about my experiences with EFT. Thank you, Veterans Stress Project. Thank you, EFT. Thank you, Marilyn, you saved my life! When asked how I feel, my only response is "I'm free!"

* * *

David's story has been repeated many times. After a slow beginning, the Stress Project now reaches thousands of veterans and family members each year. With official government channels slow to offer EFT, the Stress Project picked up the slack. Having a large number of trained professionals able to offer EFT showed that the technique had a substantial base of support. It has provided government therapists a reliable partner to which they can refer veterans under their care.

While veteran suicides, homicides, and domestic violence impact an increasing number of Americans, the need for EFT is not confined by any national boundary. It has been used with some of the most severely traumatized people in the world. Many orphaned children who survived the Rwanda genocide still live in "orphanages" though they are now in their 20s. They are unable to function socially or economically in any kind of normal manner. While mental health problems such as anxiety and depression usually have a start, middle, and end, PTSD is different. It often becomes worse over time. Veterans might seem normal after they return from a tour of duty, then start showing symptoms of PTSD years later. Similarly, genocide orphans often develop lifetime symptoms that become worse over time. EFT is one of the few rays of hope offering the promise of reversing this bleak prognosis.

In a surprising twist, the lives of some of these Rwandan orphans have become entwined with another group of traumatized families: those involved in the December 2012 shootings at Sandy Hook elementary school in Newtown, Connecticut. The shootings were one of a long and depressing string of similar events in recent American history. While shootings in countries with strict gun control laws are rare because of the lack of availability of firearms, psychotic individuals in America have little trouble getting their hands on guns. Even military-style assault weapons are easily obtained. A single one of these is more lethal than an army of warriors wielding the muzzle loaders prevalent when America's Founding Fathers wrote the Second Amendment to the country's constitution, guaranteeing the right to bear arms.

Nick Ortner happens to live in Newtown, Connecticut, where the shootings occurred. In 2007, Nick had launched the Tapping World Summit, a free annual online event that has introduced EFT to over 1,000,000 people worldwide (TWS.EFTUniverse.com). During that same year, Lori Leyden founded Create Global Healing (CGH), a nonprofit organization providing trauma healing and training based on EFT/tapping to orphan genocide survivors in Rwanda. Within a few hours of the tragedy Nick was working with Lori Leyden, me, and others to frame a response from the EFT community. Nick quickly recognized a crucial fact, that the shootings had affected thousands of people who were not directly involved. The shootings affected the entire community, and Nick and Lori developed a community-wide response over the ensuing months. Here is their account of how EFT helped the Newtown community deal with the shocking events at Sandy Hook, as well as the links with the humanitarian work in Rwanda.

From Rwanda to Newtown: Our Shared Vision for Humanity
By Lori Leyden, PhD, and Nick Ortner

Little did we know when we first began our humanitarian efforts that our paths would become so integrally connected. Although we shared a vision for how EFT could heal our world, we didn't actually connect personally until 3 years later. By then the Tapping World Summit had become enormously successful, with a percentage of the profits supporting extraordinary EFT-based projects like Deepak Mostert's Trauma Relief and Emotional Support Techniques (TREST) work with earthquake survivors in Indonesia, Deborah Miller's work with child cancer patients in Mexico, and Dawson Church's Stress Project serving U.S. Veterans.

(Nick) *When I first learned about EFT, I was so blown away with how effective it was that I absolutely knew I had to find a way to teach others the technique. Since then it's been my life's mission to show others how they can quickly learn and use EFT/tapping to make life better in every way possible. My team and I are committed to spreading a message of hope, healing, and joy through tapping.*

In the meantime, CGH trauma relief programs with over 1,000 orphans and Orphan Head of Households suffering from PTSD in Rwanda were proving to be amazingly effective. After one train-the-trainer program with 50 of the 650 students at the Remera Mbogo High School Orphanage, trauma outbreaks were reduced by 90% in 1 year.

(Lori) *Every time I return from Rwanda, my heart breaks open even wider to the possibilities for world healing if our next generation of young people are given the tools to heal, work, and lead us into a peaceful future. From my very first trip, I knew that if EFT/tapping could be this effective for those who had experienced the worst of human tragedies then anyone, anywhere in the world could heal as well.*

Nick and Lori met in early 2010 when CGH was selected as the Tapping World Summit's humanitarian cause of the year.

(Nick) *Just talking to Lori about her work in Rwanda can overwhelm you with the healing power of EFT. That such a simple practice can promote healing on every conceivable level—physical, emotional, mental, and spiritual—in a nation as deeply scarred as Rwanda makes you pause long enough to imagine the profound change tapping can effect around the globe.*

(Lori) *The vision for Project LIGHT: Rwanda began to emerge when I realized that trauma healing was not enough for these young people if they continued to live in poverty and were hopeless about their futures. As passionate as I am about my work in Rwanda, fundraising has been both magical and challenging. As my dream for global healing expanded and deepened so did my desire to attract all the right "hearts" to support our work. But how could that happen? I was just one person with a dream that oftentimes felt impossible. What if we could prove that love and the right resources could heal anyone from any circumstance?*

(Nick) *When Dr. Leyden came to me with her proposal for Project LIGHT: Rwanda, I saw its enormous potential and I knew it was in alignment with my mission to bring EFT to those who need it most around the world. Lori had essentially developed a new form of humanitarian aid based on tapping. With major backing by the Tapping Solution, Project LIGHT: Rwanda—the world's first international youth healing, heart-centered leadership and entrepreneurship program—has been operational since May 2011 and is achieving profound results.*

(Lori) *We use tapping as the basis for all elements of our program from physical and emotional healing to problem solving, creativity, productivity, focus, concentration, and more. Our first group of 13 Project LIGHT Ambassadors like Mattieu, Chantal, Yvette, Desire, and Fidel have transformed their own despair and grief into love, compassion, and joy. They have influenced the lives of thousands more by teaching tapping in their communities as well as becoming elected and appointed leaders in local government positions. Now, just as important, they are finding their way out of poverty with sponsorships for university education and developing self-sustaining microfinance businesses. Here's what I know to be true—love and the right resources, including EFT, can heal anyone, anywhere from any circumstance.*

Imagine Project LIGHT centers, based on tapping, where young people receive emotional healing and training, real opportunities for economic independence and the freedom to become heart-centered leaders. With advanced technology to have real-time interactions between these young people, students, donors, and our visionary Resource Partners in the fields of education, healing arts, business, and entrepreneurship. With a business incubator to develop products and services that will make each program self-sustainable. Now imagine Centers like this—all over the world—in Congo, Sudan, the Middle East, India, China, Russia, and right here in our own backyards, where our young people are given the opportunity to create global connections and collaborations that lead us into a peaceful future.

Then came December 14, 2012. The Sandy Hook Elementary School Shooting tragedy literally struck home for Nick and his Newtown, Connecticut–based company. Twenty-eight lives were lost, including 20 first graders. Nick called on Dr. Leyden to lead a support team to provide trauma relief for Newtown. Within days they were working with families who lost loved ones, first responders, survivors of the shooting, and other affected members of the community, and providing vital support to community mental health caregivers.

(Lori) *When Nick called, I asked myself, "Is this mine to do?" I listened to my heart and, based on my experience, I knew that if people in Rwanda could heal, so could those affected by the tragedy in Newtown.*

(Nick) *The decision to establish the Tapping Solution Foundation was an easy one. When I saw what was needed, and I knew what was possible, right here in Newtown, I knew the timing was right. So we quickly moved forward to formalize and fund our long-term commitment to charitable works here in Newtown and around the world.*

In collaboration with Create Global Healing, the Tapping Solution Foundation has developed a powerful network of local, national, and international alliances to bring train-the-trainer trauma relief and resiliency services and educational programs to Newtown. This is a new model of sustainable long-term, community-based humanitarian aid.

Embracing the legacy of Newtown's signature response, We are Newtown, we CHOOSE LOVE, the Tapping Solution Foundation and Create Global Healing joined the town in creating a new standard for changing a culture of violence to one of peace, love, and safety for all. To date we have provided effective trauma relief to hundreds of Newtowners and people in surrounding communities, as well as provided training to nearly 100 local licensed health care professionals and self-care practitioners.

(Nick) *April 27, 2013, was one of the most profound days of my life. It was a day that had me in tears more than just once...JT Lewis, the 12-year-old older brother of Jesse Lewis who died on December 14, 2012, in the Sandy Hook shootings, did something really incredible...Two months before, JT was struggling to even go to school, until he had a powerful conversation with several of the Project Light: Rwanda Ambassadors. The Ambassadors taught JT how to tap, shared with him their stories of the pain they experienced during the Rwandan genocide and the healing they now had, and JT was transformed. He returned to school the next day with a mission—to raise money to give back and help the Ambassadors for the gift of hope they had given him. Less than 2 months later, he announced on a Skype call with the Project LIGHT: Rwanda Ambassadors that he had raised enough money to send one of the ambassadors, Betty, to the university for a year!*

(Lori) *With confidence in EFT, I followed my heart to Sandy Hook, and the vision for Project LIGHT is unfolding. Now we have Project LIGHT: Pacific Grove, Project LIGHT: Newtown, Project LIGHT: New England, Project LIGHT: Hartford, and more...*

When hearts are aligned with a shared vision, everything is possible!

* * *

A different challenge confronted the humanitarian teams that used EFT in response to the 2010 Haiti earthquake. The quake orphaned an estimated 250,000 children. Several EFT practitioners traveled to Haiti as soon as the airport opened and offered EFT where they could. Then an organized team of volunteers led by Claudie Caufour and Jean-Michel Gurret of Lyons, France, visited Haiti in 2012 to train social service personnel in EFT. Haiti is a French-speaking country. They trained close to 300 new practitioners, many of them Catholic seminarians. In Haiti, the church provides many of the social services that in other countries would be provided by the government; the seminarians are the closest thing Haiti has to social workers or psychologists. They provide care to many of the children orphaned in the earthquake.

Another team visited Haiti in June of 2013. It included Yves Wauthier-Freymann, who heads the Center for Brief Therapy in Brussels, Belgium, as well as Jean-Michel. Yves heads up EFT training and certification in Francophone countries. Here are two case histories from just one of the many days during that trip.

Children of the Haiti Earthquake
By Yves Wauthier-Freymann

During our intervention in Haiti, Claudie Caufour (president of Energy Psy Sans Frontières Association) and I worked with a mother of five (three children from her deceased husband and two of her own) who had syphilis. Her choices were difficult. She could: (a) pay for the medicine for her hospitalized premature child (28 weeks); (b) pay for her own medicine, which she needs in order to be healthy enough to sell second-hand clothes to feed her children; or (c) pay the rent on a small plot of land where she has a hut made of old carpets, tents, and scraps. She doesn't have the money to pay for more than one. Her "home" poses a major health and safety risk whenever it rains. Being the sole provider for the children, her greatest fear concerns her own survival, as she doesn't know what would happen to her children should she die.

This case is far from unique. Given these desperate circumstances, a Haitian institute that trains students in psychology, as well as the neonatal and pediatric services unit of the Port-au-Prince Hospital, asked us for training in energy psychology. Their request was simple: teach them tools that are easy to use and efficient.

During the session with this mother, there were no positive resources to reinforce, except for her faith and her unswerving hope. We did round after round of EFT, naming everything she was experiencing in her daily life, acknowledging how real that was, though also acknowledging the other reality: She is alive, a survivor, and has helped her children and stepchildren survive—a huge proof of love and faith. This mother told us that she felt stronger and more courageous after the tapping rounds. Coming from someone who obviously is already very brave, considering her everyday reality, all we can do is honor this courage and feel very small and very privileged when we start to complain about trifles... his day helped me put my own "worries" in perspective and I felt grateful for the simplicity and efficiency of EFT.

While we were training about 90 students, another case came up. We had identified various treatment targets and were starting to use EFT on them. We reminded the students that personal details of what happens during the training are confidential, and warned them to choose medium-sized problems to work on. In Haiti, that itself is not easy.

I started doing a demonstration with a little 9-year-old princess, creating rapport, and slowly and respectfully bringing her to her triggering topic: the difficulty she had with certain students in school. The underlying issue was the death of her father during the earthquake, and her mother's inability to talk about it or even mention the father... Creating rapport was crucial: I started imitating Donald Duck, made a few jokes to play down the teacher's absence of reaction when the little girl experienced bullying in school and the guilt she felt when the children who bothered her cried...All this clearly hid immense suffering, a need to create a nurturing bond, and the need for acknowledgment for all the suffering that was experienced, in all the children, be they the bully or their victim.

Having this enormous amount of suffering acknowledged relieved the negative emotions, and the blocks faded away...This session healed this trigger and enabled Jean-Michel Gurret to go on in a private session with the real issue, the father's death during the 2010 earthquake and the mother's blackout (origin of the mother's trauma and her inability to talk with her children about their father). This session also allowed me to demonstrate a treatment plan for children and to answer many questions about helping children in "domesticité." This term designates child orphans or children who have been taken from their families who are used as slaves in their "adoptive" families. They spend their days cleaning, laundering, and ironing, so much so that they have never learnt how to play. These children experience great trouble when being reintroduced into the education system, as they do not know play, have a complete lack of self-confidence, a terrible self-image, and no resources.

I taught them Brain Gym and the energy routine in order to give them a basis for their learning, and to enable them to discover some resources to work on Self and self-esteem before going on to traumas and repetitive rapes. Heavy stuff! We ended the day by illustrating how we can rapidly change a belief system and free ourselves from it for an enhanced quality of life. The day brought up lots of emotions and tomorrow we will continue with a more specific attention to resources, Self, and the reconstruction of our inner qualities...Thank you, everyone!

* * *

Jean-Michel gathered data on his 2012 teaching trip to Haiti (Gurret, Caufour, Palmer-Hoffman, & Church, 2012). He measured PTSD symptoms in 77 of the seminarians to whom his team taught EFT. Before they began, 62% of them met the criteria for PTSD, but after t2wo days of EFT, 0% did. Other humanitarian teams that have gathered data echo his experience. Lori Leyden, along with Barbara Stone and Bert Fellows, published two studies of energy psychology in Rwandan orphanages (Stone, Leyden, & Fellows, 2009a-b). They found that PTSD symptoms declined significantly in both orphanages. Caroline Sakai and colleagues gathered data at other Rwandan orphanages where they used TFT (Connolly, Sakai, & Oas, 2010;

Connolly & Sakai, 2011). They measured partial or complete recoveries from PTSD resulting from their work.

Another place EFT has made a difference is the Mexican city of Nuevo Laredo. Fueled by the drug trade, levels of violence in the city are high. A team led by David MacKay taught EFT to social work groups through EFT Global, a humanitarian organization working under the umbrella of the National Institute for Integrative Healthcare. Here's their story.

EFT in Nuevo Laredo
By David MacKay

In this troubled city that borders Texas, people live in constant fear. For many people from other areas, it is hard to imagine what it means to live in a zone where violence reigns and its power exceeds the possibilities of law and order, but for people here that is their daily reality. The project was be headed by EFT practitioner David MacKay from Puebla, accompanied by Carolina Tellez from Guadalajara, and Jenny Pavisic from Mexico City. They spent 5 days training psychologists and social workers from the DIF (Integral Family Development, an official organization dedicated to the implementation of public policy regarding social welfare), as well as the health and education sectors and community volunteers. There were 34 participants in all.

Local organization was done by Maria Esther Fuentes, a psychologist who had previously studied EFT and headed a team of psychologists at a government agency. This team had its hands full attending to victims of the violence, and sorely needed a tool like EFT to deal efficiently with the overwhelming tragedy they confronted every day, as well as its impact on them. She had quite a time working this project into the political agenda and her report may be helpful to those looking to do the same.

The first 3 days (24 hours of instruction) were used to teach standard basic training in EFT (Levels 1 and 2) and the last 2 days focused on the application of EFT for treating trauma. That was our basic plan, but, right off the bat during the morning of the first day, the first demonstration, which would normally be a routine issue for didactic purposes, turned out to be a crisis intervention. One of the DIF's psychologists was suffering from posttraumatic stress caused by the disappearance 2 weeks earlier of an adolescent family member. She had slept very little since the event, as she would spend most of each night watching the street outside her window for suspicious activity. Twice she had fled in the dead of night in her car, thinking that evil-doers were meaning to enter her house, probably exposing her family to greater danger.

With about 20 minutes of tapping in front of the group, she calmed visibly. The next day she reported having slept peacefully for the first time in weeks and she was able to assist other family members similarly affected. After completing the workshop, she wrote, "Today, thanks to you David, Jenny, Caro, and EFT, I can breathe without pain, I have recovered my peace and taste for life because I know that in spite of the circumstances and the absence/loss of [name omitted], I can live, I deserve to live and enjoy life fully. EFT awakened me and my connection to the world, I am able to feel again, but above all I can work, eat, sleep, and enjoy my son, without any more fear than that which is required to protect me and my family. Today I feel very differently from the day I started the course, a course that has given me the peace I needed. And from today I promise to take EFT to the many people who need it, with the desire to draw from so much pain an opportunity that you and EFT have given me."

Some people had come to the course rather reluctantly. One woman wrote: "I arrived with total distrust regarding this technique and as the days passed, the work with specific situations changed my opinion. The first things I noticed were changes in my breathing, my sight, and changes in my temperature. I think this can become a basic tool during pregnancy, because my discomfort practically disappeared, and even with my initial distrust, I can say thank you to EFT."

With this being a fairly long training, and free for the participants, one might expect a significant number of dropouts; instead their commitment and enthusiasm grew with each passing day, and everyone completed the course with new hope to be agents for change in their troubled city. They were especially impressed with the phenomenon of Borrowing Benefits, because to heal one by one all the inhabitants of a city would be impossible. They felt in themselves the emotional healing that occurs when simply accompanying others in their tapping. One of them exclaimed on the final day: [We need to] "create an EFT epidemic." Another commented: "My life has been colored by hope!" Another: "EFT is something as important and as simple as the smiling reply from God to our questioning when faced with a raw and cruel reality that has wounded us."

There were several nuns in the course, and one said: "Speaking from the life experience of a people who coexist daily with danger, with the pain born of impotence, as a church we have committed to accompanying our brothers so they don't become perpetrators and that we may be bearers of good tidings. And this week we have received the good tidings of EFT, a tool we have tested on ourselves and found to be valuable and effective. These are tools of the future; this has opened new perspectives and by the grace of God we will continue." Following this, we taught a 3-day training for 43 participants in the Cathedral of Nuevo Laredo that put more emphasis on working with trauma.

* * *

Change Is Possible: The San Quentin Death Row Project

One of the most startling places in which EFT is used successfully is prison. The San Quentin prison north of San Francisco is one of the most notorious in the California prison system. It houses death-row and life-without-parole prisoners, among other groups. In this unpromising environment, an EFT practitioner named Hari Lubin introduced an EFT program called "Change Is Possible." Inmates would receive five sessions from Hari, and apply EFT to the anger, pain, and impulsive behavior that complicated their lives behind bars.

One said, "I understood that one thing led to another, but it didn't matter. It didn't connect to anything about how I felt or thought. Knowing it didn't change anything."

The program ran for nearly 10 years until it was cut short by Hari's death at the age of 80. The changes he saw were powerful. Men who previously believed that their only course of action was to meet violence with violence discovered new options opening up for them. One inmate described this experience as being able to "feel the emotional intensity drop to a manageable level. Then, I'd be able to make a sound decision, or take action to resolve the revealed problem." They often described their experience in grateful letters to Hari. Here's a selection from those, drawn from a clinical report Hari coauthored on the program (Lubin & Schneider, 2009).

"It was shocking. That day, and then the subsequent sessions, gave me a sense of peace and equanimity that I have never experienced before. There really could be a freedom for me here, even though I am incarcerated. I started telling everyone."

"Hari brings to the table many new ideas and makes us think through some of our preconceived notions. I've come to realize that my old communication style was very judgmental and full of fault finding. EFT empowers you to change your insight and core beliefs."

"I see now that there has never been any benefit in life by losing control of my emotions. I made some irreversible mistakes that changed my life. It's not money for me. Now, success for me is being in touch with my emotions and acting as thoughtfully as possible. How can anyone express gratitude for being helped to discover such a wonderful gift?"

"I don't resort to my old belief system, and I no longer feed on the chaos of prison life. EFT allows the old behavior patterns to crumble."

"I like this method of facing anything I may be up against. This really works and I will be tapping for the rest of my life."

* * *

Volunteering for Humanitarian Projects

As you read the previous stories, you might have felt called to explore the possibility of volunteering to offer EFT to people in need. There are many ways you can do this. You can start a local program offering EFT to a group in your area. That's how Hari Lubin started Change Is Possible. He contacted the prison authorities and volunteered to teach mindfulness meditation classes at San Quentin. After he learned EFT, he added it to his repertoire.

You can join a Tapping Circle in your area. Tapping Circles are Borrowing Benefits groups that meet periodically, such as once a month or once a week, in a particular geographic area. They're listed at TappingCircles.EFTUniverse.com. If there isn't a Tapping Circle near you, start one of your own. It will give you great support and encouragement on your EFT journey, as well as develop your skills.

You can also join one of the volunteer teams that go to disaster zones. You'll first need to go through training in order to understand the intricacies of working with vulnerable people, and the patchwork of official and nongovernmental agencies that coordinate care in the aftermath of a disaster. Contact EFTGlobal.com to find out how to prepare yourself to join a humanitarian team.

If you'd like to work with veterans, it's best to become certified first, and to develop an understanding of the special needs of people with psychological trauma. You can sign up for the Veterans Stress Project at StressProject.org under the "Scientific Research" tab.

You can also make a donation or bequest to EFT research through the National Institute for Integrative Healthcare, which has taken the lead in EFT research for the past decade. Many of the studies that validate EFT that you've seen described in this manual were funded by people like you. They may have contributed $10, or they may have contributed $10,000. When you add it all up, coupled with the countless volunteer hours people have contributed, it's resulted in dozens of studies published in peer-reviewed psychology and medical journals. If these had been done commercially, rather than through the goodwill of donors and volunteers, they would have cost over $5 million. Each dollar contributed to the National Institute for Integrative Healthcare results in about $12 of research or the delivery of services to veterans with PTSD. It's one of the smartest places you can put your tithes, bequests, and other donations. EFT really works to help those in need, and you multiply your money many times over when you donate.

Future Research

Throughout this book, you've seen how important research has been to the development of Clinical EFT. Research gives us answers to questions, and opens up new avenues of enquiry. Here's how EFT research is likely to evolve in the future.

We've done a great deal of research into psychological problems such as anxiety, depression, phobias, and PTSD. I expect that we'll now see increased research using physiological measures such as blood pressure, skin temperature, and heart rate variability. Advanced research will use devices like MRI and MEG (magnetoencephalogram) machines to determine what is happening in the brain during an EFT session.

This technology will also assist us in determining which components of EFT are most effective. Clinical experience has shown that the 9 Gamut technique is very useful for early childhood trauma that predates the formation of memory. The emotional signatures of these traumas should show up in an MRI or MEG scan, and if EFT is able to treat them successfully, those emotional signatures will change. Some parts of EFT might prove less useful, based on MRI evidence, and might be refined.

I expect research to increasingly gather data using smartphones, tablets, and similar mobile devices. Your smartphone can now measure your blood pressure and heart rate, as well as administer psychological questionnaires. Properly organized, this is likely to make data gathering much easier.

We'll also use these devices to deliver EFT. Battle Tap is an online tapping coach that interacts with veterans wanting EFT sessions. They enter the name of their problem and their SUD score. Battle Tap composes a Setup Statement, pairs it with a video image of a veteran tapping for a similar emotion, such as anger, shame, or guilt, and guides them though a tapping session. They keep track of their progress using an online journal. Battle Tap is right on the home page of the Veterans Stress Project with a big "Tap Now" button so veterans can get help right away. It's a brilliant program, made possible entirely by people like you who have volunteered their time or donated their money.

An online EFT program called FibroClear is available for fibromyalgia patients (www.FibroClear.com). This approach could be customized for other problems such as depression, anxiety, and pain.

Research will also identify how best to implement EFT in various settings. If hospital patients receive a session when they check in, how do their symptoms change? If soldiers receive EFT the day they get back from deployment, are they less likely to get PTSD later? If motor vehicle accident victims get EFT in the ambulance, do their symptoms improve? If EFT is used throughout a school system, do test scores rise, does bullying go down, and does social bonding increase? Does EFT make people more resilient?

Group research will refine our knowledge of how to use EFT with dozens or perhaps hundreds or even thousands of people at one time. What's the optimal size for a group? Research can tell us.

Problems such as depression and pain are enormously costly. The U.S. government estimates that depression costs the economy $83 billion annually (National Institute of Mental Health, 2010). How are medical costs affected when levels of costly symptoms go down? Does a 60% decrease in depression result in a 60% drop in depression treatment costs? EFT holds the promise of making people much better physically and psychologically, and lowering the cost burden to society of medical treatment by hundreds of billions of dollars a year (Church, 2010a). Measuring the financial impact of implementing EFT will become a primary target of future research.

A World Without Trauma?

Let's put all the pieces of evidence found in this chapter together, and add the evidence from the rest of EFT research on PTSD, in order to paint a picture of what happens when EFT is applied to major psychological trauma:

- Veterans received EFT for PTSD. After six sessions, 86% no longer had PTSD symptoms. Overall symptoms levels dropped by 64%.

- In a hospital setting, patients with PTSD were effectively treated in four EFT sessions.

- In Haiti, 77 Catholic seminarians were trained in EFT. Beforehand, 64% had PTSD. Afterward, none of them tested positive for PTSD.

- Veterans with PTSD had large drops in symptoms after group therapy.

- In Rwanda, orphans who had suffered high levels of PTSD symptoms for most of their lives recovered fully or partially after EFT.

- When PTSD symptoms reduced, other psychological problems such as anxiety and depression also improved.

- Physical symptoms such as pain and those associated with TBI (traumatic brain injury) went down too, by over 40%.

- Clinical reports from a prison and from a drug-riddled city indicated the value of EFT.

- The PTSD symptoms of spouses decreased alongside their veteran partners.

- EFT was effective when delivered by life coaches as well as therapists.

- Telephone sessions remediated PTSD in 67% of veterans.

Taken together, this base of evidence presents us with the very real possibility that PTSD can be largely eliminated from society in time, just the way diseases such as cholera, typhoid, and polio were eliminated. This may seem like a pipe dream laced with fairy dust to most people right now. Yet so did the elimination of other diseases in earlier eras. Big social changes like the abolition of slavery or the emancipation of women seemed like impossible tasks when they were begun. Just a few people believed they were possible; the majority did not. Huge commercial interests were arrayed against reformers, like the cotton and sugar farmers who benefited from the slave trade. Yet against all odds, the reformers succeeded. Might you and I be the people who change the global reality of psychological trauma?

In my book *The Genie in Your Genes* (Church, 2009), I have chapters chronicling these big social and medical changes. One case history I use is that of typhoid fever in the city of New York. Sarah Josephine Baker was an American doctor prominent in New York in the late 19th century. Typhoid, induced by a strain of *Salmonella* bacteria, induces headaches, high fever, and often delirium. It hits children especially hard. In New York City where Dr. Baker practiced, more than a third of all deaths were among children under 1 year old, with typhoid being a primary culprit (Matyas & Haley-Oliphant, 1997). Baker chose medicine as a profession after her father died of typhoid fever when she was 16 years old. She began working for the New York Department of Health at the turn of the century.

She was very aware of the role that hygiene played in health. At a time when preventive medicine was virtually unknown, she organized school nurses to visit the homes of mothers with newborn babies to show them how to care for their children before they became sick. Baker also innovated by creating the first infant formula, by improving standards for the sanitary storage of milk, by teaching the siblings of young children to wash their hands, and standardizing the dispensing of medicine to newborns.

Dr. Baker was particularly interested in eradicating typhoid fever, the disease that had killed her father. A colleague of hers, George Soper, analyzed seven typhoid mini-epidemics that had occurred in family groups over the previous decade. The common denominator turned out to be that they all shared the same cook, an Irish immigrant named Mary Mallon. Baker went to the house of Mallon's current employer to collect samples for laboratory testing, but when she explained her errand, the cook slammed the door in her face. The next day, Baker returned with a police escort. Mallon fled the house, but Baker found footprints in the snow that led to a neighbor's closet in which Mary Mallon was hiding. She was found to be carrying massive amounts of the typhoid bacillus, though she herself was symptom free. At that time the germ theory of disease was relatively new, and not universally accepted. The phenomenon that a person might carry a disease without being affected by it was outside the realm of current medical knowledge.

For nearly 3 years, Mallon was treated at Willard Parker Hospital, but all efforts to eradicate the typhoid in her system failed. Eventually, she was released, with the understanding that she would no longer cook meals for others. Mallon broke her promise, however, and again began working as a cook. Her special dish was iced peaches, but her unsuspecting employers were consuming more than peaches, and fresh typhoid outbreaks were soon traced to her. After Dr. Baker found her again, she was confined for good.

Typhoid fever was soon eradicated in New York City and Dr. Baker's efforts became a model for other cities around the world. Yet she faced enormous opposition to her efforts from the medical hierarchy. In testimony before a congressional committee, a disgruntled doctor said, "If we're going to save the lives of all the women and children at public expense, what incentive will there be for a young man to go into medicine?" (O'Hern, 1985). When she helped form the Bureau of Child Hygiene, a group of 30 Brooklyn physicians wrote to the mayor to demand it be abolished, saying that, "it was ruining medical practice by its results in keeping babies well."

Many other medical innovations have faced similar resistance. Skeptics have opposed the adoption of virtually every medical advance, from hand-washing (Ignaz Semmelweiss in the 1840s) to PET scans (Michel Ter-Pogossian in the 1950s), sometimes at the expense of tens of thousands of lives. In a recent paper, clinical psychologist Gary Bakker says EFT has "an unsupported and implausible theoretical basis and claims in response of representing a 'pseudoscientific' movement" (Bakker, 2013). He goes so far as to advocate the halting of all research into EFT, saying, "Further research is highly unlikely to be scientifically productive." His perspective is that, even if the large body of research shows excellent outcomes for patients and clients suffering from pain, depression, anxiety, phobias, and PTSD, the studies are methodologically flawed (by his own *ad hoc* standards rather than those of the American Psychological Association) and should stop. Of course, research will not stop, and neither will the implementation of EFT in primary care. Eventually, the barriers to widespread adoption will crumble, and it will be widely adopted in many settings, just as Dr. Sarah Josephine Baker's scientific antityphoid techniques eventually triumphed over ignorance and superstition.

Imagine if we were to dedicate ourselves to a world without psychological trauma with the same passion that Dr. Baker brought to eradicating typhoid. Imagine if EFT were in every school classroom, in every prison, in every family, in every courtroom, in every hospital, in every conflict zone, in every government, in every country. Imagine if discord and conflict were addressed immediately in every family relationship, rather than being allowed to fester unhealed for years or decades. Imagine if every child had the tools to regulate their emotions, dissipating fear, pain, and anxiety as soon as they appeared, growing up a stranger to psychological trauma. Imagine if tapping were the norm in business, and it became commonplace to solve workplace conflicts and eliminate creative blocks using EFT. Imagine if EFT were used with every patient before every operation at every hospital, and doctors included tapping in their arsenal of tools with which to fight disease.

Research shows a massive drop in symptoms of trauma after tapping. Imagine a world where such a reduction affects everyone across the globe. Imagine everyone becoming much happier, unshackled from the emotional bondage that has kept them imprisoned in their past experiences. What we are as a species, the effect we as a species have on the global ecosystem, and the history of our future, would take a radically different and far more positive trajectory.

I believe we are at precisely such a moment in global history. As a species, we're about to embark on a journey of radical and discontinuous change. Freed of the habit of acting on the basis of our past psychological wounding, we're about to help our species liberate itself from its habit of suffering. Once that old pattern is broken, we go in an entirely new and unpredictable direction. We free up intelligence and creativity that was previously frozen in suffering, and make it available to create a positive future. I am thrilled that you have chosen to join me on this journey of liberation, and I look forward to living in the world we will create together.

* * *

Resources

- Project Light: ProjectLightRwanda.com
- Research: Research.EFTUniverse.com
- Tapping Circles: TappingCircles.EFTUniverse.com

Appendix A:
The Full Basic Recipe

There are as many versions of EFT as there are people. However, there is one version of EFT that has been validated in more than 20 clinical trials, so we know it works. These studies can be evaluated using criteria for "empirically validated therapies" published by the Clinical Psychology division of the American Psychological Association (Chambless et al., 1996; Chambless et al., 1998; Chambless & Hollon, 1998). According to these criteria, EFT is an evidence-based practice that is effective for anxiety, depression, phobias, and posttraumatic stress disorder or PTSD (Feinstein, 2012a). We call this evidence-based form Clinical EFT (Church, 2013a).

There is a long and a short version of the Basic Recipe used in Clinical EFT. The short Basic Recipe is the one used throughout this book, and it is very effective, as all those studies show. Yet it's also well worth learning the long form. It's called the Full Basic Recipe. The reason for learning the long form is that it includes additional techniques that are useful for difficult issues. Most of the time, all you'll need is the short form of the Basic Recipe. Occasionally, you'll find that you don't make much progress that way, and you'll need the procedures in the Full Basic Recipe. It includes tapping points on the fingers, as well as an eye movement protocol called the 9 Gamut Procedure.

Recent research shows that eye movements are closely linked to the brain's ability to process traumatic events (Ruden, 2005; Tym, Beaumont, & Lioulios, 2009). When a memory carries no emotional charge, you can move your eyes smoothly through your field of peripheral vision. But a traumatic memory interferes with smooth eye rotation, and the eyes skip around; it's almost as if the person doesn't want to "see" the traumatic memory again. When you use EFT's 9 Gamut Procedure, eye movements show you whether or not the traumatic memory has been resolved. It's also useful (a) when a client says he or she cannot remember a specific event, (b) when working with nonverbal, preverbal or pre-birth trauma, and (c) when working on a large number of traumatic events simultaneously, for instance with a client who was beaten frequently as a child. In these three cases, the 9 Gamut can produce startlingly good results where little else is effective. This makes it an extremely important tool in your EFT toolkit. There are 48 Clinical EFT methods, which you'll find listed at the EFTUniverse. com website and summarized at ClinicalEFT.com. Familiarity with all of them is why practitioners who use Clinical EFT are so effective with a variety of clients and conditions. Clinical EFT is the method taught in *The EFT Manual* (Church, 2013c).

There are four parts to the Full Basic Recipe: The Setup, the Sequence, the 9 Gamut, and a second application of the Sequence. Here's how they're put together.

Ingredient #1: The Setup

The Full Basic Recipe begins with the Setup Statement:

Even though I have this _____, I deeply and completely accept myself.

While reciting the Setup Statement, either tap on the Karate Chop point or massage your Sore Spot.

The Sore Spot (description follows) is not part of the shortcut EFT method described in this book, but it can be substituted for the Karate Chop point at the beginning of any EFT session. Here's how to find it.

The Sore Spot

There are two Sore Spots and it doesn't matter which one you use. They are located in the upper left and right portions of the chest.

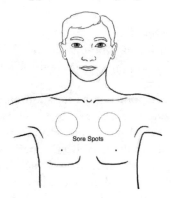

The Sore Spot.

Go to the base of the throat about where a man would knot his tie. Poke around in this area and you will find a U-shaped notch at the top of your sternum (breastbone). From the top of that notch go down 2 or 3 inches toward your navel and sideways 2 or 3 inches to your left (or right). You should now be in the upper left (or right) portion of your chest. If you press vigorously in that area (within a 2-inch radius) you will find a spot that feels sore or tender. This happens because lymphatic congestion occurs there. When you rub it, you disperse that congestion. Fortunately, after a few episodes, the congestion is all dispersed and the soreness goes away. Then you can rub it with no discomfort whatsoever.

I don't mean to overplay the soreness you may feel. You won't feel massive, intense pain by rubbing this Sore Spot. It is certainly bearable and should cause no undue discomfort. If it does, then lighten up your pressure a little.

Also, if you've had some kind of operation in that area of the chest or if there's any medical reason whatsoever why you shouldn't be probing around in that specific area, then *switch to the other side.* Both sides are equally effective. In any case, if there is any doubt, consult your health practitioner before proceeding or simply tap the Karate Chop point instead.

Ingredient #2: The Sequence

The Sequence involves tapping on the Eyebrow, Side of Eye, Under Eye, Under Nose, Chin, Collarbone, Under Arm, and Below Nipple points.

The **Below Nipple** point is a newer addition to the full sequence. It was originally left out because it's in an awkward position for women while in social situations (restaurants, etc.) as well as in workshops. Even though the EFT results have been superb without it, I include it now for completeness. For men, it is 1 inch below the nipple. For women, it's where the under-skin of the breast meets the chest wall. Some call it the "underwire" point on an underwire bra. This point is abbreviated **BN** for **B**elow **N**ipple.

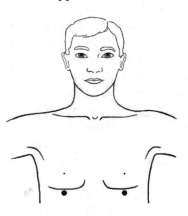

Below the Nipple (**BN**).

In addition, the Sequence in the Full Basic Recipe includes the following finger points:

Thumb (**Th**) Point.

Thumb: On the outside edge of your thumb at a point even with the base of the thumbnail. This point is abbreviated **Th** for **Th**umb.

The Index Finger (**IF**) Point.

Index Finger: On the side of your index finger (the side facing your thumb) at a point even with the base of the fingernail. This point is abbreviated **IF** for **I**ndex **F**inger.

The Middle Finger (**MF**) Point.

Middle Finger: On the side of your middle finger (the side closest to your thumb) at a point even with the base of the fingernail. This point is abbreviated **MF** for **M**iddle **F**inger.

The Baby Finger (**BF**) Point.

Baby Finger: On the inside of your baby finger (the side closest to your thumb) at a point even with the base of the fingernail. This point is abbreviated **BF** for **B**aby **F**inger.

You may have noticed that the Sequence does not include the ring finger. However, some include it for convenience, and this does not interfere with EFT's effectiveness.

The Karate Chop (**KC**) Point.

Karate Chop: The last point is the Karate Chop point, which can also be used at the beginning of the Setup.

Thus, the complete Sequence consists of the following EFT points, which are tapped while one repeats a Reminder Phrase that describes the problem, such as "This headache" or "This fear of heights."

EB = Beginning of the **E**ye**B**row

SE = **S**ide of the **E**ye

UE = **U**nder the **E**ye

UN = **U**nder the **N**ose

Ch = **Ch**in

CB = Beginning of the **C**ollar**B**one

UA = **U**nder the **A**rm

BN = **B**elow the **N**ipple

Th = **Th**umb

IF = **I**ndex **F**inger

MF = **M**iddle **F**inger

BF = **B**aby **F**inger

KC = **K**arate **C**hop

Ingredient #3: The 9 Gamut Procedure

The 9 Gamut Procedure is designed to engage parts of the brain involved in the resolution of trauma. It involves eye movements, humming, and counting. It's designed to engage both the left and right sides of the brain, through counting and music. Recent research has demonstrated a link between the processing of traumatic memories and the stability of peripheral vision, and the eye movements used in the 9 Gamut take advantage of these discoveries. Clinicians report that it is very useful in removing the emotional charge of very early trauma, such as events that occurred in the first few years of life, when there are no conscious memories accessible. The 9 Gamut is also useful for clearing the intensity of a large number of similar traumatic events simultaneously.

The 9 Gamut Procedure is a 10-second process in which nine "brain stimulating" actions are performed while you tap continuously on one of the body's energy points—the Gamut point. It has been found, after years of experience, that this routine can add efficiency to EFT and hasten your progress toward emotional freedom, especially when *sandwiched* between two trips through the Sequence.

One way to help memorize the Full Basic Recipe is to look at it as though it is a ham sandwich. The Setup is the preparation for the ham sandwich and the sandwich itself consists of two slices of bread (The Sequence) with the ham, or middle portion, as the 9 Gamut Procedure.

The Gamut Point.

To do the 9 Gamut Procedure, you must first locate the Gamut point. It is on the back of either hand and is a half inch behind the midpoint between the knuckles at the base of the ring finger and the little finger.

If you draw an imaginary line between the knuckles at the base of the ring finger and little finger and consider that line to be the base of an equilateral triangle whose other sides converge to a point (apex) in the direction of the wrist, then the Gamut point would be located at the apex of the triangle. With the index finger of your tapping hand, feel for a small indentation on the back of your tapped hand near the base of the little finger and ring finger. There is just enough room there to tap with the tips of your index and middle fingers.

Next, you must perform nine different steps while tapping the Gamut point continuously. These nine steps are:

1. Eyes closed.
2. Eyes open.
3. Eyes down hard right while holding the head steady.
4. Eyes down hard left while holding the head steady.
5. Roll the eyes in a circle as though your nose is at the center of a clock and you are trying to see all the numbers in order.
6. Roll the eyes in a circle in the reverse direction.
7. Hum two seconds of a song (I usually suggest "Happy Birthday").
8. Count rapidly from 1 to 5.
9. Hum two seconds of a song again.

Note that these nine actions are presented in a certain order and I suggest that you memorize them in the order given. However, you can mix the order up if you wish, as long as you do all nine of them *and* you perform the last three together as a unit. That is, you hum for two seconds, then count, then hum the song again, in that order. Years of experience have proven this to be important.

Also, note that for some people humming "Happy Birthday" causes resistance because it brings up memories of unhappy birthdays. In this case, you can either use EFT on those unhappy memories and resolve them or you can side-step this issue for now by substituting some other song.

Ingredient #4: The Sequence (again)

The fourth and last ingredient in the Basic Recipe is another trip through the Sequence, including the finger points.

As in the shortcut Basic Recipe, check for any remaining discomfort, in which case you'll do another round of EFT tapping using a modified Setup Statement:

Even though I still have some of this _____, I deeply and completely accept myself.

You will add "remaining" to the Reminder Phrases as you tap through the complete Sequence.

Appendix B:
Easy EFT

Now I would like to introduce you to a fast, effective, and effortless way to learn EFT. It's literally as easy as watching a video and tapping along with it. You can use one of the many Tap-Along videos at www. EFTUniverse.com for this purpose. Easy EFT is a three-step process that requires no training or experience with EFT.

1. Identify the issues.

First, write up a list of troublesome symptoms, self-improvement goals, and other problems, and rate the intensity of each on a scale of 0 to 10, with 0 being no emotional intensity, and 10 being maximum intensity. Here are some examples:

Shoulder pain: 7   Performance Stress: 5   Binge Eating: 9

You can also tap for specific events that bother you, such as:

I'm mad at my coworker who swore at me last week: 8
I'm upset that my daughter was held back from third grade by the principal: 7
I hate myself for giving in to that craving and eating a tub of ice cream: 9
When my mentor criticized me, I felt so hurt: 10

2. Tap along.

As you watch the video, tap along with the coach and client. You can pick one that closely matches your issue from the dozens available on EFTUniverse.com. Even if the issue in the Tap-Along Video isn't an exact match with yours, your brain is smart enough, and eager enough to heal, that it will associate your problem with the one you're witnessing.

3. Check your results.

Revisit your list of issues and write down their new 0-to-10 intensities. You should notice some improvement each time. The more sessions you tap along with, the better your results.

It's that simple! For the best results, review the *Questions and Answers* and *Helpful Tips* that follow.

Questions and Answers about Easy EFT

Q: How was Easy EFT discovered?

A: Therapists offering EFT to their clients began to report that their issues resolved as well. They would conduct sesssions with others and discover that an illness or phobia from which they'd previously suffered had disappeared.

We then began to put this phenomenon, called Borrowing Benefits, to an experimental test. We performed several studies, and found that just watching someone else's session while tapping along produced substantial reductions in anxiety, depression, phobias, and other psychological problems (Church & Brooks, 2010; Palmer-Hoffman & Brooks, 2011; Rowe, 2005).

Q: Why does Easy EFT work so well?

A: As you tap along with the real-life people featured on our videos, a part of your brain called the hippocampus finds similarities between your issues and the ones being addressed in the session. We also have "mirror neurons" in our brains that fire as we watch a similar experience being enacted by someone else. Mirror neurons mimic the other person's experience in our own brains.

Q: Can I really benefit from a session that deals with someone else's issue?

A: Yes. We're empathetically wired to other human beings; the ability to recognize and respond to the emotions of others is a valuable evolutionary skill. You needn't have the same experience to benefit. Just as you laugh or cry (have an emotional reaction) during a movie in which the characters are having experiences nothing like yours, your brain responds to the emotions of those you watch. You can tell if you are making progress by recording your SUD score regularly.

Q: What should I expect?

A: Your results may be dramatic improvement, incremental improvement, or no improvement. Studies suggest that substantial improvement, though not complete remission, is the norm.

Q: Are there any cautions regarding this process?

A: While Easy EFT is relatively gentle and most people experience benefits, you might feel emotional or physical stress. With EFT as with any other healing method, you should always consult your primary care provider in advance.

Helpful Tips for Getting the Most out of Easy EFT

Watch the Tap-Along videos at EFT Universe. This will acquaint you with the basic tapping points and make it easier for you to tap along.

- You do not have to read *The EFT Manual* (Church, 2013c) to benefit from Easy EFT.

- You may find that the EFT sessions vary the pace and order of the points tapped. Just follow along and don't worry about these variations.

- **At first, you may find the tapping pace in the sessions to be too fast for you to follow along.** That's okay, just do your best. The process can still help you even if you miss a tapping point here or there. Eventually, you will get used to the process and the pace will be easy to follow.

Give careful consideration to your list of issues and their 0-to-10 intensities because tracking your progress is essential to understanding the power of EFT.

- For your list, go back to childhood and write down a list of events that elicited negative emotions such as anger, guilt, and shame. Give each a SUD score of 0 to 10. Also list body sensations such as pain and score them the same way.

- If you can't find a 0-to-10 intensity, that's okay. Just estimate what the number should be. The mere fact that you remembered an issue means you have some sort of charge on it, though you might not be fully in touch with it.

- List as many issues as you want. This gives you an opportunity to determine if, as you tap on one, others diminish in intensity. The generalization effect can simulaneously reduce the charge around a number of events.

- Your list might look something like the spreadsheet below after a few tap-along sessions. This example is for illustration only and does not indicate what you should expect for the specific items listed. You might find the intensity of some issues dropping more rapidly than others.

Issue	Original 0-to-10	Session 1 0-to-10	Session 2 0-to-10	Session 3 0-to-10	Etc.
Fear of Heights	8	5	2	3	
Easily Angered	10	10	5	2	
Test Anxiety	7	7	5	7	
Knee Pain	9	2	0	0	
Digestion Problems	4	4	2	3	
Etc.					

Some of your results may be subtle and you may not notice them until later. You may also experience some pleasant "side benefits" and discover improvements that you weren't expecting. Here are some examples:

Uncle Joe's aggressive personality may no longer bother you.

You're no longer irritated by Aunt Peg's overbearing manner.

Your friends notice and comment on your reduced stress level.

You notice yourself scoring better at basketball.

Your insomnia is markedly improved.

You find yourself looking forward to each day's work.

Troublesome memories from your childhood may lose their sting.

Physical symptoms may improve.

Read your list of issues before each tap-along session just to remind your brain what you are working on. After that, put the list aside and just tap along and enjoy the session while Easy EFT goes to work.

Revisit your list after each tap-along session. Then go through each issue and carefully assess any changes in current intensity. Write them all down, even those that haven't changed. Then do another tap-along session and visit the list again.

Do your sessions on any schedule you like. You can do them daily, weekly, or at any time interval you choose. You can even do several per day or break them up so that you do a half session today and finish it tomorrow. It all depends on your schedule.

Work with a variety of Tap-Along Videos. There are many different issues represented in this collection, and you can experiment with a varied selection.

Make friends in the Weight Loss Discussion Group. You'll find many relevant topics in the discussion group at EFT Universe. You can ask your question and tap the rich vein of wisdom offered in the group.

Most important…have fun with it!

EFT doesn't have to be complicated, difficult, or totally serious. You'll find plenty to laugh about in our EFT books, at EFT workshops, and your own EFT sessions at home.

For books, classes, practitioners, tutorials, discussion groups, case histories, and Tap-Along videos, visit www.EFTUniverse.com. While there, download our free EFT starter kit, and sign up for our Weekly Health Report.

Appendix C: A Format Diagram for Using EFT

This diagram depicts a format, or flow, to use with EFT. It is a useful guide for knowing where you are in the process and becomes second nature after you have used it a few times.

BR = Basic Recipe; CBE = Collarbone Breathing Exercise.

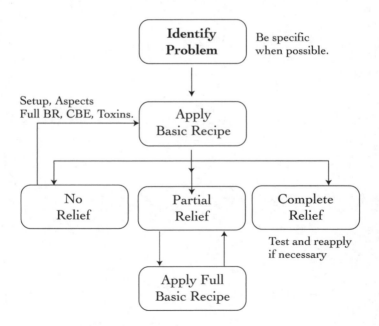

Appendix D:
The 48 Clinical EFT Techniques

One of the most common misconceptions about Emotional Freedom Techniques is the belief that EFT equals the acupoint tapping routine. Because EFT involves the very visible phenomenon of tapping with the fingertips on 12 acupressure points, it's easy to suppose that that single act is the main feature of EFT. Many people even use an incorrect name, "Emotional Freedom Technique" (singular), rather than the correct "techniques" (plural).

In fact, there are 48 distinct techniques that make up EFT, and the acupoint tapping routine is just one of those. Good EFT practitioners will use dozens of techniques, and when a particular technique is not producing results, switch to another. Here is a list of the core techniques in which certified Clinical EFT practitioners are trained, and where in this book you can find them.

A. Basic Recipe Techniques

1. Describing a Source of Emotional Distress. Ch 3
2. Obtaining a Rating for Subjective Units of Distress (SUD). Ch 3
3. Identifying Specific Events Linked to the Origin of the Problem. Ch 3

4. Creating a Setup Statement that Combines Exposure and Cognitive Shift. Ch 3

5. Focusing on the Negative First (Resisting the Urge to Caretake the Client Using Positives). Ch 6

6. Key Elements of a Reminder Phrase. Ch 3

7. Correcting for Secondary Gain and Psychological Reversal. Ch 3

8. Tapping 12 Prescribed Acupressure Points. Ch 3

9. Testing the Results. Ch 3

B. Foundational Techniques

10. The Movie Technique. Ch 3

11. The Tell the Story Technique. Ch 3

12. How to Handle Excessive Emotional Intensity. Ch 5

13. Finding Core Issues. Ch 7

14. Identifying the Writings on Your Walls. Ch 7

15. The Characteristics of Effective Affirmations. Ch 7

16. Identifying Tail-Enders. Ch 7

17. Daisy Chaining, and Tapping and Talking. Ch 7

18. The Generalization Effect: Identifying it, and Adjusting the Setup Statement. Ch 3

C. Techniques Used to Identify Target Issues

19. Identifying Aspects of the Problem. Ch 3

20. Identifying Different Categories of Aspects (Emotional, Physical, Visual, Cognitions). Ch 3

21. Shifting the Setup Statement as the Client Rapidly Shifts Aspects. Customized Setup Phrasing, and Flowing Setup Statements. Ch 7

D. The Gentle Techniques

22. The Tearless Trauma Technique. Ch 6

23. Chasing the Pain. Ch 6

24. Sneaking Up on the Problem. Ch 6

E. Techniques for Special Populations

25. Age-Appropriate Techniques for Using EFT with Children. Ch 8

26. Daily Releasing with Children. Ch 8

27. Borrowing Benefits. Ch 8

28. Working with Groups. Ch 8

29. EFT for Cravings and Addictions. Ch 8

30. Techniques for Multiple Phobias. Ch 8

31. EFT for Physical Symptoms: How the Approach Differs from EFT for Psychological Symptoms. Ch 8

32. Techniques to Use When Regular EFT Does Not Reduce SUD Level. Ch 8

F. Professional Practice Techniques

33. Reframing. Ch 9

34. Preframing. Ch 9

35. Techniques for Maintaining Client-Centered Focus. Ch 9

36. Identifying Tables and Legs. Ch 9

37. Techniques for Working on Your Own Issues. Ch 7

38. Maintaining Focus on Self-rating versus Observer-rating. Ch 9

39. Techniques for Becoming Extremely Specific. Ch 9

40. Additional Testing Methods. In Vivo Testing, Confrontive Questions. Ch 9

40. The Personal Peace Procedure. Ch 3

42. Cognitive Shifts and How to Identify Them, and the Role of Insight in EFT. Ch 6

43. Techniques to Apply When Self-acceptance Is the Problem. Ch 9

44. Telephone and Skype Delivery of EFT. Ch 5

G. Optional Physical Techniques

45. Additional Optional Tapping Points. Appendix A

46. Collarbone Breathing Exercise. Ch 9

47. The 9 Gamut Procedure, and When to Use It. Appendix A

48. The Floor to Ceiling Eye Roll. Ch 9

Appendix E: Acupuncture Meridians of the Frontal Torso

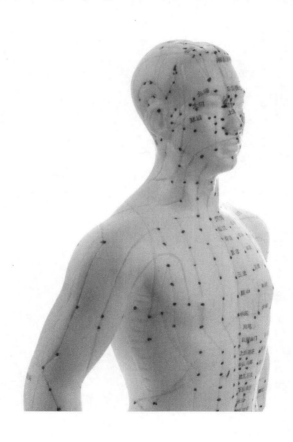

References

Adams, A., & Davidson, K. (2011). *EFT comprehensive training resource level 1.* Santa Rosa, CA: Energy Psychology Press.

American Psychiatric Association. (1994). *Diagnostic and statistical manual of mental disorders* (4th ed.). Washington, DC: Author.

American Psychological Association. (2009). *Publication manual of the American Psychological Association* (6th ed.). Washington, DC: Author.

Baker, A. H., & Siegel, M. A. (2010). Emotional Freedom Techniques (EFT) reduces intense fears: A partial replication and extension of Wells et al. *Energy Psychology: Theory, Research, and Treatment, 2*(2), 13–30. doi:10.9769.EPJ.2010.2.2.AHB

Bakker, G. M. (2013). The current status of energy psychology: Extraordinary claims with less than ordinary evidence. *Clinical Psychologist* (in press). doi: 10.1111/cp.12020

Bender, S. & Sise, M. (2007). *The energy of belief: Psychology's power tools to focus intention and release blocking beliefs.* Santa Rosa, CA: Energy Psychology Press.

Benedek, D. M., Friedman, M. J., Zatzick, D., & Ursano, R. J. (2009). Practice guideline for the treatment of patients with acute stress disorder and posttraumatic stress disorder. *Psychiatry Online.*
Retrieved from http://www.psychiatryonline.com/content.aspx?aid=156498

Benor, D. J., Ledger, K., Toussaint, L., Hett, G., & Zaccaro, D. (2009). Pilot study of Emotional Freedom Techniques, wholistic hybrid derived from Eye Movement Desensitization and Reprocessing and Emotional Freedom

Techniques, and cognitive behavioral therapy for treatment of test anxiety in university students. *Explore: The Journal of Science and Healing,* 5, 338–340. doi:10.1016/j.explore.2009.08.001

Blanchard, E. B., Jones-Alexander, J., Buckley, T. C., & Forneris, C. A. (1996). Psychometric properties of the PTSD Checklist (PCL). *Behaviour Research and Therapy, 34*(8), 669–673.

Blanton, B. (2005). *Radical honesty: How to transform your life by telling the truth.* Reston, VA: Sparrowhawk.

Blanton, B. (2011). *Some new kind of trailer trash.* Reston, VA: Sparrowhawk.

Bougea, A. M., Spandideas, N., Alexopoulos, E. C., Thomaides, T., Chrousos, G. P., & Darviri, C. (2013). Effect of the Emotional Freedom Technique on perceived stress, quality of life, and cortisol salivary levels in tension-type headache sufferers: A randomized controlled trial. Explore: *The Journal of Science and Healing, 9*(2), 91–99. doi:10.1016/j.explore.2012.12.005

Brattberg, G. (2008). Self-administered EFT (Emotional Freedom Techniques) in individuals with fibromyalgia: A randomized trial. *Integrative Medicine: A Clinician's Journal, 7*(4), 30–35.

Callahan, R. (1985). *Five minute phobia cure: Dr. Callahan's treatment for fears, phobias and self-sabotage.* Blair, NE: Enterprise.

Callahan, R. (2000). *Tapping the healer within: Using Thought Field Therapy to instantly conquer your fears, anxieties, and emotional distress.* New York, NY: McGraw-Hill.

Callahan, R. (2013). Thirty years of Thought Field Therapy. Retrieved from http://www.rogercallahan.com/news/30-years-of-thought-field-therapy/case-studies

Capacitar. (2013). Retrieved from http://capacitar.org/country.asp?CID=8&lang=1

Cardozo, B. L., Vergara, A., Agani, F., & Gotway, C. A. (2000). Mental health, social functioning, and attitudes of Kosovar Albanians following the war in Kosovo. *JAMA 284*(5), 569–577.

Carrington, P. (2000). *EFT choices training manual: Introducing the positive into EFT.* Mahwah, NJ: Pace Educational Systems.

Challis, G. B., & Stam, H. J. (1990). The spontaneous regression of cancer. A review of cases from 1900 to 1987. *Acta Oncologica 29*(5), 545–550.

Chambless, D., Baker, M. J., Baucom, D. H., Beutler, L. E., Calhoun, K. S., Crits-Christoph, P.,...Woody, S. R. (1998). Update on empirically validated therapies, II. *Clinical Psychologist, 51,* 3–16.

Chambless, D., & Hollon, S. D. (1998). Defining empirically supported therapies. *Journal of Consulting and Clinical Psychology, 66,* 7–18.

Chambless, D. L., Sanderson, W. C., Shoham, V., Bennett Johnson, S., Pope, K. S., Crits-Christoph, P.,…McCurry, C. (1996). An update on empirically validated therapies. *Clinical Psychologist, 49,* 5–18.

Cherkin, D. C., Sherman, K. J., & Avins, A. L. (2009). A randomized trial comparing acupuncture, simulated acupuncture, and usual care for chronic low back pain. *Archives of Internal Medicine, 169*(9), 858–866.

Church, D. (2009/2013). *The EFT mini-manual.* Santa Rosa, CA: Energy Psychology Press.

Church, D. (2009). *The genie in your genes.* Santa Rosa, CA: Energy Psychology Press.

Church, D. (2010a). The economic cost savings of energy psychology treatment. *Energy Psychology: Theory, Research, and Treatment, 2*(1), 9–12.

Church, D. (2010b). The treatment of combat trauma in veterans using EFT (Emotional Freedom Techniques): A pilot protocol. *Traumatology, 16*(1), 55–65. http://dx.doi.org/10.1177/1534765609347549

Church, D. (2013a). Clinical EFT as an evidence-based practice for the treatment of psychological and physiological conditions. *Psychology, 4*(8), 645–654.

Church, D. (2013b). *EFT for fibromyalgia and chronic fatigue.* Santa Rosa, CA: Energy Psychology Press.

Church, D. (2013c). *The EFT manual* (3rd ed.). Santa Rosa, CA: Energy Psychology Press.

Church, D. (2013d). *EFT for weight loss.* Santa Rosa, CA: Energy Psychology Press.

Church, D. (2014a). Clinical EFT (Emotional Freedom Techniques) as single session therapy: Research, indications, and cautions. In M. Hoyt & M. Talmon (Eds.), *Capturing the moment: Single-session therapy and walk-in services.* Bethel, CT: Crown House

Church, D. (2014b). *EFT for back pain.* Santa Rosa, CA: Energy Psychology Press.

Church, D. (2014c). *EFT for golf.* Santa Rosa, CA: Energy Psychology Press.

Church, D. (2014d). *EFT for PTSD.* Santa Rosa, CA: Energy Psychology Press.

Church, D. (2014e). Pain, depression, and anxiety after PTSD symptom remediation in veterans. Explore: *The Journal of Science and Healing* (in press).

Church, D., & Brooks, A. J. (2010). The effect of a brief EFT (Emotional Freedom Techniques) self-intervention on anxiety, depression, pain and cravings in healthcare workers. *Integrative Medicine: A Clinician's Journal, 9*(4), 40–44.

Church, D., & Brooks, A. J. (2013). The effect of EFT (Emotional Freedom Techniques) on psychological symptoms in addiction treatment: A pilot study. *International Journal of Scientific Research and Reports, 2*(2).

Church, D. & Brooks, A. J. (2014). CAM and energy psychology techniques remediate PTSD symptoms in veterans and spouses. Explore: *The Journal of Scientific Exploration* (in press).

Church, D., De Asis, M. A., & Brooks, A. J. (2012). Brief group intervention using EFT (Emotional Freedom Techniques) for depression in college students: A randomized controlled trial. *Depression Research and Treatment, 2012,* 1–7. doi:10.1155/2012/257172

Church, D., & Downs, D. (2012). Sports confidence and critical incident intensity after a brief application of Emotional Freedom Techniques: A pilot study. *Sport Journal, 15.*

Church, D., Geronilla, L., & Dinter, I. (2009). Psychological symptom change in veterans after six sessions of EFT (Emotional Freedom Techniques): An observational study. *International Journal of Healing and Caring, 9*(1).

Church, D., Hawk, C., Brooks, A., Toukolehto, O., Wren, M., Dinter, I., & Stein, P. (2013). Psychological trauma symptom improvement in veterans using EFT (Emotional Freedom Techniques): A randomized controlled trial. *Journal of Nervous and Mental Disease, 201,* 153–160.

Church, D., & Marohn, S. (Eds.). (2013). *The clinical EFT handbook: A definitive resource for practitioners, scholars, clinicians, and researchers.* Santa Rosa, CA: Energy Psychology Press.

Church, D., & Palmer-Hoffman, J. (2014). TBI symptoms improve after PTSD remediation with Emotional Freedom Techniques. *Traumatology* (in press).

Church, D., Piña, O., Reategui, C., & Brooks, A. (2012). Single session reduction of the intensity of traumatic memories in abused adolescents after EFT: A randomized controlled pilot study. *Traumatology, 18*(3), 73–79. doi:10.1177/1534765611426788

Church, D. & Wilde, N. (2013, May). Emotional eating and weight loss following Skinny Genes, a six week online program. Reported at the annual conference of the Association for Comprehensive Energy Psychology (ACEP), Reston, VA. Submitted for publication.

Connolly, S. M., & Sakai, C. (2011). Brief trauma intervention with Rwandan genocide survivors using Thought Field Therapy. *International Journal of Emergency
Mental Health, 13*(3), 161–172.

Connolly, S. M., Sakai, C. E., & Oas, P. (2010). Treatment of PTSD in Rwandan
child genocide survivors using Thought Field Therapy. *International Journal of
Emergency Mental Health, 12*(1), 41–50.

Craig, G. (2008/2010). *The EFT manual.* Santa Rosa, CA: Energy Psychology Press.

Craig, G., Bach, D., Groesbeck, G., & Benor, D. J. (2009). Emotional Freedom
Techniques (EFT) for traumatic brain injury. *International Journal of Healing
and Caring, 9*(2).

Craig, G., & Fowlie, A. (1995). *Emotional Freedom Techniques: The manual.* Sea
Ranch, CA: Gary Craig.

Craske, M. G., & Barlow, D. H. (1993). *Panic disorder and agoraphobia. Clinical
handbook of psychological disorders: A step-by-step treatment manual.* New York,
NY: Wiley.

Curioni, C. C., & Lourenco, P. M. (2005). Long-term weight loss after diet and exercise: A systematic review. *International Journal of Obesity, 29*(10), 1168–1174.

Diepold, J. H. (2000). Touch and Breathe: An alternative treatment approach with
meridian based psychotherapies. *Traumatology, 6*(2), 109–118.

Diepold, J. H., & Goldstein, D. (2008). Thought Field Therapy and qEEG changes
in the treatment of trauma: A case study. *Traumatology, 15*(1), 85–93. http://
dx.doi.org/10.1177/1534765608325304

Dispenza, J. (2013). *Breaking the habit of being yourself: How to lose your mind and
create a new one.* Carlsbad, CA: Hay House.

Ecker, B., Ticic, R., & Hulley, L. (2012). *Unlocking the emotional brain: Eliminating
symptoms at their roots using memory reconsolidation.* New York, NY: Routledge.

Eden, D. (2012). *The little book of energy medicine.* New York, NY: Tarcher Penguin.

Fang, J., Jin, Z., Wang, Y., Li, K., Kong, J., Nixon, E. E.,…Hui, K. K.-S. (2009).
The salient characteristics of the central effects of acupuncture needling:
Limbic-paralimbic-neocortical network modulation. *Human Brain Mapping,
30,* 1196–1206. doi:10.1002/hbm.20583

Fehmi, L., & Robbins, J. (2010). *Dissolving pain: Simple brain-training exercises for
overcoming chronic pain.* Boston, MA: Trumpeter.

Feinstein, D. (2008). Energy psychology: A review of the preliminary evidence.
Psychotherapy: Theory, Research, Practice, Training, 45(2), 199.

Feinstein, D. (2010). Controversies in energy psychology. *Energy Psychology: Theory, Research, and Treatment, 1*(1), 45–56.

Feinstein, D. (2011). *Ethics handbook for energy healing practitioners: A guide for the professional practice of energy medicine and energy psychology.* Fulton, CA: Energy Psychology Press.

Feinstein, D. (2012a). Acupoint stimulation in treating psychological disorders: Evidence of efficacy. *Review of General Psychology, 16,* 364–380. doi:10.1037/a0028602

Feinstein, D. (2012b). Energy psychology treatments over a distance: The curious phenomenon of "surrogate tapping" *Energy Psychology: Theory, Research, and Treatment, 5*(1), 42–53. doi:10.9769.EPJ.2013.5.1.DF

Gallo, F. P. (2000). *Energy diagnostic and treatment methods.* New York, NY: Norton.

Gallup. (2013). *State of the American workplace: 2010–2012.* Washington, DC: Gallup.

Geronilla, L., McWilliams, M., Clond, M., & Palmer-Hoffman, J. (2014). EFT (Emotional Freedom Techniques) remediates PTSD and psychological symptoms in veterans: A randomized controlled replication trial. Presented at Grand Rounds, Fort Hood, Texas, April 17. Submitted for publication.

Goodheart, G. (1991). *Applied kinesiology.* Gaylord, MI: Touch for Health

Google Trends. (2013). Retrieved from http://www.google.com/trends/explore#q=eft&tapping&cmpt=q

Gottschalk, A., & Flocke, S, (2005). Time spent in face-to-face patient care and work outside the examination room. *Annals of Family Medicine, 3*(6), 488-493.

Greenberg, G., & Rosenheck, R. (2009). Mental health and other risk factors for jail incarceration among male veterans. *Psychiatric Quarterly, 80*(1), 41–53. doi:10.1007/s11126-009-9092-8

Grossman, L. C. D., & DeGaetano, G. (2009). *Stop teaching our kids to kill: A call to action against TV, movie, and video game violence.* New York, NY: Random House Digital.

Gurret, J-M., Caufour, C., Palmer-Hoffman, J., & Church, D. (2012). post-earthquake rehabilitation of clinical PTSD in Haitian seminarians. *Energy Psychology: Theory, Research, and Treatment, 4*(2), 33–40.

Harris, R. E., Zubieta, J. K., Scott, D. J., Napadow, V., Gracely, R. H., & Clauw, D. J. (2009). Traditional Chinese acupuncture and placebo (sham) acupuncture are differentiated by their effects on μ-opioid receptors (MORs). *Neuroimage, 47*(3), 1077–1085.

Hartung, J., & Stein, P. (2012). Telephone delivery of EFT (Emotional Freedom Techniques) remediates PTSD symptoms in veterans: A randomized controlled trial. *Energy Psychology: Theory, Research, and Treatment, 4*(1), 33–42. doi:10.9769.EPJ.2012.4.1.JH

Hendricks, H. (1993). *Keeping the love you find: A personal guide.* New York, NY: Atria.

Hill, N. (1966). *Think and grow rich.* New York, NY: Hawthorn Books.

Hodge, P. M., & Jurgens, C. Y. (2010). A pilot study of the effects of Emotional Freedom Techniques in psoriasis. *Energy Psychology: Theory, Research, and Treatment, 3*(2), 13–24.

Horowitz, M., Wilner, N., & Alvarez, W. (1979). Impact of Event Scale: A measure of subjective stress. *Psychosomatic medicine, 41*(3), 209–218.

Hover-Kramer, D. (2011). *Creating healing relationships: Professional standards for energy therapy practitioners.* Santa Rosa, CA: Energy Psychology Press.

Howard, J. (2014) *EFT for sports performance.* Santa Rosa, CA: Energy Psychology Press.

Hui, K. K. S., Liu, J., Marina, O., Napadow, V., Haselgrove, C., Kwong, K. K.,… Makris, N. (2005). The integrated response of the human cerebro-cerebellar and limbic systems to acupuncture stimulation at ST 36 as evidenced by fMRI. *NeuroImage, 27,* 479–496.

Hurley, A. D. (2004). Treatment of multiple phobias and agoraphobia in a man with Down syndrome. *Mental Health Aspects of Developmental Disabilities, 7*(4), 143–147.

Institute of Medicine, Committee on Treatment of Posttraumatic Stress Disorder. (2007). *Treatment of posttraumatic stress disorder: An assessment of the evidence.* Washington DC: Institute of Medicine. Retrieved from http://www.nap.edu/catalog/11955.html

Jain, S., & Rubino, A. (2012). The effectiveness of Emotional Freedom Techniques (EFT) for optimal test performance: A randomized controlled trial. *Energy Psychology: Theory, Research, and Treatment, 4*(2), 13–24. doi:10.9769.EPJ.2012.4.2.SJ

Jemal, A., Bray, F., Center, M. M., Ferlay, J., Ward, E., & Forman, D. (2011). Global cancer statistics. *CA: A Cancer Journal for Clinicians, 61,* 69–90. doi: 10.3322/caac.20107

Johnson, D. R., Fontana, A., Lubin, H., Corn, B., & Rosenheck, R. A. (2004). Long-term course of treatment-seeking Vietnam veterans with posttraumatic stress disorder: Mortality, clinical condition, and life satisfaction. *Journal of Nervous and Mental Disease, 192,* 35–41.

Jones, S., Thornton, J., & Andrews, H. (2011). Efficacy of EFT in reducing public speaking anxiety: A randomized controlled trial. *Energy Psychology: Theory, Research, and Treatment, 3*(1), 19–32. doi:10.9769.EPJ.2011.3.1.SJ

Kandel, E. R. (1999). Biology and the future of psychoanalysis: A new intellectual framework for psychiatry revisited. *American Journal of Psychiatry, 156*(4), 505–524.

Karatzias, T., Power, K., Brown, K., McGoldrick, T., Begum, M., Young, J.,… Adams, S. (2011). A controlled comparison of the effectiveness and efficiency of two psychological therapies for posttraumatic stress disorder: Eye Movement Desensitization and Reprocessing vs. Emotional Freedom Techniques. *Journal of Nervous and Mental Disease, 199*(6), 372–378. doi:10.1097/NMD.0b013e31821cd262

Lake, D. (2013). EFT in an integrative medicine practice. In D. Church & S. Marohn (Eds.), *The clinical EFT handbook: A definitive resource for practitioners, scholars, clinicians, and researchers* (Vol. 1). Santa Rosa, CA: Energy Psychology Press.

Lambrou, P. T., Pratt, G. J., & Chevalier, G. (2003). Physiological and psychological effects of a mind/body therapy on claustrophobia. *Subtle Energies and Energy Medicine, 14,* 239–251.

Lane, J. (2009). The neurochemistry of counterconditioning: Acupressure desensitization in psychotherapy. *Energy Psychology: Theory, Research, and Treatment, 1*(1), 31–44.

Lipton, B. H. (2008). *The biology of belief: Unleashing the power of consciousness, matter, and miracles.* Carlsbad, CA: Hay House.

Llewellyn-Edwards, T., & Llewellyn-Edwards, M. (2012). The effect of Emotional Freedom Techniques (EFT) on soccer performance. *Fidelity: Journal for the National Council of Psychotherapy, 47,* 14–21.

Lubin, H., & Schneider, T. (2009). Change is possible: EFT (Emotional Freedom Techniques) with life-sentence and veteran prisoners at San Quentin State Prison. *Energy Psychology: Theory, Research, and Treatment, 1*(1), 83–33.

Maguire, E. A., Frackowiak, R. S., & Frith, C. D. (1997). Recalling routes around London: Activation of the right hippocampus in taxi drivers. *Journal of Neuroscience, 17*(18), 7103–7110.

Matyas, M. M., & Haley-Oliphant, A. E. (1997). *Women life scientists: Past, present, and future.* Bethesda, MD: American Physiological Society.

Mayo Clinic. (2013). Fibromyalgia: Definition. Retrieved from http://www.mayo-clinic.com/health/fibromyalgia/DS00079

McCallion, F. (2012). Emotional Freedom Techniques for dyslexia. *Energy Psychology: Theory, Research, and Treatment, 4*(2), 35–46.

McFarlane, A. C., & Van der Kolk, B. (1996/2007). Trauma and its challenge to society. In B. A. van der Kolk, A. C. McFarlane, & L. Weisaeth (Eds.), *Traumatic stress: The effects of overwhelming experience on mind, body, and society* (pp. 24–46). New York, NY: Guilford.

McGowan, P. O., Sasaki, A., D'Alessio, A. C., Dymov, S., Labonté, B., Szyf, M., Turecki, G., & Meaney, M. J. (2009, March). Epigenetic regulation of the glucocorticoid receptor in human brain associates with childhood abuse. *Nature Neuroscience, 12*(3), 342–348. doi:10.1038/nn.2270

Napadow, V., Kettner, N., Liu, J., Li, M., Kwong, K. K., Vangel, M., …Hui, K. K. (2007) Hypothalamus and amygdala response to acupuncture stimuli in carpal tunnel syndrome. *Pain, 130*(3), 254–266.

National Institute of Mental Health. (2010). *The numbers count: Mental disorders in America.* Retrieved from http://www.nimh.nih.gov/health/publications/the-numbers-count-mental-disorders-in-america/index.shtml

National Institutes of Health. (2008). *Depression.* Washington, DC: National Institutes of Health, Publication #08 3561.

National Institutes of Health. (2009). *Fibromyalgia.* Washington, DC: National Institutes of Health. Retrieved from http://www.ncbi.nlm.nih.gov/pubmed-health/PMH0001463

Nelson, B. S., & Wright, D. W. (1996). Understanding and treating PTSD symptoms in female partners of veterans with PTSD. *Journal of Marital and Family Therapy, 22*(4), 455–467. doi:10.1111/j.1752-0606.1996.tb00220.x

Nemiro, A. (2013, May). EFT vs CBT in the treatment of sexual gender based violence in the Democratic Republic of the Congo. Presented at the conference of the Association for Comprehensive Energy Psychology (ACEP), San Diego, CA.

Nickerson, R. S. (1998). Confirmation bias: A ubiquitous phenomenon in many guises. *Review of General Psychology, 2*(2), 175.

O'Hern, E. M. (1985). *Profiles of pioneer women scientists*. New York, NY: Acropolis Books.

Orcutt, H. K., King, L. A., & King, D. W. (2003). Male-perpetrated violence among Vietnam veteran couples: Relationships with veteran's early life characteristics, trauma history, and PTSD symptomatology. *Journal of Traumatic Stress, 16*(4), 381–390.

Oschman, J. (2000). *Energy medicine: The scientific basis*. London: Churchill Livingstone.

Oschman, J. (2003). *Energy medicine in therapeutics and human performance*. London: Butterworth Heinemann.

Ozer, E. J., Best, S. R., Lipsey, T. L., & Weiss, D. S. (2008). Predictors of post-traumatic stress disorder and symptoms in adults: A meta-analysis. *Psychological Trauma: Theory, Research, Practice, and Policy, 5*(1), 3–36.

Palmer-Hoffman, J., & Brooks, A. J. (2011). Psychological symptom change after group application of Emotional Freedom Techniques (EFT). *Energy Psychology: Theory, Research, and Treatment, 3*(1), 33–38. doi:10.9769.EPJ.2011.3.1.JPH

Pasahow, R., Callahan, R., Callahan, J., & Rapp, D. (2014). Enhancing the efficacy of energy psychology psychotherapies by neutralizing individual energy toxins. *Energy Psychology: Theory, Research, and Treatment, 5*(1), 45–57.

Qouta, S., Punamäki, R. L., & El Sarraj, E. (2003). Prevalence and determinants of PTSD among Palestinian children exposed to military violence. *European Child and Adolescent Psychiatry, 12*(6), 265–272.

Reich, W. (1927). *Die Funktion des Orgasmus: Zur Psychopathologie und zur Soziologie des Geschlechtslebens,* Vienna, Austria: Internationaler Psychoanalytischer Verlag.

Rogers, C. R. (1957). The necessary and sufficient conditions of therapeutic personality change. *Journal of Consulting Psychology, 21*(2), 95.

Rossi, E. L. (2002). *The psychobiology of gene expression: Neuroscience and neurogenesis in hypnosis and the healing arts*. New York, NY: Norton.

Rowe, J. E. (2005). The effects of EFT on long-term psychological symptoms. *Counseling and Clinical Psychology, 2,* 104–111.

Ruden, R. A. (2005). A neurological basis for the observed peripheral sensory modulation of emotional responses. *Traumatology, 11,* 145–158. doi: 10.1177/153476560501100301

Salas, M. M., Brooks, A. J., & Rowe, J. E. (2011). The immediate effect of a brief energy psychology intervention (Emotional Freedom Techniques) on specific phobias: A pilot study. *Explore: The Journal of Science and Healing, 7*(3), 255–260.

Scaer, R. C. (2007). *The body bears the burden: Trauma, dissociation, and disease* (2nd Ed.). New York, NY: Routledge.

Scaer, R. C. (2012). The dissociation capsule. Retrieved from http://www.trauma-soma.com/excerpt1.html

Seal, K. H., Maguen, S., Cohen, B., Gima, K. S., Metzler, T. J., Ren, L., Bertenthal, D., & Marmar, C. R. (2010). VA mental health services utilization in Iraq and Afghanistan veterans in the first year of receiving new mental health diagnoses. *Journal of Traumatic Stress, 23*(1), 5–16.

Sezgin, N., & Özcan, B. (2009). The effect of progressive muscular relaxation and Emotional Freedom Techniques on test anxiety in high school students: A randomized controlled trial. *Energy Psychology: Theory, Research, and Treatment, 1*(1), 23–30. doi:10.9769.EPJ.2009.1.1.NS

Shapiro, F. (1989). Efficacy of the eye movement desensitization procedure in the treatment of traumatic memories. *Journal of Traumatic Stress, 2*(2), 199–223.

Shealy, C. N., & Church, D. (2013). *Soul medicine.* Santa Rosa, CA: Energy Psychology Press.

Sheldrake, R. (2013). *Science set free: Ten paths to new discovery.* New York, NY: Chopra.

Stanley, E. A. & Jha, A. P. (2009). Mind fitness and mental armor: Enhancing performance and building warrior resilience. *Joint Force Quarterly, 55,* 144-151.

Stapleton, P., Church, D., Sheldon, T., Porter, B., & Carlopio, C. (2013). Depression symptoms improve after successful weight loss with EFT (Emotional Freedom Techniques): A randomized controlled trial. *ISRN Psychiatry* (in press).

Stapleton, P., Sheldon, T., & Porter, B. (2012). Clinical benefits of Emotional Freedom Techniques on food cravings at 12-months follow-up: A randomized controlled trial. *Energy Psychology: Theory, Research, and Treatment, 4*(1), 13–24.

Stone, B., Leyden, L., & Fellows, B. (2009a). Energy psychology treatment for orphan heads of households in Rwanda: An observational study. *Energy Psychology: Theory, Research, and Treatment, 2*(2), 73–82. doi:10.9769.EPJ.2010.2.2.BS

Stone, B., Leyden, L., & Fellows, B. (2009b). Energy psychology treatment for posttraumatic stress in genocide survivors in a Rwandan orphanage: A pilot investigation. *Energy Psychology: Theory, Research, and Treatment, 1*(1), 73–82. doi:10.9769.EPJ.2009.1.1.BS

Sutton, L. K. (2013, October). Homeward bound—guiding our veterans all the way home: Equipping communities to serve as the front lines of hope & healing. Presented October 19 at Veterans, Trauma and Treatment conference at Omega Institute, Rhinebeck, NY.

Swingle, P. (2010). EFT in the neurotherapeutic treatment of seizure disorders. *Energy Psychology: Theory, Research, and Treatment, 2*(1), 27–38.

Swingle, P. G., Pulos, L., & Swingle, M. K. (2004). Neurophysiological indicators of EFT treatment of posttraumatic stress. *Subtle Energies and Energy Medicine, 15*(1), 75–86.

Tanielian, T. L., & Jaycox, L. H. (Eds.). (2008). *Invisible wounds of war: Psychological and cognitive injuries, their consequences, and services to assist recovery.* Santa Monica, CA: Rand.

Taylor, M., Carlson, S. M., Maring, B. L., Gerow, L., & Charley, C. M. (2004). The characteristics and correlates of fantasy in school-age children: Imaginary companions, impersonation, and social understanding. *Developmental Psychology, 40*(6), 1173.

Tedeschi, R. G., & Calhoun, L. G. (2004). Posttraumatic growth: Conceptual foundations and empirical evidence. *Psychological inquiry, 15*(1), 1–18.

Traffic Estimate. (2013). Retrieved from http://www.trafficestimate.com/eft.mercola.com

TREST Aid. (2013). Trauma Relief and Emotional Support Techniques. Retrieved from http://www.trestaid.com

Tronick, E., Als, H., Adamson, L., Wise, S., & Brazelton, T. B. (1979). The infant's response to entrapment between contradictory messages in face-to-face interaction. *Journal of the American Academy of Child Psychiatry, 17*(1), 1–13.

Tronick, E. Z. (1989). Emotions and emotional communication in infants. *American Psychologist, 44*(2), 112.

Tym, R., Beaumont, P., & Lioulios, T. (2009). Two persisting pathophysiological visual phenomena following psychological trauma and their elimination with rapid eye movements: A possible refinement of construct PTSD and its visual state marker. *Traumatology, 15*(3), 23–33.

U.S. Department of Health and Human Services. (2012). *Child maltreatment 2011.* Washington, DC: Administration for Children and Families, Administration on Children, Youth and Families, Children's Bureau. Retrieved from http://www.acf.hhs.gov

Vasterling, J. J., & Brewin, C. R. (Eds.). (2005). *Neuropsychology of PTSD: Biological, cognitive, and clinical perspectives.* New York, NY: Guilford Press.

Veterans Stress Project. (2013). Retrieved from http://stressproject.org

Wells, S., Polglase, K., Andrews, H. B., Carrington, P., & Baker, A. H. (2003). Evaluation of a meridian-based intervention, Emotional Freedom Techniques (EFT), for reducing specific phobias of small animals. *Journal of Clinical Psychology, 59,* 943–966. doi:10.1002/jclp.10189

Whitaker, R. (2011). *Anatomy of an epidemic: Magic bullets, psychiatric drugs, and the astonishing rise of mental illness in America.* New York, NY: Random House.

Wise, A. (2002). *Awakening the mind: A guide to harnessing the power of your brainwaves.* New York, NY: Tarcher.

Wolpe, J. (1958). *Psychotherapy by reciprocal inhibition.* Palo Alto, CA: Stanford University Press.

Index

9 Gamut Procedure, 87, 190, 285, 329–330, 335, 350
    eye movements, 335

A

abuse, childhood, 103, 183, 200
acupoints, xvi, 73
acupuncture, xi, 59, 62, 84, 148
addiction, 251–252
    treatment of, 50, 349
affirmation, 89, 170, 201, 214, 217, 348
allergens, 291
Alzheimer's, 122
American Psychological Association (APA), xix–xxi, 327, 329
anxiety, 30, 68, 74, 267, 289
Apex Effect, 223–227
archive of EFT, xxii
arthritis, rheumatoid, 53
aspects, tapping on, 100, 227–228, 258, 283–285, 290, 348
aspirin, 80

B

Baker, Harvey, 64
Baker, Sarah Josephine, 325
Bakker, Gary, 327
Basic Recipe, xviii, 77, 85–86, 241, 272
Battle Tap, 323
Becker, Robert, 62
behavioral psychology, 75
Berger, Hans, 61
Blanton, Brad, 198
Bly, Robert, 189
body location, 86
Borrowing Benefits, 69–71, 247–249, 340, 349
brain, 76
    waves, 57
Brattberg, Gunilla, 38, 69
business, and EFT, 266–267

C

Callahan, Roger, xvii, 78, 223, 251, 291

cancer, 295
Carrington, Patricia, 230
case histories, 301
catastrophizing, 196, 259, 296
Caufour, Claudie, 313
Chasing the Pain, *see also* Gentle
    Techniques, 178, 199–200, 290,
    299, 349
child, like a, 221
children, working with, 86, 91, 120,
    241, 244, 246, 349
    daily releasing, 243, 349
    high school, 243
    self-esteem, 182
    television-watching, 245
childhood event, 102, 289
    guessing, 102, 295
Choices Method, 230–231
chronic fatigue syndrome (CFS),
    34, 38
clichés, 196, 212–214
client-centered focus, 270, 349
client reports feeling worse, 287
Clinical EFT, xvi, xix, xxii, 47, 71, 81,
    84, 87, 113, 160, 183, 208, 234,
    241, 288, 329–330, 347
coaching, 300, 302
cognitive behavior therapy (CBT), xvi,
    65, 75, 79, 87
cognitive frame, 183
cognitive reframe, 59
cognitive shift, 185–186, 348, 350
Collarbone Breathing Exercise,
    275, 350
conditioned responses, 59
confidence, 267
confirmation bias, 212
confrontive questions, 286, 349
continuing education/continuing med-
    ical education (CE/CME), 161

control groups, 70
core beliefs, 196, 209, 211–212, 282
core issues, 101, 208, 348
cortisol, 73
counterconditioning, 74
Craig, Gary, xvii
cravings, 132, 251, 349
    alcohol, 251
    chocolate, 251
    sweets, 251
Create Global Healing (CGH), 309
customized setup phrasing, 228, 348

D
Daily Peace Procedure,
    for children, 245
daisy chaining, 218–220, 261, 348
Defense Center for Excellence, 203
dehydroepiendrosterone (DHEA), 56
Department of Veterans Affairs, 306
depression, 30, 69, 74, 323
diabetes, 45
diagnosis, 158
    mental health conditions, 158
Diamond, John, xvii
Discovery Statement, 80
disease,
    lifestyle, 295
    serious, 295–296
Dispenza, Joe, 207
dissociation, 175, 188, 190–191, 193,
    259, 287
dissociative capsule, 183
domestic violence, 121
doorknob effect, 202
Downs, Darlene, 267
drug trade, 317

E
Easy EFT, 339
EEG, 84

EFT,
    explaining, 162
    for emotional trauma, 45
    for families, 118
    for pain, 42
    limitation of, 50
    research, 43, 53, 81
    stress reduction, 45
    surrogate, 355
    variants, xix
EFT Global, 317, 321
EFT on a Page, 374
ego, 51, 168–169
Einthoven, Willem, 61
electromagnetic fields, 61
emergencies, 129
emotional,
    eating, 133
    experience, 294
    intensity, excessive, 195, 348
    overwhelm, 163
    trauma, 76–77, 177, 252
empiracally validated treatment,
    xx, 329
energy fields, 62
energy psychology, xvii
energy toxins, 291
epigenetic signals, 56, 80
Erickson, Milton, 278
ethical issues, 243, 301
evidence-based treatments, xxi
expectations, 180
exposure therapy, xvi, 59, 75, 77–78,
    87, 96, 113, 231, 348
Eye Movement Desensitization and
    Reprocessing (EMDR), 65

F
Facebook, EFT Universe, 114
fear, *see also* phobias, 24

response, 62
Feinstein, David, 226, 242, 304
FibroClear, 39
fibromyalgia, 36, 38, 69, 93, 225, 297,
    200, 323
fight-or-flight, 56–57, 73, 75, 84
first aid, and EFT, 130
Flexner Report, 61
floor to ceiling eye roll, 276, 350
follow-up studies, 72
forums, 173
Frank, Alina, 198
Freud, Sigmund, 28, 273
Full Basic Recipe, xviii, 87, 275,
    329, 335
future research, 322
    through smartphones, 322

G
Gallo, Fred, xvii
Gamut point, 336
generalization effect, 100, 103, 154,
    222–223, 254, 280, 348
genes, 73
Gentle Techniques, xviii, 155,
    177–178, 190, 196
    Chasing the Pain, 178, 199–200,
        290, 299, 349
    Sneaking Up on the Problem,
        178, 196, 349
    Tearless Trauma, 178, 349
Gestalt therapy, 198, 200
Golden Rule, 169
Goodheart, George, xvii
Google, and EFT, xv, 81
groups, working with, 249, 349
Grof, Stanislav, 273
Gurret, Jean-Michel, 313
Gurwitsch, Alexander, 62

H

Haiti, 313, 316
    orphaned children, 313–314
headaches, 43
health, affirming, 215
Health Care Workers Study, 251
highly traumatized populations, 304
Hill, Napoleon, 216
hippocampus, 76, 103
hopelessness, 196
hormonal system, 73
humanitarian work, 114, 303, 321
    volunteering, 321
humor, using, 299
hypothalamus, 56

I

IEGs, 58, 74
imaginary event, 211
imagination, using, 153
imago therapy, 233
immediate early genes (IEGs), 56
in vivo testing, 286, 349
infants, working with, 242, 246
insight, 273, 350
Institute of Medicine (IOM), 78
intensifying problem, 259

J

journal, personal, 235
Jung, Carl, 189, 288

K

Kandel, Eric, 76
Karate Chop point, 93, 97, 330

L

Lake, David, 251
Leyden, Lori, 309, 316
limbic system, 55, 58, 62, 73, 103

limiting beliefs, 237
Llewellyn-Edwards,
    Tam and Mary, 266
long-term effects, 157
Look, Carol, 224, 230, 250
Lubin, Hari, 319

M

MacKay, David, 317
magnetic resonance imaging
    (MRI), 61
magnetoencephalogram (MEG), 61
massive reversal, 292
Mayo Clinic, 38, 54
McWilliams, Marilyn, 306
medical costs, 323
medical innovations, 327
meditation, 143, 169, 234, 244
meetups and hangouts, 172
memories, childhood, 68
memory,
    lack of, 49
    neutralization, of, 101
    traumatic, 61, 79, 188
memory reconsolidation, 46–47
meridians, xvi
microcurrents, 62
Middleton, Tracey, 181, 222
mirror neurons, 340
money, and EFT, 137, 140, 215
Movie Technique, 104, 188, 192,
    199, 348
muscle testng, 79

N

National Health Service (NHS), 65
National Institute for Integrative
    Health Care, 306, 317, 321–322
National Institutes of Health (NIH),
    38, 78

natural disasters and EFT, xv
negative,
    cognitions, 196
    emotion, 220, 288
    experience, 117, 244
    influence, 297
neural plasticity, 76–77, 80, 203
neuronal pathways, 219
newsletter, EFT Universe, 114

O
one-minute wonders, 255, 295
online delivery of EFT, 42, 69
Oregon State University, 72, 266
Ortner, Jessica, 226
Ortner, Nick, 226, 304, 309
outcome studies, 72
overconfidence, and EFT, 168

P
pain, 69, 81, 128, 199, 226, 255
pain, neck, 60
panacea, 49
panic attack, *see also* anxiety, 205
Pavlov, Ivan, 28, 74
peak performers, 72
peer-reviewed journals, 63
perceived threat to survival, 179
perfectionism, 280, 284
Perls, Fritz, 198, 200
persistence, 236, 295
Personal Peace Procedure, 109–110,
    234, 298, 349
phobias, *see also* fear, 24, 253, 349
    water, 78
physical symptoms, 34, 124, 156,
    255, 257, 294, 297, 349
physicians using EFT, 41, 83,
    128, 166
physiological mechanisms, 62

pituitary, 56
placebo, 72
positive thinking, 90, 170
posttraumatic growth, 203–204
posttraumatic stress disorder (PTSD),
    24, 29, 49, 64, 68, 71–72,
    77–78, 92, 203–204, 223, 247,
    302, 305, 316, 324–325
powerlessness, 180
practitioners, certified, 113, 158,
    234–235, 253, 269, 278, 281,
    287, 304, 314
preframing, 277, 349
prescribed medication, and EFT, 166
primary care, 327
professional records, 301
professional standards, 300
psoriasis, 43
psychological reversal, 88, 92–93,
    293, 348
psychotherapy, 165, 233, 244,
    247, 273
    session, 200, 231

R
referring clients, 302
reframes, xv, 276–277, 349
Reich, Wilhelm, xvi
Reminder Phrase, 96, 348
resilience, 203
resistance, 196–197
right words, finding, 147
Rogers, Carl, 90, 197
Rowe, Jack, 70, 247
Rwanda genocide, 308

S
Salas, Maria, 64
San Quentin prison, 319, 321

Sandy Hook elementary school, 309
saying the right words,
　　while tapping, 112
Scaer, Robert, 190
schools, standardized, testing, 120
scope of practice, 301–302
secondary gain, 92–93, 299, 348
self-acceptance, 91, 271–272, 350
self-care, 300
self-esteem, 209, 279–280, 289
Selye, Hans, 74
Serenity Prayer, 90
Setup Statement, 87, 89, 91, 106, 147,
　　190, 197, 222, 227–229, 242,
　　269, 272, 285, 348, 353, 355
　　Flowing, 231, 348
Sheldrake, Rupert, 241
shadow, Jungian, 190, 288
Shealy, Norman, 50
skill, developing, 48
Skype, EFT via, 306, 350
Sneaking Away from the Problem,
　　200, 202
Sneaking Up on the Problem, see also
　　Gentle Techniques, 178, 196–
　　198, 298, 349
Sore Spot, 330
special populations,
　　treating with EFT, xviii
specific events, targeting, 98, 106,
　　109, 153, 175, 197, 254, 279,
　　289, 347
　　extremely, 284
spiritual and moral development, 141
spirituality, 233
sports, and EFT, 266–267
　　baseball, 266
　　basketball, 2667
　　golf, 266–267
　　volleyball, 267

sports performance, 72
Stapleton, Peta, 71
statistical significance, xxi
still face experiments, 181, 204
stock market, 138
Stone, Barbara, 316
stress, 84, 112, 267
　　releasing, 59, 62, 82, 144
subconscious mind, 189, 245
subjective units of distress (SUD), 47,
　　85–86, 96–97, 149–150, 183,
　　188, 199, 258, 271, 275, 276,
　　280, 286, 291, 347, 349
suffering, 115, 118
supervision, 169, 234, 301
surrogate tapping, 242–243
Sutton, Loree, 203
sympathetic nervous system, 57, 74

T
table and legs, 278, 280, 349
　　distinguishing, 281
tail-enders, 216–217, 348
talk therapy, 73
Tap-Along videos, 339, 341, 344
tapping, xvi
　　and Talking, 218–219, 348
　　circle, 114, 172, 248, 321
　　mental, 263
　　on others, 98
　　scripts, 113
　　secret, 265
　　sequence, 94
Tapping Deep Intimacy course, 236
tapping points, 59
　　optional, 350
Tapping Solution movie, 226
Tapping World Summit, 309

Tearless Trauma, *see also* Gentle
    Techniques, 178, 190–192,
    195, 349
telephone, delivery of EFT, 350
Tell the Story Technique, 104, 188,
    192, 199, 348
testing, 107, 286, 348–349
Thought Field Therapy
    (TFT), xvii, 79, 202, 291, 316
tinnitus, 50
Touch and Breathe (TAB), 202, 242
transferred PTSD, 29
trauma, psychological, 175
trauma capsule, 183–186, 188,
    190, 284
traumatic brain injury (TBI), 44, 71
traumatic events, 177–178, 183–184,
    228, 255, 330, 335
    eye movements linked to, 330
traumatic life experience, 85
    and children, 58, 178, 180, 189,
    192, 238
typhoid, 325
    children's deaths from, 325

U–V
validity of cognition (VOC),
    213–214, 217
veterans, 28–29, 49, 202–204, 223,
    247, 305
    domestic violence, 308
    spouses of, 29, 204
    suicides, 308
Veterans Stress Project, 27,
    305–306, 308
volunteering, 114

W–Y
Warburton, Greg, 266

water, drinking, 171, 259
Watkins, Jan, 281
Wauthier-Freyman, Yves, 314
weight loss, 71, 131, 236
Wells, Steve, 63, 192
Wolpe, Joseph, xvii, 28, 75, 271, 286
work, and EFT, 133
    productivity, 134
working on your own issues, 233, 349
workshops, in EFT, 114, 214, 249,
    253, 281
worst and/or the first, 254, 289
writings on our/your walls, 211–214,
    217, 348
YouTube, 81

EFT on a Page

1. **Where in your body** do you feel the emotional issue most strongly?

2. **Determine the distress level** in that place in your body on a scale of 0 to 10, where 10 is maximum intensity and 0 is no intensity:

   10, 9, 8, 7, 6, 5, 4, 3, 2, 1, 0

3. **The Setup:** Repeat this statement three times, while continuously tapping the Karate Chop point on the side of the hand (large dot on hand diagram below):

   "Even though I have _____ (name the problem), I deeply and completely accept myself."

4. **The Tapping Sequence:** Tap about 7 times on each of the energy points in these two diagrams, while repeating a brief phrase that reminds you of the problem.

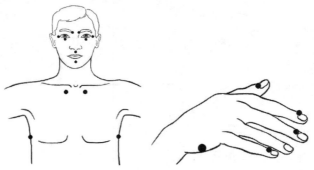

5. **Determine your distress level** again on a scale of 0 to 10 again. **If it's still high, say:**

   "Even though I have some remaining _____ (problem), I deeply and completely accept myself."

6. **Repeat from Step 1** till your distress level is as close to 0 as possible.

   Find dozens of Tap-Along videos at EFTUniverse.com